FOUNDATION S

NORTHWICK PUBLISHERS
14, BEVERE CLOSE, WORCESTER, WR3 7QH, ENGLAND
Telephone Number: 0905-56876/56529

FOUNDATION SERIES

Other books in the series:

LAW
Author P. GERRARD B.Sc., Ph.D., A.C.I.B.

FINANCIAL ACCOUNTING
Author W. HARRISON, F.C.I.B., Cert.Ed.

COST ACCOUNTING
Author G. J. WILKINSON-RIDDLE, B.A., F.C.A.

FOUNDATION SERIES

ECONOMICS
Second Edition

R. G. WINFIELD, B.Sc.(Econ.)Hons., F.C.I.B.

*Principal Lecturer at the
City of London Polytechnic*

NORTHWICK PUBLISHERS

NORTHWICK PUBLISHERS

© R. G. WINFIELD 1985, 1990

ISBN 0 907135 58 7

Printed in England by Clays Ltd, St Ives plc

First Edition 1985

Second Edition 1990

CONTENTS

IX ECONOMIC MANAGEMENT

X INTERNATIONAL ECONOMICS

FOREWORD TO THE SECOND EDITION

This book has been written for the student with no prior knowledge of Economics whatever. I have covered the requirements of the "A" level syllabus and also all the topics required by students on professional courses such as those of The Chartered Institute of Bankers, the various Accountancy bodies, the Insurance institutes and the Institute of Chartered Secretaries and Administrators.

The aim of this book is to provide the student with a text on Economics that can be studied on its own without reference to other books on the subject. Unlike some textbooks on Economics it does not dwell at great length on matters which are more properly in the province of commerce; but I have not treated Economics purely as an academic subject and there are references throughout the text to things which are happening in the real world – in particular in the U.K.

The student is encouraged to read as widely as his time permits. The macro-economic part of the text will be much more relevant to him if accompanied by the reading of a good newspaper. Indeed, there is much to be said for keeping a "scrap book" of newspaper cuttings on topics of economic interest.

I wish to record my thanks to several individuals, firms and organisations who have helped to make the second edition of this book possible. In particular I must thank Keith Bird for his careful reading of the text and much of the updating, in particular the tables and charts, and Mary Cartwright and Marc Wood who provided the graphics. My thanks are also due to my colleagues at City of London Polytechnic including those in the Library; and to the excellent staff of the City Business Library in London Wall.

Finally I would like to record my thanks to the Bank of England, the Central Statistical Office, The Treasury and the Department of Employment for permission to quote various statistics. Other organisations who have provided useful data include Lloyds Bank, Midland Bank, the stockbrokers W. Greenwell & Co. and The Chartered Institute of Bankers. Like all writers on Economics I rely heavily on good newspapers to keep myself up-to-date and I am happy to acknowledge my debt, in particular, to The *Financial Times* and *The Observer*.

June 1990   Roderick Winfield

CHAPTER 1

WHAT IS ECONOMICS ALL ABOUT?

WHAT IS ECONOMICS?

Economics is one of the so-called *social sciences*, a group of disciplines which include sociology, political science and social psychology. It is a social science because it is concerned in large measure with human behaviour and is not, therefore, capable of the same degree of exactitude as physical sciences such as mathematics and chemistry.

Economics, as distinct from the other social sciences, is concerned with three principal matters:

1. The behaviour of prices
2. The forces which determine income and employment
3. The creation and distribution of wealth

Prices, incomes, wealth – all of these are measurable in money terms; yet economics is really concerned with much more than money matters. Economics is a broad field of study and includes such specialist areas as monetary economics, industrial economics, labour economics and so on. There are also specialists who deal with economics-related subjects such as economic history and economic geography. Then there is the separate but closely related discipline of econometrics which is concerned with the mathematical and statistical analysis of economic relationships.

Economics then is central to the study of the world as it is today and is related to a number of other disciplines too. It is at the heart of any course on business studies.

THE MEANING OF "ECONOMICS"

Economics is derived from a Greek word meaning the management of a household. At the domestic level this means setting aside a part of one's income for the various expenses necessary to the smooth running of the home – food, clothing, cleaning materials, mortgage payments or rent – and a host of other things. Since we never seem to have enough money to provide all the things we would like, we have to economise, that is we try to make the best use of our scarce resources; in short to use them efficiently.

FREE AND SCARCE GOODS

Nearly all goods and services are scarce in the sense that the supply of them is limited. The air we breathe may seem to be an exception, but huge sums of money have been spent to keep the air as clean as it is. Many areas are today designated "smokeless zones" and there is a continuing campaign to remove pollutants from petrol and other toxic substances. So even the air we breathe involves a substantial cost in economic terms.

There are, however, some genuinely free goods. In the autumn blackberries are in the hedgerows for the taking, and if you know where to look you can find abundant supplies of mushrooms growing wild. Even commercially produced goods may occasionally be free as, for example, when an abundant harvest causes a glut. Some stables find it easier to give away horse manure than to sell it! In this book the use of the term "goods" means economic (i.e. scarce) goods – *goods and services* which are bought and sold.

THE ECONOMIC PROBLEM – SCARCITY AND CHOICE

Economics can be seen basically as the study of human behaviour in the context of limited resources, and the allocation of those scarce resources among competing ends. As individuals or firms our income is finite, our wants potentially infinite. Except for a few ascetic people, our wants – not the same as our needs – nearly always exceed our available resources (Figure 1.1(a)). This is a truism not only for individuals but for businesses and governments too. It is true for rich and poor alike, although the starkness of choice for the very poor – between sufficient food and adequate clothing – is more striking (Figure 1.1(b)). An already wealthy businessman will not necessarily jump at the chance of making more money. For him time is a scarce resource. For the government the budget is its annual exercise in reconciling scarcity and choice for the nation as a whole.

Human beings may choose things for a variety of reasons – for security, to promote health or even to increase their self-esteem. These underlying reasons are not really the concern of the economist who is more interested, for example, in how the individual's income and/or the price of a commodity influences his choice – whether to buy at all, and if so in what quantity? Nevertheless, because the dividing lines between economics and other disciplines are not sharply drawn there are areas of overlap. Economic analysis can be fruitful in many areas of sociology, and can help the political scientist to better understand the nature of the

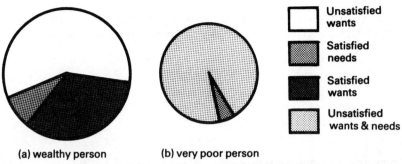

(a) wealthy person   (b) very poor person

Figure 1.1: Wants, Needs and Scarce Resources.

demands placed on governments by people whether in a democracy or in a totalitarian regime.

THE POLITICO-LEGAL FRAMEWORK

Because economics is a social science operating within a human context there are bound to be constraints upon what individuals and firms can do. Indeed this is more true today than it has ever been before. Today's corporate state is a far cry from the laissez-faire ideals of the 19th century liberals.

Some of the rules are broadly construed such as that which prevents the government from seizing private property withot due compensation. The existence and the characteristics of various taxes have a great deal to do with determining economic behaviour. The Monopolies and Mergers Act, 1965 limits monopolistic tendencies in industry and commerce.

Other rules may be imposed within society. Thus trade unions may operate "closed shop" agreements while doctors and accountants may restrict entry by one means or another to their respective professions.

Such rules may limit the choices of people affected by them: in a democratic society, however, there will always be ways of changing the rules. However, notwithstanding even statute law some rules may be deliberately flouted as, for example, in the fight by some retailers against restrictions on Sunday trading.

BASIC ECONOMIC CONCEPTS

Economists, as we have said, are concerned with a broad range of subject matter – scarcity and choice, prices and markets and international trade, for example; and economists have their own peculiar terminology or jargon. Some of these terms – and the ideas behind them – are so fundamental to economics that we will consider them briefly now.

1. Opportunity cost
2. The margin
3. Efficiency
4. Utility
5. Transactions costs

OPPORTUNITY COST

Experts mean a variety of things when they talk about *cost*. Accountants, for instance, distinguish "direct", "indirect" and "sunk" costs to mention only a few examples. In everyday life we tend to use the word quite loosely but nearly always its meaning is closely associated with the spending of money.

Economists use the word "cost" in a number of different ways too, but the central idea of the word for the economist is known as *opportunity cost*. This is defined as the cost of doing something as measured in terms of the value of the lost opportunity to pursue the best alternative activity with the same time and resources. We are constantly confronted with the need to make such choices.

Sometimes the choices presented are obviously in money terms. For example, a farmer may choose to use additional land he has recently acquired for pigs rather than poultry. The opportunity cost of his pig farming is the raising of poultry. However, we can also use the term where one alternative involves no money cost at all – choosing to work overtime is, after all, at the expense – the opportunity cost – of leisure.

THE MARGIN

In economics you will find the word *margin* (and *marginal*) used in various contexts – cost, productivity, utility etc. – to refer to a small (unit) increase or decrease in some economic activity. The marginal cost of producing a TV set will be the additional cost involved in making one more set – the materials and labour, but not the "overhead" costs, those such as rent and salaries. To the economist, if the *marginal revenue* (i.e. the selling price) exceeds the *marginal cost* the additional, production will be worthwhile.

As we shall see more clearly later many economic decisions are really adjustments at the margin. That is, we do not necessarily simply reject one good in favour of another but rather decide to buy a little more of one at the opportunity cost of rather less of the other. Thus the concepts of opportunity cost and the margin are closely related.

EFFICIENCY

Because of the prevailing scarcity of all economic goods, economists are naturally concerned that these should be made or provided with the minimum of cost and effort consonant with the need for quality. To the extent that production and distribution are efficient it may be possible to provide more goods and services at lower prices and thus enable people to have more control over their lives, giving them more time for family commitments as well as increased leisure activities.

Table 1.1: Production possibility schedule for Food and Cloth

Units of	
Cloth	Food
0	20
1	18
2	14
3	8
4	4
5	0

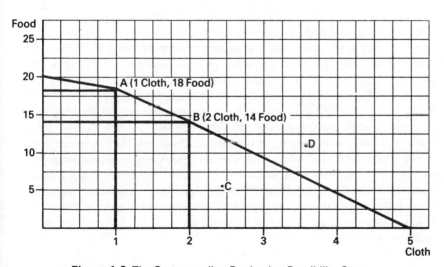

Figure 1.2: The Corresponding Production Possibility Curve.

Efficiency can be looked at in a very simplified way by producing a *production possibility* schedule or curve which shows the different combinations which can be produced by fully employing all the resources at its disposal using the best technology available.

Table 1.1 shows what a very simple society might produce – at one extreme no cloth and twenty units of food, and at the other five units of cloth and no food. It will be seen that to produce one unit of cloth entails giving up two units of food but to produce a second unit of cloth society must forgo a further four units of food. Production possibilities are very closely allied to the concept of opportunity cost.

In Figure 1.2 note also points C and D. Point C lies within the curve and indicates that production of food and cloth at this level represents a failure to employ all the resources available. Point D, on the other hand, being outside the production possibility "frontier" represents an impossible position given the existing level of economic resources. Any relevant development in technology for improvement in organisational capability would allow the production possibility curve to shift to the right.

In a closed society (i.e. one without imports or exports) the relative production possibilities will be important determinants of price, but in the real world countries will tend to specialise in producing those goods and services which they produce most efficiently relative to other countries.

We are all intuitively aware that if the price of something we desire goes down we are more likely to buy it in greater quantities. Economists use the term utility to describe the need, fulfilment or enjoyment we gain from the consumption of goods and services. We are also aware that as we consume more and more of a particular item we generally derive less satisfaction from it. After strenuous physical activity, for instance, the first drink is invariably the most welcome with each successive drink less so. This is known as the principle of diminishing marginal utility.

In the real world consumers must choose between different goods offered at different prices out of their limited incomes. As we have observed previously they must economise. Although they may not consciously aim to do so, most consumers are attempting to maximise utility when they make economic decisions. A state of consumer equilibrium is said to exist when consumers' expenditures are distributed amongst alternative goods in such a way that the marginal utility of £1 spent on food is exactly equal to that of £1 spent on clothing or £1 on anything else for that matter.

TRANSACTIONS COSTS

Perfect economic efficiency requires that there can be no way to make one person better off except at the expense of another. However, because of imperfections in the market this is rarely the case in practice. The market is a system for getting people together to make mutually agreeable transactions. But dealings themselves incur costs and these may hinder the execution of mutually beneficial transactions. The chief *transactions costs* are:

1. Information costs.
2. Negotiation costs.
3. Taxes.

All these costs can be illustrated if we look at the selling of a house which is a complex, time-consuming and often frustrating business for those involved. Most people are happy to leave the sale in the hands of a professional estate agent even though the costs of doing so are usually considerable. However, since no agent could possibly provide information about the property to be sold to every potential buyer – advertising costs could in no way be justified – there can never be a perfect match between buyer and seller.

Negotiation is rarely completely straightforward either, and because discussions often break down the estate agent endeavours to protect his sale by pressing for an early completion, playing off potential buyers against each other and using other forms of "gamesmanship". Solicitors' and building societies' costs also add considerably to the costs of negotiation.

Finally taxes – in the shape of stamp duty and capital gains tax – may also interfere with the smooth operation of economic forces. The impost of transfer stamp duty is certainly a prime factor in discouraging people from moving house.

ECONOMIC ANALYSIS – METHODS AND TOOLS

As we have seen economic science faces certain difficulties. Because economics is concerned with human behaviour, economists face certain problems which other scientists do not encounter, for example:

1. They cannot really experiment with people.
2. The economy as a whole is so vast and complex that it is not possible to follow the results of individual changes except to a very limited extent.

3. Because economists only measure things in money terms occupations such as housework, the labour involved in decorating one's own home and voluntary work are treated as having no economic significance.

4. Economic findings, to be useful, may have to be examined in conjunction with other social sciences.

Notwithstanding these difficulties economists nevertheless attempt, and in many cases achieve a measure of success in interpreting economic phen-

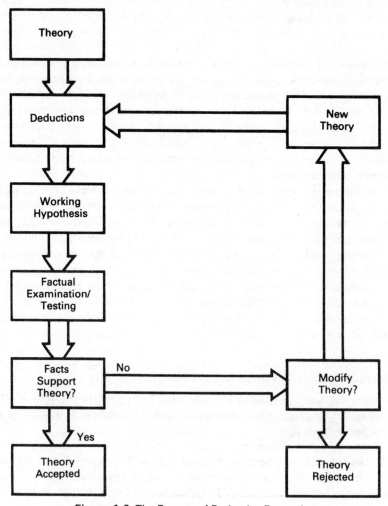

Figure 1.3: The Process of Deductive Reasoning.

omena. In their analysis they apply the same methods as scientists in other disciplines – inductive and deductive reasoning.

Inductive reasoning is the process of thought whereby general conclusions are drawn from a set of premises based mainly on experience. Thus, for example, because tomatoes are cheap in August we conclude that this is because the supply of them is greatest at this time. But there could be other reasons. So economists, like other scientists, also use the more rigorous method of analysis known as deductive reasoning. Following this approach the economist is able to draw specific conclusions from a set of general premises. The economist builds a "model", selects certain variables and then looks at changes in these one at a time, observing and noting the results. Eventually he may prove or disprove his original theory (Figure 1.3). One of the commonest phrases in the literature of economics is "ceteris paribus" – other things being equal. It is a most important qualification for, in the real world which economics seeks to penetrate, other things rarely are equal.

POSITIVE AND NORMATIVE ECONOMICS

Economists cannot foretell the future. Their training does, however, enable them to make reasonable predictions of the if/then variety, e.g. if the government reduces taxes then the increased spending available to the community will stimulate consumption and thus further economic growth. Such a statement is an example of *positive economics* even though different economists might argue about the extent of its validity.

Individual economists might interpret the outcome in several ways. One might assume that the consequent fall in unemployment would be a good thing: another that the risk that government spending might fuel inflation cannot be justified. Both these economists are making value judgements in contrast to the if/then predictions of positive economics. We call this *normative economics* because it makes assumptions about norms.

Statements of positive economics may be regarded as intellectually superior but this is not necessarily so. The statement "If government reduces taxes, unemployment will rise", although unquestionably wrong. (given the ceteris paribus assumption) is nonetheless a statement of positive economics!

Normative economics may sometimes be politically biased or merely emotional and must therefore be looked at with a degree of circumspection. However, few economists worthy of the name would never make any statements of this kind: to do so would be to divorce themselves from the real world. Economics is about the real world however much economic models may sometimes seem to belie this. Both positive and normative economic statements have a role in economics. It is important, however, to be able to differentiate the two kinds of thinking.

THE "LAWS" OF ECONOMICS

It was stated earlier that economics is not a precise science in the same way that, for example, chemistry or physics is: we cannot isolate or control data under laboratory standards. Nevertheless, it is possible in a few cases to formulate what can be called "laws of economics". Very often these may seem to be no more than "dressed-up" versions of things we tend to know intuitively anyway. Thus we recognise that if the price of something goes up we are less likely to buy it than before – one of the laws of demand. Another example is the case of diminishing returns. If a farmer uses chemicals he can increase his yield but after a certain time each additional unit produces less benefit – reduced marginal productivity – than before. You will meet this law too in a later stage of your studies.

MICRO- AND MACRO-ECONOMICS

Positive and normative statements pervade much of economics but they are not divisions of its subject matter. As stated previously economics is a vast subject with branches and connections with other disciplines. The central part of economics, however, is broadly divided into two areas.

Microeconomics ("micro" – Greek for small) is concerned with the behaviour of small economic units – individuals, households, and firms; and the determination of prices under various conditions. *Macroeconomics* ("macro" – Greek for large), on the other hand, is the study of large scale economic phenomena such as production, economic growth, inflation and employment.

Certain topics, however, do not fit easily into either category, e.g. economic development and international trade, so it would be misleading to think of all economics as being either micro- or macro-oriented.

QUESTIONS

1. "Economics is about scarcity and choice." Comment on this statement.

2. What do you understand by the terms "opportunity cost" and the "margin" in economics?

3. Distinguish between inductive and deductive reasoning and their applicability in economics.

4. Comment on the statement: "Positive economics is superior to normative economics".

5. Discuss "utility" and "efficiency" as these words are used by economists.

CHAPTER 2

THE ALLOCATION OF RESOURCES

FUNDAMENTAL ECONOMIC DECISIONS

In any country the economic system exists to meet society's aims and desirably to meet those aims as efficiently and effectively as possible. The relatively limited means of production together with relatively unlimited wants results in a need to choose between alternatives. In effect, a society has to take three basic economic decisions:

(a) Which goods shall be produced and in what quantities? This is concerned with the make-up of a country's total production, including the range of goods and services which are to be produced. It necessarily requires a mechanism for determining the orders of priority, to operate either at an individual or collective level.

(b) How should the various goods and services be produced? This is concerned with methods of production and organisational arrangements for achieving an efficient and effective use of resources. It involves the way in which different resources are combined, e.g. labour-intensive or capital intensive means of production, as well as the scale on which production takes place.

(c) How should the goods and services which have been produced be distributed among the population?

Whereas decisions (a) + (b) above are regarded as being about "resource allocation", decision (c) is about the sharing of the output among the members of the community. This is termed the "distribution of goods and services" and is dealt with in Chapter 16.

These economic decisions will be continually subject to the processes of change: developments in technology and new methods of production together with changes in consumer preference will necessitate frequent review and updating of economic decisions. Moreover, economic policy and decisions will be constrained by political and social considerations. Thus, awareness of the "greenhouse effect" and of the need to combat the effects of pollution is placing burdens on manufacturing industry as well as individual members of society.

FACTORS OF PRODUCTION

Economic resources can include anything that can be utilised in the production or distribution of goods or services. Three basic categories generally agreed upon are land, labour and capital. Some economists include a fourth factor of production – entrepreneurship.

LAND

The term *land* should really be extended to include all natural resources – mines, fishing grounds, exploration rights and so on. At national level land is fixed in quantity although some countries, notably Holland and South Africa have reclaimed land from the sea on quite a large scale. Land can also be "lost" due to exhaustive mining or serious and damaging flooding or by soil erosion. Sometimes changes in land occur as a result of good or bad farming; large scale forestry can even improve the climate and thus the value of the land; and improved communications can open up hitherto inaccessible areas and make them productive. The building of a second bridge over the River Severn will greatly assist industry and have an appreciable impact on property prices in the surrounding area.

LABOUR

Labour, like land, is also limited in quantity at any given time, although in practice there are nearly always more people available for work than there are jobs available. Over time, the size of the working population changes relative to the total population. In the U.K. the working population irrespective of the higher level of unemployment, is becoming relatively small because of the increasing number of elderly people in the population. Against this trend, however, must be set the continuing increase in the number of married women seeking work.

Social pressures such as the pressures on women to go out to work (or stay at home) and the provision of welfare services (pensions, unemployment benefit, etc.) also affect the total amount of labour available.

Some countries have deliberately made efforts to increase their populations. In the U.K. this was done in the 1950s by the active encouragement of West Indian immigration; in Germany by the employment of Turkish workers on a large scale; while Australia, Canada and South Africa have at different times opened their doors to people with the requisite skills.

The nature and quality of the labour force will vary greatly from country to country. Educational differences and the opportunities for post-school education and training are important factors in determining the quality of labour. A feature of labour as a factor of production is its mobility – greatest in western democracies and most apparent among the better educated. Labour, however, is relatively immobile when compared to capital because of the need to consider housing and other social provisions.

CAPITAL

Capital is any material resource other than land used in production. Although we may speak of a sum of money saved as capital, money is not what economists call capital. Money is not inherently useful but is important as a lubricant of the economic system.

Economists frequently use the word *"real"* in contrast to *"nominal"* to differentiate tangible from money values. So real capital includes factories, plant and machinery, and motor vehicles used in production and distribution. Stocks of raw materials, work-in-progress and finished goods prior to sale are also classified as capital goods.

In economic terms whilst the motor car, for instance, might be regarded as part of his capital by the individual, to the economist the car in this case must be classified as a consumer good. The essential property of capital (goods) is that they must be used in production. Capital is much more mobile than labour so when a multi-national firm builds a hospital or a power station it may use equipment and raw materials purchased from several different countries, while most of its labour will be recruited locally.

Capital is, in large measure, dependent on human inputs. Machinery and vehicles of all kinds are constantly being improved and updated in the interests of greater efficiency. Hence, greater productivity is achieved at lower cost.

Those factors of production are also to some extent interchangeable. Under-developed countries with large resources of labour sometimes choose methods of production that utilise their indigenous labour instead of relying heavily on plant and machinery which would probably have to be imported anyway. Such production methods are described as labour-intensive in contrast to production in the industrialised world which is much more capital intensive.

ENTREPRENEURSHIP

The rewards of labour are wages and salaries, and benefits in kind such as company cars and subsidised mortgages. Some individuals, however, seek greater rewards by going into business on their own account. They may draw salaries but the raison d'etre for their decision is the chance to make profits. Economists call such people entrepreneurs. Entrepreneurs initiate decisions, invent new ways of doing things and overcome constraints. In short, they take risks. For this reason *entrepreneurship* is sometimes considered to be a separate factor – a fourth factor of production.

There is and must be a substantial overlap between entrepreneurship and labour as factors or production. Is the small jobbing builder or smallholder really what we mean by an entrepreneur – a risk-taker? Some senior (and not so senior) managers employed in industry on a salaried basis may more properly be considered entrepreneurial even though they may have little if any money invested in the business which employs them. For these reasons it may be misleading to consider entrepreneurship as a separate factor of production. As a factor in economic thinking it is, however, very important indeed.

ECONOMIC UNITS

Microeconomics studies the behaviour of small economic units, traditionally *households* and *firms*. With the continuing importance of public spending – by governments, local authorities and nationalised industries – a third unit, that of *government* has to be considered too.

HOUSEHOLDS

A *household* is a group of individuals who pool their incomes, own property in common and make economic decisions jointly. These assumptions are based on the ties of kinship and affection. It is at best a half-truth as others, in particular the sociologists, have pointed out. Nevertheless, whatever its deficiencies the household is a useful concept for the economist.

Within the economic system as a whole households are buyers of goods and services. They are also known as consumers – and consumer expenditure is one of the great yardsticks used in macroeconomics. They also enter the market as sellers of factors of production – labour, land and capital.

FIRMS

Firms purchase factors of production from households and use them to produce finished goods and services which they sell either directly or

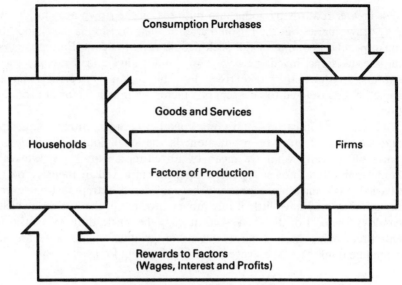

Figure 2.1: Factors of Production: Movements and Rewards.

more probably through a network of intermediaries – wholesalers, retailers and agents of all kinds. A simple model of the movement of
factors of production is given in Figure 2.1.

There are many different kinds of firm but the three most frequently
met with are sole-proprietorships, partnerships and limited companies.
The latter, though far less numerous, account for the vast majority of
the goods and services produced in Britain today. Indeed, some large
multi-national companies have a total output that far exceeds the total
national product of some of the countries in which they operate.

Internally firms are structured hierarchically, the owners appointing
managers, and the managers employees. Although there is often a degree
of overlap between ownership and control in a small firm this may be
almost totally absent in the large company as an examination of the
accounts of the big banks and insurance companies will usually reveal. It
is very rare indeed certainly to find public companies where a majority
of the shares is vested in a single individual or family. Ownership of such
enterprises is well spread today, institutional investors such as insurance
companies and pension funds becoming dominant. The one assumption
that economists make about the firm is that it is run so as to earn the
maximum profits for its shareholders: in short the firm is a profit
maximiser.

GOVERNMENT

Traditional microeconomics treated only firms and households and government was regarded as outside its scope. Because of the increased importance of government expenditure and its impact on production and consumption, *government* is now brought explicitly into the consideration of microeconomics.

ECONOMIC SYSTEMS

Every government has to determine broadly what it aims to do on the economic front. It is assumed that the government aims, in a similar way to firms, to achieve the maximum degree of satisfaction – utility – with a minimum of waste. In short it seeks economic efficiency. Governments of different political persuasions will of course, differ about priorities. In particular each government must decide to what extent, if at all, it wishes to determine:

1. What goods are to be produced – and in what quantities.
2. How are the resources available (the factors of production) going to be best deployed to achieve this aim.
3. Who is to benefit, and to what degree, from the production of the goods and services produced.

How these matters are decided varies from country to country. In the western world the private enterprise system holds sway, even though the state together with the public corporations, controls major parts of the economy. In the communist world, on the other hand, the state plays the dominant role with private enterprise a relatively minor part. All countries, however, have something of a mixed economy and there is increasing recognition in command economies (e.g. the Soviet Union) of the importance of an adequate market mechanism. Before looking at things as they are, in the real world, however, let us take a look at the two systems in their "pure" form.

PRIVATE ENTERPRISE

Under private enterprise the state exists to provide only the traditional services – defence of the realm, a system of justice and so on. Taxation, therefore, in such a situation is minimal. In Britain this system operated less than two hundred years ago and was still very largely intact as recently as 1900.

In the private enterprise system economic decisions are made primarily by individuals (households) and firms. Firms, as suppliers of goods and services tend to respond to the demands of customers and not the other way around. Prices are determined by the relative scarcity of goods. If a good is in short supply the price will be driven up. This will encourage further production of the scarce good. The reverse will happen if the supply of goods is in excess of the demand for them.

Such an economy is self-regulating. Resources are allocated where they are most needed: there are no controls on the movement of labour or of capital, and no subsidies or incentives are given to firms to encourage them to invest in certain capital goods or establish operations in specific areas. In short, the consumer is sovereign. It is they who, in the last resort, determine what shall be produced and in what quantities, and no judgement is made by the central authority about whether a good is "useful" or not. Adam Smith (1723–90), one of the great pioneers of modern economics, described this process as the "invisible hand":

> "It is not from the benevolence of the butcher, the brewer or the baker that we expect our dinner, but from their regard to their own interest ... Every individual is continually exerting himself to find out the most advantageous employment for whatever capital he can command ... By directing that industry in such a manner as its produce may be of the greatest value, he intends only his own gain, and he is in this, as in many other cases, led by an invisible hand to promote an end which was no part of his intention"
> "An Inquiry into the Nature and Causes of the Wealth of Nations" 1766.

Most economists today would consider this to be a gross oversimplification; but like all great ideas it has more than a germ of truth in it. However, irrespective of political considerations the chief economic defects of private entreprise can be summarised as follows:

1. Some goods and services may not be produced in sufficient quantities by private enterprise, e.g. education, railways and the postal services.

2. Factors of production do sometimes remain idle as high levels of unemployment bear witness.

3. The price mechanism does not always operate smoothly and thus supply cannot always adapt quickly to changes in demand.

4. Private enterprise perpetuates and exacerbates differences in wealth. Thus the rich have most influence over what is produced; and luxuries are produced at the expense of necessities.

5. Private enterprise involves a large number of small relatively inefficient units of production – large scale state production is more efficient.

6. Excessive competition e.g. by advertising may lead to higher unit costs.

7. Private enterprise takes no account of the public good. Thus a factory may dispose of its waste products into a nearby river making life unpleasant or even dangerous for people living close by.

STATE CONTROL

In the world today there is no country where untrammelled private enterprise exists: equally there is no country where the opposite situation – absolute state control – exists either. In a totally planned economy the government through its huge bureaucracy determines what should be produced and in what quantities. If labour is in short supply in one area workers will be moved where there is work to be done, scant attention being paid to considerations of feeling or comfort. As a result there is no real unemployment to speak of. Economic efficiency depends on the making of the right decisions in all these matters. The state machine replaces the "invisible hand". Thus some of the disadvantages of the capitalist system are ameliorated. The state ensures that resources are "not wasted" on the production of luxury goods. Major industries – important to the infrastructure of the country – are properly financed and every employable person is found work. Unfortunately, however, central planning alone is not the solution to the problem of resolving scarcity and choice. Some of its disadvantages are:

1. The profit motive being absent, effort and initiative go unrewarded. This leads to inefficiency.

2. Many officials have to be employed to determine what goods and services are needed and in what quantities.

3. Decisions may be taken by committees and not by trained managers.

4. The greater prevalence of shortages and surpluses – resulting from bureaucratic decisions – would suggest that the allocation of resources is inefficient.

Many other criticisms can be levelled at the rigidly imposed state system: excessive form-filling, opportunities for corruption, an impersonal approach – all generate poor morale among consumers as well as employees and so lead to inefficiency in the operation of the system.

THE MIXED ECONOMY

We have looked briefly at two theoretical, and widely contrasting, models of the economy. It must be reiterated, however, that the totally

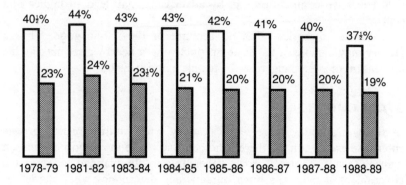

1978-79 1981-82 1983-84 1984-85 1985-86 1986-87 1987-88 1988-89

☐ Total expenditure including net debt interest

▓ of which: expenditure on goods and services

Figure 2.2: Public Expenditure as a Percentage of Gross Domestic Product.

planned economy is just as much a myth today as one which is completely free from the fetters of any controls whatsoever. Individual countries have a tendency to favour one approach more than the other. In the U.K., despite the considerable differences in emphasis by different political parties we tend more towards the private enterprise system. Nevertheless, something of the order of 40 per cent of spending is still in the public sector (Figure 2.2) – that area of the economy which includes several of our major industries and deals with the vast majority of the provision for education and health care (see Figure 2.3). The ratios for 1988–89 in particular are affected by the increase in the Gross Domestic Product rather than by any fall in real terms (allowing for inflation) in the total of public expenditure.

The great economist John Maynard Keynes (1883–1946) showed in the 1930s that the capitalist system was not self-regulating in the way Adam Smith had believed it to be. In most western economies, therefore, there is a pragmatic approach to the economy. The benefits of public ownership may seem obvious in the case of the post office and electricity supply but less obvious, perhaps, in the case of coal or transport for instance. The privatisation of several U.K. companies has even extended to telecommunications, once regarded as a "natural monopoly". In the U.S.A. some prisons are now run on private enterprise lines, the management companies being rewarded, inter alia, on their success at rehabilitation. In such areas as banking and insurance nationalisation is seen by many as being not only unnecessary but even counter-productive.

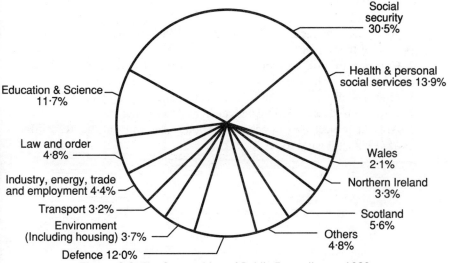

Figure 2.3: The Composition of Public Expenditure – 1989.

The main objectives of economic policy in a mixed economy were set out in the Radcliffe Report (1959):

1. Price stability.
2. Increased production.
3. Full employment.
4. Balance of payments equilibrium.

Governments of whatever complexion would generally agree on these aims but are likely to approach them in different ways. Increased production, for example, is likely to be good for employment but as we have found it can have adverse effects upon prices and on the balance of payments. Any government, therefore, has to formulate policies that contain a fine balance of these aims; or to accept the economic and political consequences.

Whilst governments may be agreed on the general aims they may use very different means to achieve them. Among the factors which will influence them will be the distribution of wealth and incomes. An egalitarian government will clearly have different objectives from one which assumes the primacy of the risk-taker in the economy. A more right-wing government may seek only minimal legislation even though this may cause inequality, lack of opportunity and even individual hardship. Such differences in philosophy are root causes of different approaches to the management of the western-style mixed economy.

QUESTIONS

1. What are the factors of production? What special characteristics does each of them have?

2. Contrast private enterprise with a system of state control. What system is found in the U.K.?

3. How well does Adam Smith's "invisible hand" operate today?

4. Is it true to describe all businessmen as entrepreneurs?

5. Are the objectives of economic policy set out in the Radcliffe Report (1959) still valid today?

CHAPTER 3

DEMAND AND SUPPLY – BASIC CONSIDERATIONS

INTRODUCTION

In August when tomatoes are abundant their price is low and the average housewife will buy more of them than she would earlier in the year. A businessman knows intuitively that one way of increasing sales is for him to reduce his price; he also knows that if market supply is currently being outstripped by demand there are further opportunities for sales (and profits) and he will want to make a contribution to increasing the supply!

It is only in the last one hundred years, however, that economists – notably Alfred Marshall (1842–1924) – have made systematic use of these ideas and have analysed demand and supply in depth.

PRICES

Prices, as we shall see, are determined by the contrary forces of *supply* and *demand*. High prices discourage the purchase of goods: producers and manufacturers, on the other hand, are stimulated by higher prices to supply goods in greater quantity. The *price mechanism*, applies not only to the goods we buy and sell but also to wages and salaries, rent – indeed all the factors of production.

Sometimes prices are controlled without reference to market forces. This is a highly artificial process and during such periods the price mechanism is suspended – officially. In practice, because demand outstrips supply, shortages occur and a black market develops with its own unofficial pricing mechanism in operation. The price mechanism therefore is found operating in all economies, not only in the market-oriented economies of the western world.

If the market is a large one, with many buyers and sellers, then there is a tendency for there to be a single price for goods of the same kind, and there is little, if any, room for negotiation – what Adam Smith, the father of modern economics, called a "higgling" of the market. Where the good has a degree of "specialness" about it – e.g. a thatched cottage, the fee of a famous actor – the price is only arrived at after negotiation, but in all such cases the forces of supply and demand come into play.

Prices perform an important social function, they reflect our values of what things are worth in relation to their relative scarcity or abundance. Thus, in normal circumstances a diamond is extremely valuable; to one dying of thirst in the desert, its value would be as nothing to a glass of water.

The price mechanism does not always work perfectly of course. Within a town three shops may all price the same article differently, but not every purchaser will compare the prices in each shop before making a decision to buy; indeed the vast majority will not. More especially is this the case if the good concerned is inexpensive. Also many products have an element of the unique about them. Thus, while there are several makes of vacuum cleaner, the name of Hoover has a special appeal for many consumers. In such cases prices will, especially if supply is restricted, be higher than they might otherwise be. In monopoly situations the price may be determined by the producer or supplier, but he then has no control over the quantity demanded. Alternatively he may decide on the quantity he will supply, but in this case the price will be determined by the consumer.

VALUE

Price and value are closely related but they are not the same. If, for example, oranges cost 10p, apples 5p and plums 2p each then we can say that one orange is worth two apples or five plums and so on. If apples double in price then the ratio changes, apples becoming worth more in relation to both oranges and plums. We say that there has been a change in the relative prices of these commodities. If, however, prices generally double so that an orange costs 20p and an apple 8p with plums 4p each then the exchange value of the fruits is unaltered. All that is changed is the money value. Economics is more concerned with changes in *exchange value* than with those in *money value*. Although we speak of exchange value this does not imply that we engage in barter to acquire goods. Instead we use money as a medium of exchange. This serves to quantify in common terms the value of a great many commodities.

DEMAND – BASIC CONSIDERATIONS

The law of demand states that for any particular commodity the quantity demanded by buyers tends to increase as the price of the good decreases and to decrease as the price of the good increases, other things being equal.

Quantity demanded should not be confused with want or need. You may want a new car but if the current price of your chosen model is too high for you then your quantity demanded at that time and at that price is zero. A poor person in the Third World may have an urgent need for a new roof but cannot afford it. Although his need is desperate, in economic terms his quantity demanded is likewise zero.

The phrase, "other things being equal" (Latin – ceteris paribus), also needs some explanation. It is the most important qualifying condition in economics. In the present context it implies that if some circumstance were to change then so might the quantity demanded. If, for example, your income increased you might be able to afford the car you want, but you could instead use the additional income to increase expenditure in other directions.

QUANTITY DEMANDED

Before looking at demand in the aggregate, i.e. total market demand, it is useful to consider the demand pattern of a single individual. For some

Table 3.1: An Individual's Demand Schedule for Commodity X.

Price (P)	1	2	3	4	5	6
Quantity Demanded (Qd)	70	60	49	36	32	30

people a particular commodity may be of no interest to them whatsoever. For a teetotaller the quantity of whiskey demanded will be zero whatever the price. For most goods, however, the situation is different. If the price of a good falls we demand more of it, and if its price rises we shall demand less. Table 3.1 shows an individual demand schedule for commodity X.

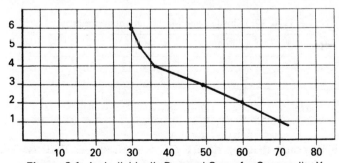

Figure 3.1: An Individual's Demand Curve for Commodity X.

When this data is presented in a graph (Figure 3.1) it will be noted that the individual's demand curve slopes downwards from left to right. This is the standard pattern for demand curves generally although the precise shape may vary considerably.

Economists, however, are much more concerned with *aggregate* or *market* demand.

MARKET DEMAND

Market demand for a consumer good is made up of the total of household demand; and it is the level of market demand which is one of the important determinants of price. The factors which determine the volume of aggregate demand are:

1. Population – its size, structure and rate of growth.
2. The extent and distribution of the national income.

Clearly, the actual size of the population is important but so also is its composition. During the 1930s the birth rate was very low and this has occurred again more recently. Periodically there are "bulges" in population growth which give rise to demand for particular kinds of product – e.g. baby foods and toys. Today people live longer than they used to and this increases the demand for medical care and the provision of old people's homes.

The absolute level of national income is also an important factor, but more important still is the way in which wealth is distributed amongst the population. Taxes and subsidies are used by governments to influence the level of aggregate demand.

Market demand consists of the aggregation of all the individual demand schedules of the population. A very simplified example will make this clear. Consider a market which consists of just three individuals – A, B and C – whose very different preferences are shown in Table 3.2.

Table 3.2: Individual and Market Demand Schedules.

Price	1	2	3	4	5	6
A	30	22	17	12	10	9
B	55	40	32	24	20	18
C	70	60	49	36	32	30
Market	155	122	98	72	62	57

It will be noted that the data for C is the same as that used in our previous example. We can also show this data graphically (Figure 3.2). It

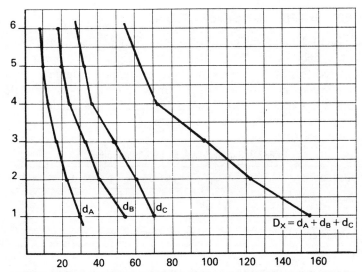

Figure 3.2: Individual and Market Demand Curves for Commodity X.

will be observed that the demand curve for C looks very different from that shown in Figure 3.1 but this is only because we have used a different scale.

Note how all the curves are *negative* – i.e. they slope downwards from left to right – reflecting the increased quantity demanded as prices fall. When the price is £3 A will purchase 17 units, B 32 and C 49 units – 98 units in all. At the lower price of £2 they will buy 22, 40 and 60 units respectively – a total of 122 units. These points are highlighted in the market demand curve.

MOVEMENTS ALONG THE DEMAND CURVE

The market demand curve may slope steeply or may fall only gently, but as explained earlier the apparent slope depends upon the scale of the graph. Except in a very special case (to be discussed in Chapter 4) the demand curve always slopes downwards from left to right. Its slope is negative in that as price increases so quantity demanded decreases. Each of the points on the demand curve represents a combination of *price* and *quantity demanded*. In our example 98 units will be purchased when the price is £3 but this will be increased to 122 units if the price falls to £2. This is known as an *increase in the quantity demanded*. Increases and decreases in quantity demanded are represented by movements along the demand curve.

SUPPLY – BASIC CONSIDERATIONS

In the case of demand the quantity demanded depended on the price. So it is with supply; except that in this case the higher the price consumers are prepared to pay the greater will be the quantity supplied by firms. We begin, as we did with demand, by drawing up a supply schedule for commodity X – more precisely two individual supply schedules and the market supply schedule derived from them.

Table 3.3: Supply Schedules for Commodity X.

Price (£)	1	2	3	4	5	6
Quantity Supplied						
–A	0	5	10	20	30	35
–B	10	20	40	52	55	57
–Market	10	25	50	72	85	92

As our example shows the manufacturers will be prepared to make 85 units when the price is £5 but only 10 units when the price is £1 – indeed one of them will not produce any at all at this price level. The individual and market supply curves are shown in Figure 3.3.

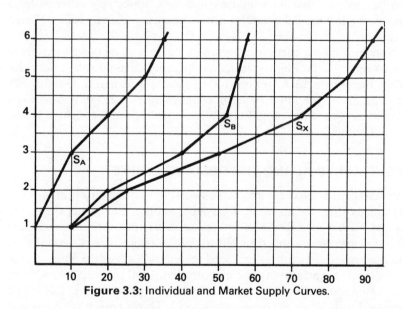

Figure 3.3: Individual and Market Supply Curves.

As in the case of demand a change in the price of the good, other things being equal, will bring about a change in the quantity supplied.

This is represented in Figure 3.3 by a *movement along the supply curve*. In contrast to demand curves supply curves have a *positive* slope – that is supply is increased as price is increased and the typical supply curve therefore slopes upwards from left to right.

MARKET EQUILIBRIUM

We have seen that, in general, consumers demand more of a good the lower the price, while producers will supply it in greater quantities the higher the price. Market research, competition and experience will guide producers in determining what to produce and at what prices it should market its goods, but in the last resort market forces themselves determine prices in a free economy.

Table 3.4: Market Supply and Demand Schedules.

Price (£)	1	2	3	4	5	6
Quantity Demanded	155	122	98	72	62	57
Quantity Supplied	10	25	50	72	85	92

Freely determined market prices result when supply and demand are in equilibrium. At this point there will be no shortage (in the economic sense) and no surplus. All production will be sold at the equilibrium

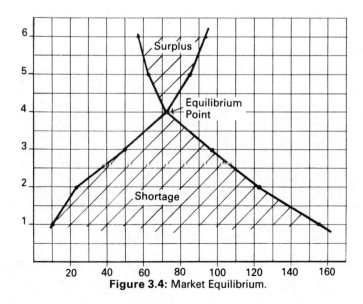

Figure 3.4: Market Equilibrium.

price. In our example, shown in Table 3.4, this will occur at the price of £4 – when the quantity demanded and supplied is 72 units. The price of £4 where *the supply and demand curves intersect* (Figure 3.4) is the *equilibrium price*. At this price the manufacturers will supply 72 units and consumers will be prepared to purchase all of the goods supplied.

If, however, producers attempt to achieve a better price than the equilibrium price they will be left with unsold stocks as buyers hold back – the area marked surplus in Figure 3.4. At prices lower than the equilibrium level, on the other hand, shortages will occur. Thus producers are forced to adjust their prices so that equilibrium is achieved.

QUESTIONS

1. Distinguish between price and value.
2. What do you understand by the phrase "other things being equal"?
3. Why are demand curves normally negative while supply curves have a positive slope?
4. What factors determine the level of individual and market demand?
5. What is meant by market equilibrium? Is it always achieved?

CHAPTER 4

CHANGES IN DEMAND AND SUPPLY

INTRODUCTION

In the previous chapter we considered the bases of demand and supply. It was observed that changes in the quantity demanded and in the quantity supplied were reflected by movements along their respective curves. Market demand was greater the lower the price while market supply was greater the higher the price.

We now go on to consider *changes in demand and supply* in contradistinction to changes in the quantities demanded and supplied. The quantities demanded and supplied *vary with the price* but changes in demand and supply are brought about by *external factors*.

CHANGES IN DEMAND

Changes in demand may occur for a number of reasons:

1. A change in consumer incomes.
2. Changes in the prices of other goods.
3. Expectations regarding future prices.
4. Changes in taste and fashion.

Whenever any of these conditions occur then we would expect there to be a change in demand. Economists call this a shift in demand because the whole demand curve shifts in direction. The quantity of peaches demanded, for example, is greatest in summer when prices are lower, but when a person's income increases he will be more inclined to purchase them out of season. In Table 4.1 we look at the market demand schedules for commodity X both before and after a change in consumer incomes.

Table 4.1: A shift in demand for commodity X.

Price (£)	1	2	3	4	5	6
Quantity Demanded	100	80	60	40	20	0
Quantity Demanded	120	100	80	60	40	20

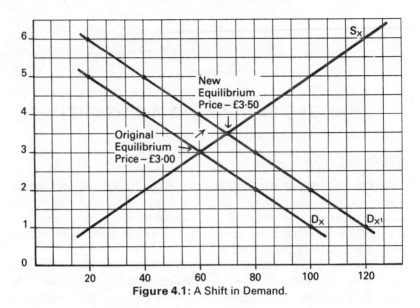

Figure 4.1: A Shift in Demand.

Thus as consumer incomes increase market demand shifts upwards. Other things remain equal i.e. there is no other external factor involved and the supply is also assumed to remain unchanged. The increase in demand pushes the price of X up to £3·50 as shown in Figure 4.1.

It will be observed that the demand curve shifts *upwards and to the right*. It now intersects the supply curve at a *new point of equilibrium*. Conversely, if consumer incomes fell then the demand curve would shift downwards and to the left of the original curve. We will now turn our consideration to the reasons for changes in demand.

CHANGES IN CONSUMER INCOMES

The level of consumer incomes is a very important influence on demand. The higher a person's income the more likely he is to purchase a particular product and, in most cases, to do so in larger quantities. As was explained earlier many of us desire things we cannot afford but this is not the same thing as demand in the sense that the term is employed in economics. Economic demand must be *effective* demand.

CHANGES IN THE PRICES OF OTHER GOODS

Availability of substitute goods is an important factor in determining changes in demand. For some goods there are a number of substitutes.

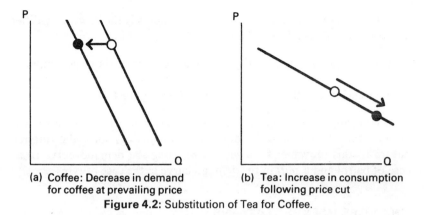

(a) Coffee: Decrease in demand
for coffee at prevailing price

(b) Tea: Increase in consumption
following price cut

Figure 4.2: Substitution of Tea for Coffee.

Instant coffee is for many people a cheaper and more convenient form of coffee than ground coffee. The most popular real alternative though is tea. If tea is reduced in price relative to coffee (i.e. the price of coffee remains unchanged) this will result in:

(a) an increase in the *quantity demanded* of tea and
(b) a decrease in the *demand* for coffee

In the case of tea this is represented by a movement along the demand curve while in the case of coffee a shift in demand occurs.

Tea and coffee, butter and margarine, can be regarded as *substitutes* for each other. They are said to be in *competitive demand*. Other goods are *complements* of each other – one cannot be used without the other. If, for eample, motoring increases then not only will petrol sales rise but so also will sales of related products such as tyres, batteries and even

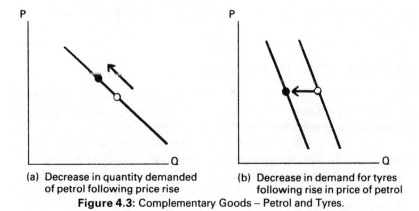

(a) Decrease in quantity demanded
of petrol following price rise

(b) Decrease in demand for tyres
following rise in price of petrol

Figure 4.3: Complementary Goods – Petrol and Tyres.

A.A. membership. The demand for complements is therefore very different from that of substitutes. Thus:

    (a) A decrease in the quantity demanded of petrol will be accompanied by
    (b) A decrease in the demand for tyres (see Figure 4.3).

Thus consumption of complementary goods is represented by movements in the same direction. It is important though to realise the different nature of this movement – a *movement along* the demand curve in the case of petrol and a *shift* in the demand curve in the case of tyres.

CHANGES IN EXPECTATIONS

A third reason for changes in demand is when consumers expect price changes to occur in the near future. If, for example, the coffee crop fails in Brazil – the world's leading producer – this will give rise to stockpiling by wholesalers, while some consumers may buy coffee in excess of their normal requirements. Such a shift in demand is likely to be only temporary and in due course consumers will revert to their familiar pattern of damand – lower consumption at higher prices.

CHANGES IN TASTE AND FASHION

Finally, changes due to taste or fashion can be important causes of shifts in demand. Some tastes change quickly and frequently, e.g. ladies' fashions, pop music and some toys, while others develop much more slowly. Coffee consumption is a good example of the latter, consumption having increased steadily – and not only relative to tea – over many years. Advertising may also play an important part in influencing demand.

THE CONDITIONS OF DEMAND

Demand varies in accordance with changes in conditions. As costs of production of many of today's products have declined so there has been an increase in the demand for them. In many cases the price has fallen *relative* to other goods or in *real terms* (after allowance for inflation), e.g. domestic appliances and transatlantic telephone calls, while in a few cases the fall in price has been absolute – e.g. ball point pens and computers.

    The main determinants of changes in demand are, at one level, the micro-economic factors which affect individual consumers and households, and at the macro-economic level those which combined all these factors to affect the working of economy as a whole.

NORMAL, INFERIOR AND GIFFEN GOODS

In most cases we purchase more of a commodity as the price falls. However this is not always the case. A number of goods are called *inferior goods* because, as our income rises we buy less of them. Many basic foods – bread and potatoes for example – come into this category. The demand curve for inferior goods, however, slopes downwards from left to right in normal fashion.

A special kind of inferior goods exist in the case of *Giffen goods* (after Robert Giffen (1837–1910)). He noted the tendency for certain goods to be consumed in greater quantities the higher the price within a limited range of the demand curve. He observed that when people were very poor this tended to happen in the case of the most basic commodities. In Ireland during the 1840s this occurred with potatoes because the poor could no longer afford to purchase certain other foods at all. Figure 4.4 shows an example of the Giffen phenomenon.

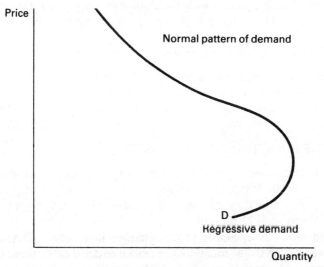

Figure 4.4: Demand Curve for a Giffen Good.

CHANGES IN SUPPLY

As in the case of demand we must distinguish changes in supply from changes in the quantity supplied – *shifts in supply* in contrast to *move-*

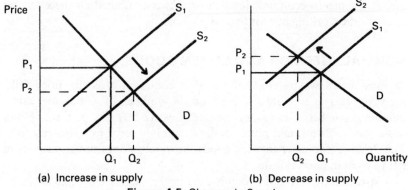

(a) Increase in supply   (b) Decrease in supply

Figure 4.5: Changes in Supply.

ments along the supply curve. An increase in supply will be evidenced by a shift in the curve downwards while a decrease in supply will see the supply curve shift upwards.

A change in supply, other things being equal, will mean a change in price as consumers adjust their quantity demanded – a movement along the demand curve – in line with the change in price which the change in supply causes. How changes in supply affect the equilibrium price is shown in Figure 4.5.

The chief causes of changes in supply are as follows:

1. Changes in production costs.
2. Changes in expectations.
3. Changes in the prices of other goods.

CHANGES IN PRODUCTION COSTS

By far the most important reason for changes in supply are changes in production costs. Producers combine the various factors of production in such a way that they minimise their total costs, and they are always exploring new ways of reducing costs.

Lower costs means higher profits for the entrepreneur. He may also reduce his prices if he considers this will lead to greater profits but he may be forced to do this anyway by his competitors.

An important cause of cost reductions is new technology. If technological changes reduce production costs the producer will be willing to supply more goods at the same price. This will cause the supply curve to shift to the right. Once the new technology is in place, however, a change in price will cause a movement up or down the new supply curve.

CHANGES IN EXPECTATIONS

Even more important than in the case of demand are changes in producers' expectations about future demand and prices. Following the great shortage of potatoes a few years ago many growers increased the acreage given over to this staple crop in anticipation of greater profits. However, too many of them thought along similar lines with the result that the market suffered a glut the next year.

CHANGES IN THE PRICES OF OTHER GOODS

Producers will, like consumers, also be affected by the prices of other goods. Production of one category of goods must always be at the expense of the production of other goods – the *opportunity cost* of producing those other goods. If the market becomes oversupplied with a particular product, perhaps because of changes in consumer tastes, the entrepreneur is likely to turn his attention to the production of other goods.

As with demand special considerations apply to goods which may be substitutes for each other or to those which complement each other. An increase in the supply of butter, for example, will reduce the price of butter and pull down the price of margarine with it. An increase in the supply of petrol will be followed by a reduction in its price reflected by a movement along the market demand curve. The consequent increase in motoring will cause an increase in demand for complementary products such as tyres and batteries.

JOINT SUPPLY

A special situation arises in the case of what is known as *joint supply* – where two or more products are produced jointly, one of which may be little more than a by-product of the other. Lamb and wool, petrol and paraffin are examples of joint supply. If the demand for petrol rises, perhaps as a result of an increase in consumer incomes, the demand curve for petrol will shift to the right causing a rise in both price and quantity demanded. Ceteris paribus, there will be no change in the demand for paraffin so the increase in supply will cause a movement along the demand curve for paraffin and a greater quantity will be sold at the new lower equilibrium price.

SUPPLY – THE TIME FACTOR

Consumers can be very fickle in regard to some products but it takes

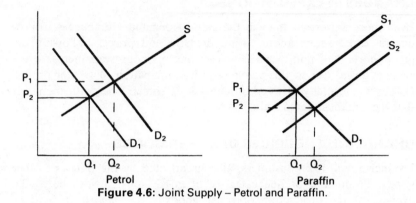

Figure 4.6: Joint Supply – Petrol and Paraffin.

time for producers to respond to changes in consumer taste. Those producers who earliest anticipate market changes are therefore the ones who can take best advantage of changes in the market. Nevertheless, for most of them increases or decreases in production take time and planning. Supply is much slower in responding to demand than is demand in response to supply. Indeed, in the short run – defined in economics as the period during which fixed costs cannot be varied – supply cannot be increased at all.

QUESTIONS

1. Distinguish between a change in the quantity demanded and a change in demand.
2. What factors cause changes in market demand?
3. What are Giffen goods? How are they different from normal goods and inferior goods?
4. What are the chief factors determining supply?
5. Discuss the special case of joint supply.

CHAPTER 5

ELASTICITY OF DEMAND

We take it as commonplace that a reduction in price results in an increase in the quantity demanded. From this point it is but a short step to understand that some price changes may affect supply and demand more than others. Some things we regard as essentials: we would buy them at almost any price – salt is such a case. The demand for luxury goods, on the other hand, may be much more sensitive to price changes. This sensitivity is referred to in economics as elasticity of demand – or more correctly, for there are other elasticities – as *price elasticity of demand.*

PRICE ELASTICITY OF DEMAND

The concept of elasticity is a very useful one in economics. Consider the London Underground System: like most such systems throughout the world it loses money. Many of its costs are fixed costs – costs which are unrelated to the actual volume of traffic. To minimise loss, therefore, management will endeavour to fix prices at such a level that total revenue is maximised. If they decide to increase prices and thereby achieve an increase in total revenue this would suggest that over the price range in question demand is *inelastic* i.e. relatively unresponsive to the price change. If, on the other hand, a reduction in price led to an increase in total revenue we would describe demand as *price elastic.*

Clearly, therefore, an understanding of elasticity is of fundamental importance to the manager whether in the private sector or in the public sector.

INELASTIC DEMAND

The quantity demanded of Product X at various prices and the total revenue therefrom is shown in Table 5.1.

An increase in the price from £1 to £2 has very little effect upon the quantity demanded and as a result the substantial increase in price is almost matched by revenue. At higher prices the fall in price relative to

Table 5.1: Inelastic Demand.

Price (£)	1	2	3	4	5
Quantity	12	11	10	9	8
Total Revenue (£)	12	22	30	36	40

quantity is less but overall there is still an increase in total revenue. Thus the whole of this demand curve is inelastic.

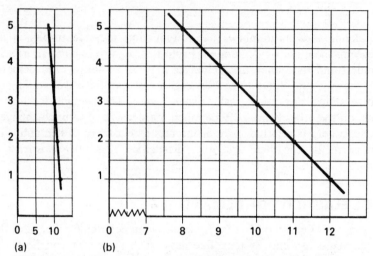

(a)   (b)

Figure 5.1: Inelastic Demand – Different presentations of the Same Data.

Generally speaking steep demand curves are inelastic but as Figure 5.1 shows we can present the above data graphically in different ways.

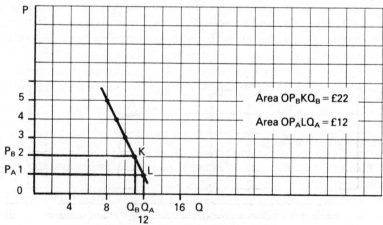

Figure 5.2: An Inelastic Demand Curve.

Both graphs are accurate descriptions of the data given in Table 5.1. The first of them, however, tends to overstress the degree of inelasticity while the second looks, at first sight, more like an elastic demand curve.

An altogether clearer representation of the same data is shown in Figure 5.2. All the possible points of price and quantity are included on the graph and there is no "gap" as in (b) above where the lowest quantity shown is 7 units. The extent of the elasticity is shown by comparing the area OPALQA where the price is £1 and the quantity demanded 12 units, total revenue being £12, with the area OPBKQB where 11 units will be demanded at a price of £2, producing revenue of £22.

ELASTIC DEMAND

Table 5.2 shows the demand schedule for Product Y. In this case each

Table 5.2

Price (£)	7	8	9	10	11	12
Quantity	28	24	20	16	12	8
Total Revenue (£)	196	192	180	160	121	96

increase in price leads to a fall in total revenue or to put it the other way round every reduction in price results in an increase in total revenue. Hence demand is elastic, the area OPBMQB in Figure 5.3 below being much smaller than that of OPANQA.

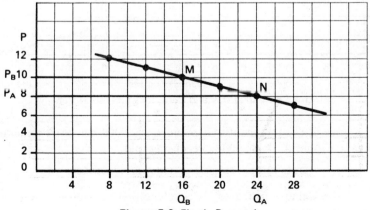

Figure 5.3: Elastic Demand.

MEASURING ELASTICITY

It will be observed that when demand is elastic total revenue changes in the opposite direction to the change in price. When, on the other hand, demand is inelastic a change in price is followed by a change in total revenue in the same direction.

Price	Revenue	Demand
Up	Up	Inelastic
Up	Down	Elastic
Down	Down	Inelastic
Down	Up	Elastic

It is not sufficient, however, merely to know whether demand is elastic or inelastic. We must be able to measure it scientifically. We cannot assume that for a given product elasticity will always be the same. Most demand curves will be partly elastic and partly inelastic. Nevertheless there are some products (e.g. tobacco and petrol) which are notoriously inelastic.

In order to examine the measurement of elasticity let us now turn our attention to the prices of "cup final" tickets ignoring the special non-price factors which in practice lead to shortages and the activities of ticket touts.

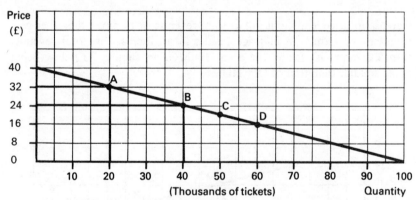

Figure 5.4: Market Demand Curve for Cup Final Tickets.

At a price of £32 the quantity demanded is 20,000 tickets. A reduction in price to £24 results in 40,000 tickets being sold:

$$20,000 @ £32 = £640,000 \quad 40,000 @ £24 = £960,000$$

Since total revenue is increased we conclude that demand is elastic over this range of prices.

POINT ELASTICITY OF DEMAND

We can measure elasticity at a particular *point* on the curve by means of the following formula.

$$\text{Price elasticity of demand} = \frac{\% \text{ change in quantity demanded}}{\% \text{ change in price}}$$

$$= \frac{+100}{-25}$$

$$= -4$$

Now let us look at the situation in reverse, that is we assume the original price of £24 is increased to £32

$$= \frac{-50}{+33\cdot3}$$

$$= -1\cdot5$$

Apart from the special case where elasticity is zero elasticity is always negative. We can highlight five situations:

Elasticity	
0	Infinitely inelastic
less than -1	Inelastic demand
-1	Unitary elasticity
more than -1	Elastic demand
$-$ Infinity	Infinitely elastic

It is usual, however, to ignore the minus sign. Price elasticity is *unitary* (i.e. 1) when a change in price results in no change whatsoever in total revenue i.e. where consumer demand corresponds exactly with the change in price. In the present case this occurs over the price range £16 to £24

60,000 @ £16 = £960,000   40,000 @ £24 = £960,000

If, however, we measure elasticity using the above formula we get:

$$\frac{33\cdot33}{50} = 0\cdot67 \qquad \frac{50}{33\cdot33} = 1\cdot5$$

We now proceed to consider this apparent contradiction.

ARC ELASTICITY OF DEMAND

As we saw above elasticity over a range of prices depends upon which way one is looking at things. In Figure 5.4 elasticity measured from point A to point B is 4 whilst from B to A it is 1·5. One way of getting over this problem is to measure instead the *arc elasticity of demand*. To do this we have to first ascertain the average quantity and the average price over the range of prices we are examining. Thus over the range £24–32:

Average Quantity = (20,000 + 40,000)/2 = 30,000
Average Price = (£24 + £32)/2 = £28

Then arc elasticity of demand is measured by the following formula:

$$\frac{\text{change in quantity/Average quantity}}{\text{change in price/Average Price}}$$

$$\frac{20,000/30,000}{8/\text{£}28} = 2.33$$

On a straight line curve there is only one point where elasticity is unitary – at the central point on the curve. In this case where price is £20 and the quantity demanded 50,000 units (C). If, for example, we measure arc elasticity between points B (40,000 units) and D (60,000 units) arc elasticity of demand will be unity (i.e. 1) but measurement in each direction (as we saw above) will produce point elasticities of 1·5 and 0·67 respectively.

SPECIAL CASES OF ELASTICITY

As we have seen the degree of elasticity will usually vary along the length of the curve. In three largely theoretical cases, however, elasticity will be constant throughout the whole length of the curve:

1. Where price elasticity of demand is zero, i.e. demand is absolutely inelastic (Ed = 0).
2. Where price elasticity of demand is infinite, i.e. demand is absolutely elastic (Ed = α).
3. The case we have already touched on – where elasticity is always unitary (Ed = 1).

These three cases are illustrated in Figure 5.5 below.

It is impossible to think of any good for which the quantity demanded would be the same whatever the price (absolutely inelastic demand), and equally one where the quantity demanded would fall to zero let alone rise to infinity! Nevertheless, under conditions of perfect competition (see Chapter 13), a situation sometimes approximated in the real world, it is possible to get something like absolutely elastic demand although only for a limited quantity of goods. Thus if I ask my broker to sell some shares and I set a limit 1p above the going price I will not sell any at all.

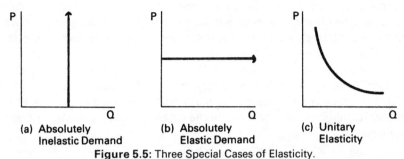

(a) Absolutely   (b) Absolutely   (c) Unitary
   Inelastic Demand   Elastic Demand   Elasticity
Figure 5.5: Three Special Cases of Elasticity.

If I drop my price 1p I shall have no difficulty selling all of them. Finally, unitary elasticity, when it does exist, usually only occurs in a very small portion of the demand curve.

THE DETERMINANTS OF ELASTICITY

The chief factors which determine elasticity are:

1. The degree of substitutability.
2. The price of the good relative to income.

The most important determinant is the extent to which substitutes are available for the good in question. The demand for food in general is inelastic for we all need a certain basic diet to survive, but within the food market there are very many substitutes and much competition to sell them. If the price of lamb rises then chicken or fish or cheese may all be purchased as substitutes. So the demand for individual food items may be relatively elastic. In contrast the demand for items such as tobacco and petrol for which there are no close substitutes is relatively inelastic.

With some goods substitutes may be of two kinds. In the case, for example, of cornflakes a number of other breakfast cereals may be substituted, or altogether different foods may be eaten instead. We must also, however, consider substitutability on a narrower basis: there are a number of different brands of cornflakes each of them competing in terms of price and quality. And so, within this narrower field substitutability is an important factor in the determination of price elasticity. Indeed the price elasticity of demand for a particular brand of cornflakes may be very high.

Less important is the price of the good in relation to total income. Some commodities cost very little, e.g. salt, newspapers, etc., so that

even a large increase or a decrease in price will not make much difference
to total expenditure. Washing machines and video recorders on the other
hand, are relatively expensive items for most people and there are often
many different brands to choose from.

Ultimately consumer tastes are important in determining price elasticity of demand. Nobody would claim that a video recorder was essential
but it is clearly a high priority for many people today, and a fall in price
brings its purchase or rental within the means of a larger number of consumers.

WHY ELASTICITY OF DEMAND IS IMPORTANT

Many business and government decisions are affected by the price elasticity
of demand for a good. If therefore, a businessman does not appreciate the
extent to which elasticity affects the demand for his product he may
increase the price and find that sales drop to a level at which total revenue is
also lower. Orders may fall, he may have to lay off workers and losses may
ensue. Demand for tobacco may be relatively inelastic but if the Chancellor
of the Exchequer imposes too rapid an increase in the duty payable he
could find a lot of people give up smoking altogether and tax revenues fall.

For most things elasticity is different at each price level, and it is not
possible to forecast with any degree of certainty just how people will
react to a change in price.

Even the monopolist cannot ignore the pattern of demand. He can fix
the price but he cannot, at the same time, also determine the quantity he
will sell at that price. If he decides how much he will sell then he loses
control of price, so the elasticity of demand is an important concept for
public utilities such as the Post Office and the gas industry.

INCOME ELASTICITY OF DEMAND

At the beginning of this chapter we defined the concept of elasticity in
general terms and then proceeded to deal exclusively with price elasticity
of demand. But there are other elasticities too. *Income elasticity of
demand* is especially important. Earlier it was stated that the relative
price of a good was an important determinant of elasticity. In defining
the income elasticity of demand we are concerned with the extent to
which a change in real incomes influences the demand for a particular
product. If, for example, real incomes rise by 10 per cent but there is
only a 1 per cent change in the demand for that product demand is
clearly inelastic as to income. If, on the other hand, demand increased by
as much as 30 per cent demand would be said to be income-elastic.

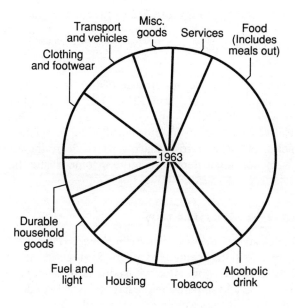

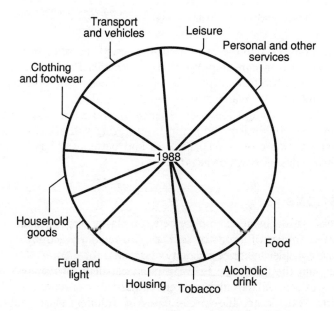

Source: Department of Employment.
Figure 5.6: Changes in Consumer Spending 1963–1988.

Income elasticity of demand is measured by the formula:

$$\text{Income elasticity of demand} = \frac{\%\text{ change in quantity demanded}}{\%\text{ change in real incomes}}$$

Figure 5.6 shows the relative importance of food and other items in total consumer spending in 1963 and 1988. Over this twenty-five year period incomes rose substantially not only in money terms but also in real terms. Relative spending on food declined while spending on transport and vehicles and leisure rose sharply. It is clear, therefore, that spending on many consumer items was more income-elastic than it was on food.

CROSS ELASTICITY OF DEMAND

Another kind of elasticity is *cross elasticity of demand*. Demand for some goods is closely related to the demand for others. Some goods we substitute, e.g. margarine for butter, tea for coffee, whilst others are complements, e.g. petrol and tyres, razors and shaving cream. Cross elasticity of demand may be positive or negative. It is measured by the formula:

$$\text{Cross elasticity of demand} = \frac{\%\text{ change in quantity demanded of X}}{\%\text{ change in price of Y}}$$

Let us first examine the case of substitutes. If the price of coffee rises relative to tea then consumption of tea will increase while that of coffee will decrease. Therefore, in the case of substitutes cross elasticity will be positive and may be greater or less than unity i.e. 1.

On the other hand, if the price of petrol rises there will be a decline in sales and the consequent reduction in motoring will affect the sales of complementary products such as tyres and batteries. Thus for complements cross elasticity will be negative.

QUESTIONS

1. Distinguish, using examples, between elastic and inelastic demand. Give six examples of goods or services you regularly acquire or use. In each case consider the price elasticity of demand for them.

2. Explain the difference between point elasticity of demand and arc elasticity of demand. Are they ever the same?

3. How realistic are the special cases of infinitely elastic, absolutely inelastic and unit-elastic demand?

4. What factors determine (a) price elasticity of demand and (b) income elasticity of demand?

CHAPTER 6

UTILITY

INTRODUCTION

As we have seen people demand goods for a number of reasons – necessity, want, taste or perhaps just to keep up with the Joneses! In short we require goods which yield satisfaction or, to use the economic term, utility. *Utility* is an economic concept and is not measurable in the same way that we might measure prices or quantities. However it is a useful one in that it does help to shed some light on demand theory.

The theory of demand is based very much on the idea that as we increase our utility by purchasing successive units of products so each additional unit purchased actually yields less utility than the previous one. In general total utility is increased while marginal utility decreases. After a certain time total utility may actually decline. From this point onwards marginal utility becomes negative.

MARGINAL AND TOTAL UTILITY

Total utility is the cumulative measure of the satisfaction we receive from a certain economic good. *Marginal utility* is the satisfaction received from the last unit consumed. Consider the date in Table 6.1 below.

Table 6.1.

Quantity	Total Utility	Marginal Utility
0	0	8
1	8	7
2	15	4
3	19	1
4	20	0
5	20	−1
6	19	

In this example each of the first four units consumed add to total utility while the fifth unit adds nothing and the sixth results in a diminution of

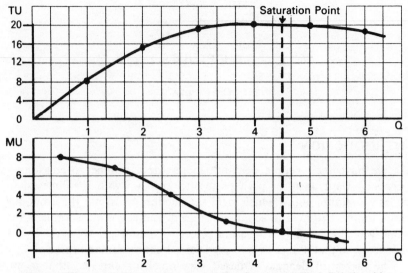

Figure 6.1: Total Utility and Marginal Utility Curves and Their Relationship.

total utility, marginal utility being negative. The relationship between total utility and marginal utility is shown in Figure 6.1.

CONSUMER EQUILIBRIUM

In individual cases we may reach a saturation point whether of cream buns, beer or even expensive products such as cars. The economist would argue, however, that the rational consumer endeavours at all times to maximise his total utility over the very wide range of choices he can make. This inevitably means that, because economic goods are always in short supply, we can never reach a saturation point still less a point where marginal utility becomes negative.

Equilibrium is achieved when we obtain an equal degree of satisfaction from the last pound spent on Product A as from that spent on Product B and indeed on every other economic good besides. This idea is expressed by means of the following equation:

$$\frac{\text{Marginal utility of A}}{\text{Price of A}} = \frac{\text{Marginal utility of B}}{\text{Price of B}} = \text{Etc}$$

In Table 6.2 we show a marginal utility schedule for two products X and Y both of which cost £8. We assume that the individual's income is £80 per time period and is spent only on these two products. In this case he will maximise his total utility by purchasing 6 units of X but only 4 units of Y:

$$\frac{MUx}{Px} = \frac{MUy}{Py} = \frac{17}{£8}$$

If he purchases one more unit of X and thus one less unit of Y he would receive 2 units less satisfaction -15 more of X but 17 less of Y. Increasing his consumption of Y at the expense of X would be less satisfactory still.

Table 6.2: Marginal utility schedule for two commodities X and Y each costing £8.

Quantity	1	2	3	4	5	6	7	8	9	10
Marginal Utility (X)	33	29	23	21	19	*17*	15	13	9	3
Marginal Utility (Y)	31	28	24	*17*	12	10	8	5	2	0

THE WATER-DIAMOND "PARADOX"

Marginal utility theory explains why it is that water which is essential to life is cheap while diamonds, which are not, are very expensive. The total utility of water certainly exceeds that of diamonds but because we consume so much water the marginal utility of the last unit consumed is very low. Diamonds, on the other hand, because they are rare have a very high marginal utility.

The classical economists who first grappled with the concept of utility did not distinguish between total utility and marginal utility and hence could not explain what was to them paradoxical.

UTILITY AND EXCHANGE

Individuals will have different marginal utility schedules and may face different prices for commodities in the areas in which they live. Indeed, international trade is based on the premise that exchange is possible if there are differences in the cost structures of industries in different countries.

Consider now an example where two consumers A and B who live in different countries each has £12 to spend. In Table 6.3 A is in equilibrium when he purchases 3 units of X (at £2) and 6 units of Y (at £1). B, for whom the prices are reversed, will acquire 6 units of X and only 3 of Y. If A now gives up one unit of Y and receives from B one unit of X:

A will increase his total utility by 4 ($-6 + 10$).
B will increase his total utility by 5 ($-8 + 13$).

But this is not the end of the mutually beneficial exchange. If A gives up a further unit of Y in exchange for one of X he will make a further gain

Table 6.3: The Possibility of Exchange.

Quantity	A X = £2 MUx	A Y = £1 MUy	B X = £1 MUx	B Y = £2 MUy
1	16	11	18	20
2	14	10	16	18
3	12	9	14	16
4	10	8	12	13
5	8	7	10	12
6	6	6	8	11
7	4	5	6	3
8	3	4	4	1

in total utility and so will B. A will then derive marginal utility of 8 units and B 12 units respectively from X and Y.

THE INDIVIDUAL'S DEMAND PATTERN

Using the principle of diminishing marginal utility and the concept of consumer equilibrium it is possible to derive the consumer's demand schedule. We will now examine this to see how it is made up. In the case we have just examined A initially purchased 3 units of X at £2 and 6 units of Y at £1. If, however, the price of X fell to £1 he would maximise his utility by purchasing 6 units of each.

Thus we have derived two points on the demand schedule (and hence the demand curve) for X.

Price	Quantity Demanded	Total Expenditure
1	6	6
2	3	6

Over this range of prices there is no difference in total expenditure and price elasticity of demand is unitary. If the fall in price had led to greater spending on X, i.e. if demand for X had been elastic, then less of Y would have been demanded.

These are just two of the many points which could make up the consumer's demand curve. If we assume the price of the commodity to change this will disturb the equilibrium position resulting in a change in the quantity demanded and a new equilibrium position will be reached.

INCOME AND SUBSTITUTION EFFECTS

The movement from one point of consumer equilibrium to another can normally be broken down into an *income* and a *substitution* effect.

In the very simplified case we have examined the movement can be explained wholly in terms of the income effect. In this instance the price of X fell from £2 to £1 and this resulted in an increase in consumption of X with no change whatsoever in that of Y. The individual's purchasing power and thus his real income increased.

Suppose though that the price of X had doubled while that of Y remained the same. The equilibrium position for A would now be:

$$\frac{MUx}{Px} = \frac{16}{£4} = \frac{MUy}{Py} = \frac{4}{£1}$$

and A will purchase only 1 unit of X as against 8 of Y. A has substituted part of his spending on X for that of Y.

When the price of a commodity rises the quantity demanded falls and the consumer's real income falls too. The income effect then reinforces the substitution effect.

INFERIOR AND GIFFEN GOODS

Up to this point we have considered only normal goods. When there is a rise in the price of an inferior good (e.g. coach as against rail travel) the substitution effect tends to reduce demand for the inferior good but the income effect does not reinforce it but works in the opposite direction. Because the substitution effect is stronger than the income effect the demand curve remains conventional i.e. it slopes downwards from left to right. With Giffen goods, on the other hand, the income effect overwhelms the substitution effect and we get instead the uncharacteristic, positive (i.e. upwards sloping) demand curve.

ALLOCATIVE EFFICIENCY

The production possibility "curve" described in Chapter 1 demonstrates the possibilities and limits of "technical efficiency". Allocative efficiency refers to the representation of society's preferences (as expressed through demand for goods and services) within the constraints of technical efficiency.

Society's demand for goods and services can be simplified into two products, X and Y. Opportunity cost means that if more of either of these products is consumed, less of the alternative can be obtained: this "trading off" principle applies in Figure 6.2. Any combination of X and

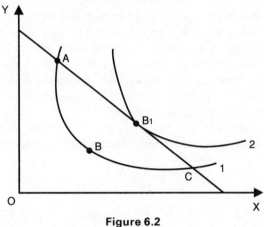

Figure 6.2

Y results in an equal level of total satisfaction: thus, there is indifference in utility terms between points A, B, C. Increased satisfaction could only be achieved by moving onto a higher indifference curve. Society is, however, constrained by production possibilities. If we were at point A, the allocation of resources could be improved in the shorter term by moving factors of production away from Y towards X. This could be taken as far as point B1, which, within the technological constraints, represents the optimum allocation of resources. With technological advance, the production possibility curve would shift to the right, facilitating greater total combinations of X and Y.

QUESTIONS

1. Why is marginal utility so much more important than total utility? Explain, in terms of utility, why a necessity such as salt is cheap while luxuries we can easily manage without are so expensive. What other reasons can you suggest?

2. How do rational consumers obtain an equilibrium leval of utility?

3. How is that a person's total utility can be increased by exchanging goods with another person?

CHAPTER 7

PRODUCTION AND SPECIALISATION

WHAT IS PRODUCTION?

Production to the economist means the *creation of goods and services to satisfy wants*. It is not limited to those activities more obviously associated with production in the physical sense – farming, manufacturing and mining – but includes banking, insurance, travel and the provision of holidays, the social services, the police and the armed forces. In other words, production includes any activity for which we individually, or society in general, are prepared to pay. However, this definition excludes many useful activities. The work of the housewife is not classified as having economic value nor is the house or car maintenance performed by her husband. The same is true of the valuable voluntary work undertaken by many people.

PRODUCTION – A COMBINATION OF FACTORS

Production is hardly ever dependent on a single factor of production – even the self-employed writer must buy paper and typewriter. Production depends on a *combination* of the various *factors of production* – land, labour, capital and the entrepreneur. One or more of these factors may be used than any of the others. Farming in the U.K. for example, uses a relatively small amount of labour, placing considerable reliance on machinery in addition, of course, to the land itself. Across the Atlantic agriculture is frequently more capital-intensive but in the less developed world labour is plentiful and machinery much less used.

DIRECT AND INDIRECT PRODUCTION

If a person works only to satisfy his own and his family's wants he is said to engage in *direct production*. Robinson Crusoe's experience is the classic case. In the modern world, however, direct production is only to be found among primitive people whose agriculture, fishing and hunting does not extend beyond mere subsistence. Production in such societies is very low. What surplus there is will be bartered, exchanged or sold for the surplus production of other subsistence producers.

In all more advanced countries there is a greater or lesser degree of *indirect production*. Many of us still produce a few of our own wants – some vegetables and clothing, for example; and "do-it-yourself" has never been more popular. Most of us, however, earn a living in some specialised branch of the economy. What we "produce" is useful but perhaps not at all to ourselves. For our labours we receive a wage or salary and we use this money freely on those goods and services which satisfy our needs. In advanced economies, therefore, economic activity is based upon indirect production.

TYPES OF PRODUCTION

Indirect production can be conveniently divided into *three* groups – primary, secondary and tertiary production.

Primary production is, as the term suggests, the most natural and basic form of production known to man. In primitive societies it is virtually the only form of production, whilst in advanced societies although still absolutely vital it is economically less important. Indeed, in the UK we depend for a great deal of our food and raw materials on primary producers overseas. Examples of primary production are:

1. Agriculture.   4. Mining.
2. Forestry.   5. Quarrying.
3. Fishing.   6. Oil drilling.

Much more important in advanced economies is *secondary production* which encompasses the vast range of practical trades and the whole of manufacturing industry. Secondary production is wholly dependent on one or more forms of primary production. Good manufacture and tractor production, for example, are completely dependent for their existence on primary products.

In the most advanced societies of all, certainly in the U.K., a third kind of production – *tertiary production* – is becoming increasingly important. Tertiary production covers all forms of economic activity that are not included under either of the two other categories. Examples of tertiary production are:

1. Traders – wholesale and retail; importers and exporters.
2. Transport and communications – road, rail and air networks; postal and telecommunications services.
3. Financial – banks, insurance companies, accountants, etc.
4. Social – police, medicine, education, etc.

The predominance of tertiary industry in Britain today is shown in Figure 7.1.

(a) In terms of the number of persons employed

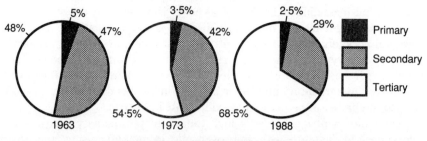

CSO: Annual Abstract of Statistics

(b) In terms of the Gross Domestic Product for 1988:

The comparable figures for 1988 reflect the increasing capital-intensiveness of primary activities (oil extraction and, increasingly, in coal mining).
The service activities in the tertiary are heavily labour-intensive.

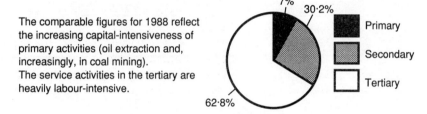

Figure 7.1: Primary, Secondary and Tertiary Industry in the U.K.

These "industries" are sometimes organised into firms or other forms of organisation, some of which are very large. On the other hand, many

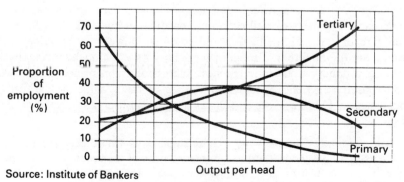

Source: Institute of Bankers

Figure 7.2: Types of Industry and Productivity.

of those engaged in tertiary production provide a service which is essentially personal. Often these are self-employed people or they may work in business units in fields such as advertising or estate agency.

An important feature of industrialisation is the cumulative nature of technological change. In this country the movement away from primary and secondary production has resulted in an enormous increase in output per head (Figure 7.2). Not only has the percentage of people employed in agriculture and other primary industries declined by so has the total number of people employed in those industries.

Unemployment may be very high today but productivity per person continues to increase with improvements in manufacturing and the expansion of tertiary activities (Table 7.1).

Table 7.1: Manufacturing Output 1984–1989
(1985 = 100)

	Total production	Production per person
1984	97·6	97·1
1985	100·0	100·0
1986	100·8	103·0
1987	106·6	109·8
1988	114·1	115·9
1989	119·6	121·8

Source: CSO-Economic Trends

DIVISION OF LABOUR

Indirect production then – whether primary, secondary or tertiary – involves the uses of factors of production in combinations which produce the required goods and services. Since time immemorial mankind has, to a varying degree, been aware, perhaps intuitively, that indirect production leads to greater overall economic production and thus to a higher standard of material satisfaction and comfort. However, it remained to Adam Smith, the father of modern economics, to explain why it was that indirect production was so much more successful. In his principal treatise "An Inquiry into the Nature and Causes of the Wealth of Nations" published in 1776 he wrote as follows about his observations at a small factory:

"One man draws out the wire, another straights it, a third cuts it, a fourth points it, a fifth grinds it at the top (for receiving of the head). To make the head requires two or three distinct operations. To put it on is a peculiar business, to whiten the pins is another. It is even a trade by itself to put them into the paper, and the important business of making the pin is divided in this way into 80 different processes, which in some manufactories are all performed by distinct hands.

I have seen a small manufactory of this kind where ten men only were employed, and where some of them consequently performed two or three distinct operations. But although they were very poor and therefore but indifferently accommodated with the necessary machinery they could, when they exerted themselves, make among the 12 lb of pins a day ... But if they wrought separately, without having been educated in this peculiar business they certainly could not have made twenty, and possibly not even one."

The chief features of the *division of labour* which Adam Smith noted were:

1. *Each worker is used to optimum advantage*
In a very simple situation suppose that Jones being a robust man can dig six trenches in one hour to Smith's three. Smith, on the other hand, can plant out cabbages much more rapidly than Jones. Obviously they will get more done if each man concentrates on what he can do best. Even if Jones were to be superior in both activities some division of labour would still be possible if Jones's relative output was greater. If, for example, Jones could dig six trenches to Smith's three but planted out only a few more cabbages than Smith it would still be sensible for Jones to do the digging and for Smith to do the planting.

2. *Economic use of tools*
The men Adam Smith saw working used a variety of tools each one specific to the needs of a particular operation. Each tool was thus used efficiently.

3. *Repetitive Processes*
Manufacture is most efficient when each activity can be broken down into separate stages. Production will be maximised and costs will be lowest when each worker does repetitively the same operation. The more repetitive the activity the easier it is to mechanise or (these days) to computerise it.

Out of these principal features – beneficial to the division of labour – there arise several other obvious advantages.

4. *It reduces costs per unit* which leads to:
(a) greater profit for the manufacturer
(b) higher wages and/or increased leisure time for the workforce.

5. *Quicker production* releases labour and other resources for other industries which improves the national output.

6. *More effective estimation and measurement of costs*
Some measure of the continuing benefits of specialisation in the modern economy may be seen in Table 7.1.

DIVISION OF LABOUR – THE DISADVANTAGES

In terms of economic efficiency, i.e. reduced costs and increased profits the case for division of labour is really unanswerable. However, there are some drawbacks associated with the very high degree of specialisation which is a feature of advanced economies. These may be divided into two groups:

1. disadvantages to labour
2. disadvantages to the firm.

DISADVANTAGES TO LABOUR

1. Many factory and office jobs are dull and repetitive.
2. Standardised production leads to
   (a) decline of craftmanship causing dissatisfaction
   (b) high productivity leading to redundancies and unemployment.
3. Resulting from all of these disadvantages labour relations can suffer.

DISADVANTAGES TO THE FIRM

The business may also suffer disadvantages due to specialisation.

1. Poorer labour relations caused by the problems enumerated above.
2. Inflexibility on the part of the workers and a greater need for retraining and replacement.
3. Inter-dependence within the factory, the firm or the industry leading to bottlenecks in production.

Considerable although all these disadvantages may appear to be, in the last resort they are probably a small price to pay for the many advantages which everyone – entrepreneurs, managers and workers – derives from the benefits of the division of labour.

SPECIALISATION AND MASS PRODUCTION

The expression "division of labour" may appear to imply only that each unit of labour is highly specialised. The term *specialisation* is perhaps more suitable. Smith noted that workers, tools and machines could all be highly specialised. So too are the factors of production. Land may be highly valued because of the mineral wealth it contains or because of its special position next to the sea or in the City of London. In each case it may be suited to some special kind of production. In today's world too the entrepreneur is often a specialist: thus Robert Maxwell in publishing and Mark Weinberg in financial services.

When work is sub-divided amongst a large variety of workers, each of them doing only a small part, and particularly when the manufacture involves one process after another we have classic examples of mass production. Large car producers, for example, keep their factories going day and night throughout the year, closing only for a uniform holiday period, while steel mills are in constant use because the cost of shutting down altogether is too great.

INTRA-FIRM SPECIALISATION

Within the firm specialisation may take place at different plants or factories. Each plant is a *unit of production* – a cost or profit centre for the firm as a whole. Individual plants will sometimes be used only to make one or two components of the final product. Rover Group for example has its factories scattered over different parts of Britain, and in Birmingham alone there are many specialised plants, each dependent on one or more of the others.

INTER-FIRM SPECIALISATION

With the growth of industry, and its subsequent *localisation* i.e. its concentration within a particular geographical area, firms themselves, as we have seen, become specialised. Ford's long ago, ceased to try and manufacture a complete motor car. Specialist firms make many of the individual components which go to make the modern mass-produced vehicle.

REGIONAL SPECIALISATION

Regional specialisation can be a great strength. However, in our consideration of the localisation of industry it was noted that some regions become very highly dependent on one industry; and that when there is a long-standing or permanent decline in the demand for its products this can have very severe consequences for those industries and thus employment prospects.

Regions, originally because of natural advantages such as the presence of raw materials or proximity to power, have often become specialised. Sheffield and its association with steel; Stoke and its concentration on pottery and china are two prime examples.

INTERNATIONAL SPECIALISATION

Natural advantages such as climate and the possession of raw materials make certain areas of the world naturally specialised. Thus rice grown in the Far East and corn in the U.S.A.; uranium is found in Australia and gold in South Africa. Some countries have very little by way of natural resources whilst others have them in abundance. Each country can, however, specialise by producing those goods (and services) in which it has the greatest comparative advantage over other countries.

LIMITATIONS ON SPECIALISATION

There are three major limits on specialisation or the division of labour: technological, monetary and those associated with the size of the market.

As Adam Smith's classic example shows, even in the making of as simple an object as a pin, scope for specialisation, even in the 18th century, was very considerable. Today, given the state of our technology, the manufacture of pins is a good deal simpler and involves virtually no manual labour. The making of a vastly more complex object might only involve a few processes but might be even more efficient if the processes were subdivided further. There must, however, come a point where further subdivision of a process will not be worthwhile or is simply impossible. Thus the most natural constraint upon specialisation is the technological one.

If the monetary system is weak because people fear devaluation, or because as in the Germany of the 1920s hyper-inflation had taken over, then people will trust in goods rather than money. This will seriously hamper the exchange of goods for money, and barter – a primitive form of exchange – will become rampant. A sound monetary system is a prerequisite of specialisation.

Finally and most important of all, it is the size of the market which determines the degree of specialisation possible. Briefly, the market for a product can increase in five ways:

1. By an increase in population either by natural means or by immigration.

2. Improved communications.
3. Increased incomes.
4. Changes in consumer tastes.
5. Changes in political boundaries.

A small isolated community must be more self-sufficient than a larger one. An island nation such as Britain has therefore, traditionally placed greater emphasis on agriculture than might have been the case given our historic role as the leader of the Industrial Revolution. In recent years our own markets have been greatly enlarged as a result of our entry into the European Community.

QUESTIONS

1. What is meant by the term "production"?
2. What benefits does the growth of tertiary industry provide? What problems may be associated with this phenomenon?
3. "Division of labour is a narrow term". Discuss.
4. Contrast inter-firm and intra-firm specialisation.
5. Are there any limits to specialisation?

CHAPTER 8

THE FIRM – TYPES OF BUSINESS UNIT

INTRODUCTION

As we have seen, the economy consists of three main elements – house-holds, firms and government. Households provide the factors of produc-tion – land, labour, capital and entrepreneurship – and firms are organised to produce goods and services to satisfy consumer demand using combinations of the various factors. Some firms make producer goods (otherwise capital goods) such as factory buildings, plant and machinery. Such goods are required by other firms to enable them to produce the goods ultimately required by consumers.

Firms vary both in size and type of ownership from the individual working on his own to the multi-national corporation or state-owned industry. The chief kinds of firm are as follows:

1. The sole proprietor.
2. The partnership.
3. The limited company
    (a) private.
    (b) public.
4. Co-operatives.
5. Nationalised industries.

We shall look briefly at each of these and then return to a consideration of the firm generally, making one or two assumptions which, however, may not always be true for all firms.

RISK AND PROFIT

In the western world the free, capitalist system is based on profit. Businessmen (entrepreneurs) decide what goods to produce or which services they will provide on the basis of the least cost and the highest selling price consistent with the maximisation of profit. As previously states it is a *fundamental assumption* of economics that the businessman is a *profit-maximiser*.

The predominant theory of profit is that profits are the *reward* to the entrepreneur for taking *risks*. Every business is subject to failure and that risk or failure, greatest in the earlier years, is implicit in the demands of those who provide the factors of production. Employees must be paid whether the business makes a profit or not; so must its suppliers; and its bankers are likely to require not merely a higher rate of interest but also a pledge of the firm's assets against risk of default.

So any business must build into its budget not merely a *margin of safety* so that all these claims can be met but also a margin of profit over and above that necessary to compensate it for the undoubted risks involved. In general the more speculative the project the greater will be the potential profit.

Most people dislike risk. If a man can earn £20,000 a year without financial risk he should not consider engaging in a business venture with a 50/50 chance of failure unless that business promises profits of at least £40,000. Profit is the residue that goes to the owners after allowing for all the costs of the business. If the owner gives up employment worth £20,000 (his opportunity cost) to start his own business then he must earn more than that amount before he can truly be said to be making a profit. Net earnings from employment are usually taken in cash. Profits and cash are not the same, however, and most businessmen retain some of their profits in the business. They need to do this to expand, and in inflationary times simply to replace stocks and worn out equipment and machinery.

THE SOLE PROPRIETOR

Individuals trading on their own comprise the vast majority of businesses in existence. The sole proprietorship is the oldest, most natural form of business enterprise and very many great businesses were started in this modest way. Many types of business are particularly suited to this mode of ownership. These businesses are concerned mainly with providing an individual service in a particular locality. Examples abound – hairdressers, sweeps, farmers and small shopkeepers; most of them are sole proprietors.

The success of the sole proprietor depends entirely on the enterprise of the individual. While some of them become highly successful, others do just enough business to satisfy their fairly modest ambitions. Many others who start up on their own subsequently fail and return to working as an employee of a larger firm. Many individuals, however, prefer to work for themselves and do not measure success entirely in terms of profit or loss.

In law the business of a sole proprietor has no separate existence of its own. Thus if a person decides to establish a business putting into it £5,000 of his own savings and incurs debts which have come to exceed his assets the firm's creditors will be able to claim the amount due to them from his personal resources. This may lead to the sole proprietor having to sell his or her home to meet the debts and obligations of the business.

THE PARTNERSHIP

Some of these problems can be overcome by the formation of a partnership – "the relationship which subsists between persons carrying on a business in common with a view to profit", as it is defined in the Partnership Act, 1890. The normal limitation on the size of a partnership is 20 persons but most partnerships are much smaller businesses and consist of just two or three individuals.

In a partnership decision making is shared and the success or failure of the business is not, therefore wholly dependent on one person. In law the death or bankruptcy of one person brings the relationship formally to an end. So although the remaining partners could continue as before this might only be after much trouble and expense. Many partnerships, in fact, do not survive long. Because many of them are informal disagreements abound and problems frequently arise.

With a partnership structure a larger amount of capital can be raised and the partners can agree to share profits and losses on whatever basis they choose, but capital raising is still largely restricted because of the small scale of the business. However, perhaps the main disadvantage of the partnership is that it too suffers from unlimited liability. Indeed, the position is even worse, for partners are jointly and severally (i.e. individually) liable for the debts of the firm. This means that if a partnership fails its creditors could successfully sue any single partner for the whole of the amount due.

A few partnerships are formed under the Limited Partnership Act, 1907. Under this statute one or more partners may be granted limited liability but there must always be one general partner who bears the full unlimited exposure to risk.

SMALL SCALE FIRMS – THE DISADVANTAGES

The disadvantages of sole proprietorship or partnership as a basis of production can be summarised as follows:

1. Dependence on a single person, or a few people, provides limited scope for specialisation.

2. Limited capital restricts growth.
3. The ability to borrow is likewise limited.
4. Illness or death may disrupt or destroy the business.
5. Unlimited liability.

LIMITED COMPANIES

Although some partners may be "sleeping" partners, i.e. partners who share the risks but not the running of the business, in the small firm there is nearly always some combination of ownership and control. Centuries ago, however, it was realised that some businesses needed substantial amounts of capital quite beyond the ability of a few people (unless also very rich) to provide. Furthermore, it was not possible to organise such businesses on a small scale. Thus joint stock companies were formed whereby each individual investor acquired shares in a joint enterprise and shared profits or losses in relation to the amount contributed. However, it was not until 1855 – when the Industrial Revolution was well advanced – that an Act of Parliament enabled companies to be formed giving investors the privilege of limited liability.

Today, although greatly outnumbered by sole proprietors and partnerships the limited company is by far the most important form of business entity. Its advantages can be summarised as follows:

1. Separation of management and ownership.
2. Limited liability.
3. Continuity.
4. Transfer of ownership simple.
5. Raising of capital easier.
6. Borrowing is facilitated.
7. Larger scale operations possible.

A limited company is owned by its shareholders and managed by its directors. In small companies these may well be, and often are, identical. In the larger company, however, there is often all but total separation of these two functions. Look at the accounts of almost any major company: some of the directors may hold some shares but frequently the proportion they hold is minute in relation to the size of the company's assets.

Because of limited liability companies will generally find it easier to raise share capital, individual subscribers knowing that the amount that they pay up (together with any amount outstanding) limits the extent of their liability. Companies raise two main types of share capital – ordinary shares which carry the most risk but also offer the best prospect of reward, and preference shares. Preference shareholders usually receive a fixed dividend, and there is normally a requirement that until all arrears of dividends have been paid the company cannot pay a dividend on its ordinary shares.

It does not follow that lenders will necessarily find limited companies more attractive lending propositions. In the case of the small "one man company" (one where nearly all the shares are owned by a single individual) limited liability will be a disadvantage to the lender. Banks therefore will frequently require the principal shareholder to add his personal guarantee, or even to mortgage his own home, in support of the borrowing. Larger advances, however, will usually be by means of the issue of debentures or other forms of loan capital at fixed rates of interest. Interest must be paid – as a debt – and in due course the loan must be repaid in accordance with the redemption provisions. Holders of loan capital carry less risk than either category of shareholder and have no say in the running of the business. In the event of the failure of the company they rank as creditors (perhaps with security) in any subsequent winding-up.

Table 8.1: The Effects of Gearing

	Low Geared Company £000s	High Geared Company £000s
Share Capital	800	200
10 per cent Loan Capital	200	800
	1,000	1,000
Debt/Equity Ratio	0·25	4·00
Profits (High)	300	300
less Interest	20	80
	280	220
Pre-tax Profits	$^{280}/_{800} = 35\%$	$^{220}/_{200} = 110\%$
Profits (Low)	40	40
less Interest	20	80
	20	(40)
Pre-tax Earnings	$^{20}/_{800} = 2\cdot5\%$	$^{(40)}/_{200} = 20\%$ (Loss)

Only a very few companies have no borrowings whatsoever. Companies which borrow are said to have *gearing*: they are relatively more risky than those companies which do not borrow; and this risk is increased to the extent of the borrowing. If the company's profits are poor – or worse if losses ensue – the interest burden can be a harsh one. Companies, however, naturally hope for the opposite result: that the cost of servicing their borrowings will be more than outweighed by additional profits (see Table 8.1). Companies with considerable dependence on loan capital are said to be "high geared" whilst those with small borrowings are "low geared".

PRIVATE AND PUBLIC COMPANIES

Public companies must have a minimum authorised share capital of £50,000 and the words "public limited company" or the initials p.l.c. must appear after its name. The minimum number of shareholders is set at two and there is no maximum.

The private limited company has no prescribed minimum limit as to capital but must include the word "limited" or the abbreviation "Ltd" in its name. It cannot have more than 50 shareholders excluding employees and former employees. It can, and usually does, restrict the right of shareholders to transfer their shares.

TAXATION OF PROFITS

Sole proprietors and partners are subject to income tax as traders. The whole of their profits, whether distributed or otherwise, will be subject to tax in the hands of the individuals concerned. It is the individual partners rather than the business of the partnership which are taxed. A limited company, on the other hand, will be subject to tax on its profits after interest. Thus:

		£
Profits before interest		150,000
less interest		10,000
		140,000
less Corporation Tax		40,500
		99,500
	£	
less Preference dividend –	7,500	
Ordinary dividend –	20,500	28,000
Retained profits		71,500

In the case of loan capital the interest will be paid to holders net of income tax at the basic rate. Thus in the above case (assuming basic rate of 25 per cent) £7,500 will be paid to the holders of the loan stock and £2,500 to the Inland Revenue.

Dividends, on the other hand, are paid after the imposition of corporation tax. This makes share capital relatively more expensive to the company than loan capital, and explains why preference shares are not so popular today. Dividends are payable in full to the shareholders who also receive a tax credit relieving them of liability to basic rate tax. Thus, in the above case, the preference shareholders' £7,500 dividend is, in cash terms, the same as the loan stockholders' £10,000. However, because the interest is paid before the imposition of corporation tax the servicing of loan capital is less expensive than that of share capital.

ADDITIONAL FINANCE

So far we have looked at share capital and loan capital as the only means of company finance but there are other means too. Companies frequently borrow from banks by means of overdrafts – for short term needs – or on loan account over the longer term. Very important sources of funds for companies are their creditors. To the extent that the company receives supplies on credit this relieves them of the need to provide alternative finance or to rely still more on their bankers.

Funds for expansion, if they do not come from ploughed-back profits, must come from outside the business. The most obvious source will be existing shareholders. If the company wishes to raise additional share capital then it must do so by means of a rights issue, so-called because the ordinary shareholders (the members of the company), have the right to provide new equity funds (i.e. ordinary shares) in priority to all other parties. Three alternative kinds of issue may be made:

1. A further issue of shares.
2. An issue of convertible loan stock – an unsecured stock carrying fixed terms for conversion into ordinary shares.
3. An issue of warrants. These carry no interest or dividend rights but may also be converted into ordinary shares at a later date.

In practice a rights issue may consist of a combination of two of the above. Both public and private companies make such issues but there may come a time for the private company when it cannot raise all the capital it needs in this way. The business may have great potential but the directors, their family and friends together do not have the resources to acquire more shares or stock.

Many private companies are now able to take advantage of some government schemes to raise additional finance. One such is the Small Firms Loan Guarantee Scheme whereby 70 per cent of the loan subject to a stipulated maximum amount, is guaranteed by the government. This scheme, however, is relatively costly to the borrower. Another, the Business Expansion Scheme, enables high rate taxpayers to invest substantial amounts in some unquoted businesses setting off the cost of their investment for tax purposes. A number of special funds have been created to channel money into smaller businesses in this way.

Banks which used to consider virtually all their lending as short term are now more inclined to lend over the medium and even the long term. Some finance may also be available from organisations such as ICFC, the small loans division of Investors in Industry.*

In addition many of the merchant banks, either themselves or through their subsidiaries, are prepared to assist growing companies. These lenders, however, usually require part of the company's equity if they are asked to provide a major part of the funds.

A successful approach to a merchant bank will often pave the way for a listing on the Stock Exchange. To obtain a quotation the company, if still private, must be converted into a public company. Flotation may be on the Stock Exchange's Unlisted Securities Market or by means of a full listing. Today the company "going public" will usually do so by means of a quotation on the nursery market in the first instance because this is considerably less expensive.

Coming to the market can take several forms. On the major market the offer for sale is the most favoured method. Such issues must be advertised in the national press, and anybody can apply for the shares which may be sold at a fixed price or by tender. A placing, on the other hand, much more common on the U.S.M., is made privately mainly to the clients of the issuing house or dealers responsible for the issue. Placings are considerably less expensive than offers for sale and are only permitted for relatively small company issues.

CO-OPERATIVES

In a primitive sense the co-operative is probably even older than the joint stock company but, the co-operative movement as such was born in Rochdale in 1844. It was then that a group of some 20 cotton workers banded together, rented a shop and started trading in groceries and other basic commodities. The Rochdale Society of Equitable Pioneers

* ICFC − formerly Industrial and Commercial Finance Corporation.

was formed not to satisfy the profit motive of its founders. Instead the
cash surplus was distributed to members in relation to their purchases.
Within a few decades the movement was international in scope and
outlook and was engaged in both the retail and wholesale trade. In the
U.K. the individual retail societies are each members of the Co-operative
Wholesale Society and so all of its surplus is divided between them.

In comparatively recent years the complex book-keeping system necessary to record dividends on every single purchase became increasingly
unworkable as the co-ops faced stiffer competition from the major
supermarket groups. The old "divi" system was abolished, and customers
– whether members or otherwise – receive trading stamps instead. These
are redeemable in cash or in goods and a bonus is allocated to those
customers who are also members.

Another type of co-operative is the producer co-operative. These are
typically established by relatively small farmers as in Denmark and New
Zealand. Purchasing co-operatives concentrate their efforts on buying
raw materials such as seed and fertilisers, while marketing co-operatives
specialise in the sale and distribution of crops, livestock and animal
products.

Friendly societies, building societies and mutual insurance companies
also operate on broadly co-operative principles.

MANAGEMENT BUY-OUTS (MBOs)

A noticeable feature of recent years has been a surge in the number of

Table 8.2: Estimate of Total UK MBOs.

	Number	Value (£m)	Average size (£m)
1980	100	40	0·4
1981	180	130	0·7
1982	200	550	2·8
1983	220	240	1·1
1984	200	270	1·4
1985	250	1,070	4·3
1986	300	1,320	4·4
1987	350	3,270	9·3
1988	400	5,000	12·5
1989*	300	5,570	18·6
	2,500	17,460	7·0

* First nine months
Accountancy: February 1990

Table 8.3: Management Buy-Outs.

	Number Sold	Number floated on Stock Exchange
1988	48	34
1989	72	11

Centre for Management Buy-Out Research,
University of Nottingham.

"management buy-outs". The companies became available for management acquisition either as ailing subsidiaries of a parent company or as still prosperous companies which are part of a strategic disinvestment programme by the parent organisation. Typically, the senior managers provide, say, £60,000 each to obtain a disproportionate share of the equity. The bulk of the funding then comes from bank loans secured as assets, making the business vulnerable to the consequences of high "leverage" if there is a down-turn in the product market. If the business is successful, the managers' eventual return is likely to be proportionally much more than the increase in the value of the business.

Advocates of MBOs contend that extra management effort, including the enforcing of strict control systems, is at the heart of any success. Moreover, all employees of the business soon become aware that the business is no longer cocooned within a much larger organisation.

The risks to the individual investing managers are high, especially in periods of economic recession. There has, indeed, been a marked increase in the number of buy-outs which choose to sell themselves subsequently to another company, rather than retain their independence – though by no means all of these were suffering from poor trading results.

NATIONALISED INDUSTRIES

A part of U.K. industry is today still partly or wholly under the control of public corporations – bodies established by Act of Parliament to organise and run specific industries. Some of these provide a service but do not trade. These include the B.B.C. and the U.K. Atomic Energy Authority. We are concerned here with those that provide a service or sell a product like any other business.

The government appoints members to the boards of each of the nationalised industries but refrains from day to day involvement in the running of them. However from time to time, especially when it is also a major customer, the government does take a more active interest in their affairs, as indeed it should.

The aims of the nationalised industries are more complex than those of commercial undertakings. For the latter, profit is the chief, if not the only, criterion of success. Many nationalised industries were formed, however, because under private ownership they were no longer profitable and thus could not find the investment necessary for the replacement of assets, still less any for expansion. A very important consideration is the need for continuing investment in strategic areas of the economy. Left to private enterprise alone it is conceivable that the railway system today would be very much smaller with consequently even more traffic congestion on our roads.

Some of the nationalised industries may be considered "natural monopolies" because the average cost of their product or service is much lower than it would be if competition were allowed. Electricity generation and supply and the Post Office are two such examples. If I post a letter to another person in the same town it will cost me the same as if I posted it to him on a remote Scottish island. Left to private enterprise inter-city postage rates would be cheaper but a letter to the Outer Hebrides might cost £1 or more.

The proponents of the state ownership of industry can put forward a number of arguments in favour of nationalisation.

1. It guarantees the supply of essential goods and services at fair prices.
2. It ensures adequate and continuing investment because:
   (a) Capital can be provided out of taxation or borrowed funds.
   (b) Profitability is not the only criterion for investment.
3. Economies of Scale (see Chapter 7).
4. Avoidance of competition based on the grounds that:
   (a) Advertising is wasteful.
   (b) Competition leads to higher prices or, on the other hand,
   (c) It can lead to price cutting and hence unsafe or otherwise unsatisfactory products.

Some of these arguments may be considered tendentious e.g. that competition necessarily leads to higher prices. Often the very reverse is the case. A strong case, however, can be made on the first two grounds.

A number of disadvantages must also be cited:

1. Diseconomies of scale. Whilst there are many advantages of large scale organisation there usually comes a time when diminishing returns are achieved. An excessively bureaucratic management might be one such diseconomy.

2. Profit-making being of secondary importance, nationalised industries may be run less efficiently in terms of:
   (a) Control of costs and thus also prices.
   (b) Decision making may be either careless or excessively cautious.
   (c) Business decisions may be influenced by politicians and civil servants.

To a very large extent nationalisation is a political football – a panacea to those on the political left but anathema to those on the right. What is important, however, is to be able to see both sides of the argument. Even in capitalist strongholds like the United States there is a measure of public ownership. In many cases it is agreed that it is an essential part of the economy, and given the constraints imposed upon them, nationalised industries are probably run as effectively as many, if not most, large corporations.

PRIVATISATION

In recent decades some industries have been denationalised or "privatised". The recent trend, "privatisation", means that the public is invited to subscribe for shares and the company becomes a public limited company with a stock exchange quotation. British Aerospace in 1980, and the hiving off of British Telecom from the Post Office and the privatisation of British Gas are cases in point.

Privatisation includes, inter alia, (a) the selling of nationalised industries (as mentioned above); (b) the contracting out of services, such as cleaning and catering in the health service; and (c) the deregulation of other nationalised industries.

There are many motives for the public sale of nationalised industries, including:

1. The claimed improvement in efficiency that should result, on the grounds that the private sector operates more efficiently than the public sector. This claim is also made to support the contracting out of services.
2. The proceeds can be used to assist government financing.
3. The means of extending share ownership among a wider public.

Any discussion of whether private concerns are more efficient turns on the recognition of two types of inefficiency: allocative inefficiency, where an enterprise operates with prices higher than marginal cost (see Chapters 6 and 14); and production inefficiency, where the costs of production are higher under one type of operation compared with another.

Allocative inefficiency, as an aspect of monopoly, may occur in publicly or privately owned concerns. By retaining essentially the same natural monopoly structures in privatised enterprises, allocative inefficiency may remain. Hence the importance of the regulatory mechanisms which the government has introduced e.g. OFTEL in the case of BT, and the Director General of Water Services in the case of the privatised water industry. It remains to be seen how effective these are.

Production inefficiency may occur in both the public and private sectors. Operating inefficiency is much more likely to be supported by State subsidies in the public than the private sector. Moreover, those running a privately owned enterprise (and having a Stock Exchange quotation) could be the subject of a take-over bid if the performance level is unreasonably low – a pressure not placed upon the managements of nationalised concerns.

De-regulation has not been so extensively carried out. Bus companies have been given greater freedom to operate; while in 1983 electricity supply was deregulated so that private suppliers could operate and make use of the publicly owned distribution network. The take-up in the latter case has been minimal. Mercury is, however, providing lively competition for British Telecom PLC in some parts of the telecommunications market.

QUESTIONS

1. Discuss the relationship between profit and risk.

2. What advantages does the limited compnay have in small scale enterprise?

3. Contrast the cooperatives with the nationalised industries. Are their aims similar?

4. Why is borrowing both a risk and an opportunity?

5. Where might an expanding company look for further finance?

CHAPTER 9

THEORY OF PRODUCTION

THE SHORT RUN AND THE LONG RUN

In economics the term the *short run* is used to denote the period during which a *fixed factor of production cannot be increased*. Some factors of production are typically fixed. Land certainly comes into this category. So it follows that the cost of using this factor – rent – must be regarded as a long run cost. The number of people employed within the firm can, however, be varied much more easily so labour costs are usually regarded as short run costs. Managerial costs, on the other hand, cannot be altered in the short run and therefore have the properties of fixed costs – and therefore *long run* costs.

It is important to recognise that the short run is not a specific time period and that it will vary from industry to industry. In North Sea exploration, capital (equipment) is clearly a long run cost, while for the firm engaged in vehicle hire new cars may be obtained readily and immediately put into use. Likewise the long run is not a specific period. Indeed, by its very nature it is indeterminate. Although defined as the period during which fixed costs can be increased, the long run is continuously being extended and, as we shall see later, is made up of an indefinite number of short run periods.

In the long run all factors of production are variable. Thus a firm can either employ more units of a particular factor or vary the combination of factors to achieve the desired level of production.

THE FACTOR MIX

In most enterprises all of the factors of production will be used to a greater or lesser degree. As we have seen each factor may be to some extent a substitute for one or more of the others. Thus if I have a smallholding (land) I can exploit this more fully by applying fertiliser (capital) in addition to the use of my own labour. A farmer will use units of land, labour and capital in those proportions which he believes will give him the most abundant return.

There are, however, limits to which factors can be productively

Table 9.1: Production with one fixed and one variable factor of production.

Units of Labour	Total Product	Marginal Production	Average Product
0	0		0
1	2	2	2
2	5	3	2·5
3	9	4	3
4	12	3	3
5	14	2	2·8
6	15	1	2·5
7	15	0	2·14
8	14	−1	1·75

employed. In each case there will come a point when taking on another worker or using another tonne of fertiliser will yield a less than worth-while return – the point of *diminishing returns* will have been reached.

The only way output can be changed in the short run is by changing the inputs of the variable factors of production. For the sake of simplicity let us consider a situation where there is only one variable factor, labour. Output can be changed in the short run only by varying the inputs of this factor.

In Table 9.1 we show some hypothetical data for agricultural produc-tion. To one unit of land is added successive quantities of labour, each of them of equal value. In column 2 we show the total production achieved and in column 3 what we call the marginal product – the increase (or decrease) in production which results from employing one more man. Column 4 shows the average product (Column 2/Column 1).

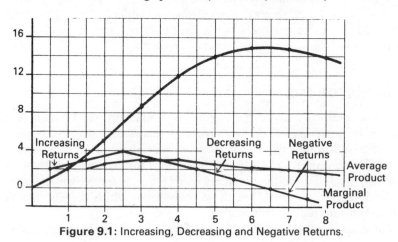

Figure 9.1: Increasing, Decreasing and Negative Returns.

As the table shows the addition of a second and then a third man results in an increase in the marginal product and the three of them together produce 9 units. Thereafter the marginal product begins to fall and finally, as the land becomes increasingly overworked, the marginal product becomes negative. In Figure 9.1 the same information is presented graphically. It shows clearly the *three* possible stages of production – *increasing* returns, *diminishing* returns and finally *negative* returns. Of course the producer will not knowing continue production to a level at which total production actually falls.

THE MARGINAL PRODUCT

It must be realised that the additional product in each case is not necessarily the work of the additional man. Each unit of production is assumed to be of equal worth. Production increases because of the greater degree of specialisation possible. When the marginal product declines this is not due to the inefficiency of one man. A point of diminishing returns inevitably results and this has given rise to what is known as the *law of diminishing returns*. This explains, in some measure, the poverty of some third world countries where the land is overworked or overgrazed and hence impoverished.

The *average product*, it will be noted, does not rise as rapidly as the *marginal product* but neither does it fall so rapidly once diminishing returns set in. The relationship between the average product and the marginal product is such that they are *equal* when the average product is at its *maximum*. So long as the marginal product is greater than the average product then the latter must also be rising even though the marginal product itself may be falling. If, on the other hand, the marginal cost has sunk below average cost then it will pull down average cost with it.

In an economics textbook it is convenient to use an agricultural example to demonstrate the law of diminishing returns but the law most certainly applies in all other fields of economic activity too.

DIMINISHING RETURNS

This universal phenomenon is the basis of one of the fundamental laws of economics – the *law of diminishing returns*. The law states that the marginal productivity of a factor will at some level of production begin to fall. It is even possible for it to be negative as in the proverbial "too many cooks spoil the broth" situation. The following assumptions underlie the law of diminishing returns.

1. At least one factor is assumed to be fixed.

2. The units of the variable factor are homogenous.

3. The law does not apply if certain factors must be applied in proportions.

4. There are no changes in production techniques.

Thus, in the above example, the land is fixed and all the workers are assumed to have equal abilities. Each man must use the same tools or equipment and each will employ the same method of using them throughout.

Usually factors other than just land and labour will also be used. How then do we compare the productivity of labour with that of capital? Should the farmer have used more labourers or more fertiliser and machinery? Fundamental to this consideration are the different prices he must pay for each of these factors. To achieve equilibrium production he will vary the factors until the following relationship applies.

$$\frac{\text{Marginal Product of Product A}}{\text{Price of Factor A}} = \frac{\text{Marginal Product of Product B}}{\text{Price of Factor B}}$$

If the price of one of the factors rises then clearly this relationship no longer holds true and it will pay the farmer to substitute some other factor for it until this equilibrium is restored.

RETURNS TO SCALE

We have looked at a very simple example where one factor of production was fixed and another variable. It is important to realise that while there may be only four identifiable factors of production there are many different forms of land, capital etc. Seed, fertilisers and tractors are all forms of capital to the farmer, and as we have seen the farmer or any other entrepreneur will endeavour to use each of them as efficiently as possible.

Another means of increasing output is by increasing the scale of production. This is quite a different matter because it involves increasing all the inputs in the same proportions. Table 9.2 shows the three possible cases of returns to scale.

Increasing returns to scale. Just as increasing returns are first encountered in the employment of a single variable factor so it may also be with an increase in the scale of production. In such cases all of the factors are increased proportionately with the aim of achieving a greater than proportionate increase in output.

Constant returns to scale. In this case total output increases in exactly

Table 9.2: Returns to Scale.

Units of Capital	Units of Labour	PRODUCTIVITY		
		Increasing Returns	Constant Returns	Decreasing Returns
1	3	100	100	100
2	6	210	200	190
3	9	330	300	270
4	12	460	400	340

the same proportion as the inputs. This situation is fairly commonly found in the real world as firms approach optimum size.

Decreasing returns to scale. The inevitable price which will have to be paid for over-expansion will be decreasing returns to scale. It is, of course, something which is sometimes achieved by accident rather than design.

In the next chapter we shall consider the economies of scale which will bring about increasing returns to scale, but also those diseconomies which frequently arise when firms become too large – when, in fact, diminishing returns to scale begin to occur.

QUESTIONS

1. What is the important difference between the short run and the long run in economics?

2. What do you understand by the law of diminishing returns?

3. Distinguish increasing, decreasing and negative returns. When could returns to scale be constant? How likely is this situation in real life?

CHAPTER 10

THE SCALE OF PRODUCTION

As we have seen modern large scale production is based upon the principles of specialisation. Traditionally, specialisation has meant the division of labour but today, when industry is even more capital-intensive, it is machines too that are highly specialised. As we have also seen in our study of the location of industry, certain geographical areas have become associated with particular industries, and hence have become specialised.

The advantages of producing on a large scale may seem obvious. However, in many areas of activity, even in manufacturing small scale producers remain, and so we must ask the question why this is so. We shall examine in detail the economies (and the diseconomies) of scale and the methods by which firms expand sometimes into multi-national corporations.

ECONOMIES OF SCALE

It is self-evident that the larger firm has some advantages which are not enjoyed by the smaller firm. Indeed the chief motive for the expansion of a plant or a firm will be to reduce costs and hence to increase the opportunity for profit.

The economies of scale are of two main kinds. Internal economies of scale arise *within the firm* and benefit that firm only. External economies of scale, on the other hand, arise *outside the firm* and benefit the industry.

INTERNAL ECONOMIES OF SCALE

The advantages of large scale production over which the individual firm can exercise control are known as the internal economies of scale. These may be divided into seven broad categories:

1. Technical.
2. Administrative and managerial.
3. Commercial.

4. Financial.
5. Research and development.
6. Social (welfare).
7. Risk-bearing.

TECHNICAL ECONOMIES

These are achieved mainly at plant level and typically relate to the size of the business unit. It may, for example, be possible to double the size of the plant, the associated costs of operation increasing by a smaller proportion. A major cost element for most businesses will be the fixed costs. These remain, in the short run, the same whatever the level of output. Therefore, if output will be increased average fixed costs can be reduced.

ADMINISTRATIVE AND MANAGERIAL ECONOMIES

The management of a large firm will be specialised, in contrast to that of a sole proprietor where everything – production, sales, accountants etc. – must be attended to by the same person. Larger companies can afford to employ staff with expertise in each of these and many other areas. They can also employ specialist staff in every field – e.g. accountants, surveyors, research engineers and computer analysts. The smaller firm, if it needs such services must avail itself of them on a consultancy basis at higher cost.

COMMERCIAL ECONOMIES

These are the economies associated with the purchase of raw materials and the sale of goods. The larger firm will purchase its raw materials in bigger quantities than the smaller firm. It will obtain substantial discounts and be given better credit terms. It should never have to reduce its scale of operations owing to a shortage of raw materials.

On the sales side of the business labour will be exclusively (and more fully) used in specialised functions – selling, packing, invoicing and advertising. Good debtor control should minimise the extent of bad debts.

FINANCIAL ECONOMIES

A large firm will be able to raise both equity and loan capital more readily and at lower cost than the smaller firm. It will pay interest on its borrowings at lower rates, and equity investors will not require as big a return because the risks will generally be lower. Moreover the actual costs of raising the finance are likely to be less.

RESEARCH AND DEVELOPMENT EXPENDITURE

This is one kind of expenditure that will normally only be incurred by the larger firm. The purpose of such expenditure is to improve existing products or to develop new ones, and to the extent that it is successful R & D expenditure can give firms a very great advantage over their competitors.

WELFARE ECONOMIES

The larger firm can usually boast a wider variety of employee benefits – a pension scheme, health insurance, housing and car allowances, sports facilities and so on. These will enable it to attract and retain good staff who will remain loyal to the company.

RISK-BEARING ECONOMIES

The large organisation may sometimes be able to be its own insurer. If, for example, it owns a large number of vehicles it may take out only the basic insurance cover in the expectation that its "claims" experience will average out close to the expectations of the insurance market. This policy is followed by some local authorities in regard to the insurance of public buildings.

Quite another form of "risk insurance" is the diversification of a company's product lines so that if market demand declines for certain products this may be compensated by increased demand for some of its other products. Large company profits for this reason are, on average, less volatile than those of smaller firms.

EXTERNAL ECONOMIES OF SCALE

Firms may also achieve what we call external economies of scale. These economies have nothing to do with the savings and benefits obtained within the firm but arise because certain economies benefit all the firms in an industry or in the same area.

External economies of scale may be divided into four main categories:

1. Concentration.
2. Service.
3. Information.
4. Welfare.

ECONOMIES OF CONCENTRATION

These arise from the concentration of an industry in a particular locality, sometimes long after the intial reasons for its establishment there have passed (i.e. industrial inertia). These will include the supply of skilled labour, the existence of specialist training facilities and the reputation of the region for the products of the industry. The steel industry in Sheffield and the manufacture of bone china around Stoke-on-Trent are two classic examples of this kind of concentration.

SERVICE ECONOMIES

Closely related to the economies of concentration are what are called "service economies". When an industry is well established in an area other firms set themselves up there to take advantage of the market which the larger firms provide. Thus, in the West Midlands, for instance, there are very many small firms whose existence is dependent on the motor industry; and in the City of London a large number of firms – from sandwich bars to stationers – cater for the big banks and other City institutions and their staffs. Service economies are mutually beneficial.

INFORMATION ECONOMIES

Larger firms in the same industry usually band together to form trade associations to advance their mutual interests. They prescribe standards of workmanship and behaviour. Such associations are frequently national in character and so are not necessarily to be found near to the location of the industry, and many are based in London.

Through membership of such associations individual firms may be able to do some things together that they could not do as well on their own. "Woolmark" advertising, for example, aims not to advance the sales of a particular brand of clothing or carpets but to generate and increase interest in wool products generally.

WELFARE ECONOMIES

In addition to those benefits provided by the firm there are some advantages which are associated with the place. Closely related to the economies of concentration these include the provision of roads, schools, hospitals and parks, all of which go to make the area a more attractive one in which to live. The level of rate demands – local taxation – is another factor the industrialist must bear in mind. Areas that are pleasant to live in more easily attract staff. The author recalls having his removal expenses paid when he moved to Birmingham but not on his transfer to Worcester!

DISECONOMIES OF SCALE

Generally speaking large-scale production is advantageous where suitable markets exist. However, as output rises and the organisation of the firm gets more complex some operations of the firm may become less efficient.

We probably all know the experience of making an enquiry and being passed from one person to another until someone who can deal with our enquiry can be found! It is frustrating for us and wasteful of the firm's time and resources. We can divide the diseconomies of scale into internal diseconomies and external diseconomies of scale.

INTERNAL DISECONOMIES OF SCALE

These may arise in almost any area of larger businesses – technical, managerial, commercial, etc. but will usually be more than outweighed by the benefits of the internal economies of scale.

TECHNICAL DISECONOMIES OF SCALE

There may be some disadvantages to doubling plant size. It makes the firm more heavily dependent on the plant than if it were based in two separate locations. In some cases larger capacity may involve heavier costs because better quality materials are necessitated by the method of production.

MANAGERIAL DISECONOMIES OF SCALE

Relations between management and staff, and with the general public, may become impersonal and strained. Decision making becomes more complex, involving more people – perhaps a committee – and, above all, the organisation tends to become more bureaucratic. This is one of the criticisms sometimes levelled at the nationalised industries.

EXTERNAL DISCECONOMIES OF SCALE

Whilst the concentration of an industry within a region is usually an advantage there may also be some disadvantages. When the degree of concentration becomes excessive and leads to traffic congestion, over-crowding and a shortage of satisfactory amenities some of the benefits of growth are lost. Some firms have decentralised – have moved their operations out of the capital – because of these problems. If the industry is subject to changes in tastes and fashion then the whole area can become depressed, and many smaller firms – and even some larger ones – may fail.

RETURNS TO SCALE – THE OPTIMUM FIRM

As a firm grows in size units costs will normally fall. There is however a limit to this process. At some point in its development, a firm may achieve constant costs where an increase in inputs is reflected by an equivalent increase in output. When a firm has achieved this position, and before its costs begin to escalate, it is said to be operating at optimum size. Most firms, however, do not make a single product or provide only one service so the process of optimisation is really one of optimising each separate area of the firm's operations. In practice, ascertaining whether a firm is operating at optimum capacity is extremely difficult.

Since small firms co-exist with large ones it is clearly possible for firms to survive which have not achieved an optimal scale of operations. It is therefore appropriate to consider whether optimisation is not a relative rather than an absolute state. Within an industry there is probably an optimum size for small firms, another for medium-sized firms and yet another for those which are very large. The smallest firms have not yet achieved minimisation of their technical and managerial costs whilst the largest of them all is quite likely to be affected by the diseconomies of scale.

THE SURVIVAL OF THE SMALL FIRM

In almost every field of activity the small firm exists. Although such firms individually do not employ many people, nevertheless together they make a substantial impact on total output. The Bolton Committee on Small Firms (1971) defined "small" in a number of ways. In retailing a turnover of £50,000 or less and in manufacturing 200 employees or less, were two of the bases used. However, in manufacturing industry – as well as in industry – there are many more small firms (i.e. with less

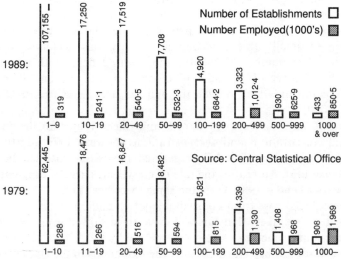

Figure 10.1: Size of Manufacturing Units – 1989 and 1979.

than 20 employees) than all the rest put together. Figure 10.1 shows the figures for 1989 together with comparative figures for 1979.

A number of reasons can be advanced for this phenomenon – in manufacturing, retailing and in the service industries generally.

1. SIZE OF THE MARKET

If demand is small or extremely localised there is no economic justification for large scale production.

2. PERSONAL SERVICE

Corner shops, hairdressers and printers all survive because they can offer individual service. This is also true of small manufacturers who provide a "service" to larger companies within their area of operations.

3. ENTREPRENEURIAL LIMITATION

The major of small businessmen do not have the capability to run a large scale business, and some of those who have such ability may in any case prefer to keep their business small.

Some benefits may arise from smallness – personal supervision, speed of decision making and better employer/employee relationships for instance. Even in the field of innovation small businessmen sometimes outshine their better equipped competitors notwithstanding the substantial expenditure on research and development by larger firms.

DEVELOPMENT OF SMALL FIRMS

A notable feature of the 1980s was the growth in the number of small businesses and of self-employed persons. Up to the mid-1960s the contribution of small firms to economic activity was declining in most industries. The number of small manufacturing firms with under 200 staff halved between 1924 and 1963 before stabilising around 82,000. In the six years from 1980 to 1986 the number rose again from 87,000 to over 128,000.

Figure 10.2 shows Department of Employment figures for the number of V.A.T. registrations and de-registrations. Between 1979 and the end of 1988 the number of V.A.T. registered businesses rose by 285,000, some 22 per cent. Moreover, the rate of growth was accelerating over the three years to end – 1988. Over the same three-year period the numbers of self-employed rose from approximately two million to just over three million. It seems likely that this will leave since slowed given the effects of the economic squeeze.

This growth has been facilitated by the reductions in the rate of "small company" Corporation Tax to 25 per cent as well as by tax-effective

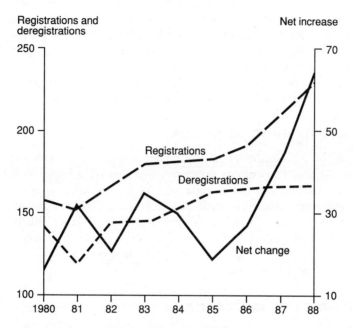

Figure 10.2. Business Registering for VAT. Source: Economic Progress Report, December 1989.

finance through the Business Expansion Scheme. Help is also provided to unemployed people to set up their own businesses. The Enterprise Allowance Scheme pays an allowance of £40 per week for a year.

Since 1983 over 450,000 people have been assisted. Of those who complete a year on the scheme, 65 per cent are still trading three years after starting (Oct. 1989).

Small firms are undoubtedly of importance in the development of the economy.

(a) they make a disproportionate contribution to job creation. Between 1982 and 1984, for instance, very small firms (employing fewer than 20 people), including the self-employed, created around 1 million additional jobs.

(b) they are a major part of the "seedbed" for future business growth.

FACTORIES AND PLANT: FIRMS AND THE INDUSTRY

A factory is a place where goods are manufactured. It is a term we all understand but is perhaps a little vague for economists who prefer the term plant which encompasses all forms of production – goods and services. The plant is a production unit based in a particular geographical location. It may produce a range of products or services or it may be highly specialised, concentrating on only one kind of output.

The firm is the business unit – sole trader, limited company etc. – and it may control one or more plants in one or more industries.

THE SIZE OF PRODUCTION UNITS

The size of production units will be influenced by technological and market factors. Thus motor manufacturing and oil refining need to be undertaken on a large scale while jobs such as welding or glazing are more frequently done by small business units. Similar considerations apply to services. A village may have but a single bank which opens twice a week and offers a limited service during restricted hours. On the other hand, banks in large cities may have branches wholly devoted to foreign or trustee business.

HOW FIRM SIZE IS MEASURED

It might be thought that it is easy to measure the size of firms. There are a number of ways this can be done. None of them alone, however, would appear to be completely satisfactory. Some measures may be suitable for a single industry but would be quite inadequate for making comparisons between different industries.

Three methods may be considered seriously defective:

1. NUMBER OF EMPLOYEES – because some firms are less labour intensive than others and because of differences in hours worked. This method is, however, widely used to measure the relative sizes of small firms.

2. CAPITAL EMPLOYED – because there is no general consensus among economists or accountants about the measning of the term. Three commonly adopted measures are:

    (a) Equity capital – i.e. ordinary shares and reserves
    (b) Long term funds – i.e. all share capital and loan capital
    (c) Total assets.

3. PROFITABILITY – Like capital employed, profit is not a precise concept and again several yardsticks may be used. Furthermore, profits can be very volatile – a profit in one year may turn into a loss in the next. On its own, therefore, this is a very unsatisfactory means of measuring firm size.

Two rather more satisfactory methods are market capitalisation and turnover.

MARKET CAPITALISATION

This is the method used by the *Financial Times* in its annual survey of U.K. and European companies. It is a more sophisticated yardstick than capital employed because it does take into account market values. However, it only takes into account the value of the ordinary shareholders' funds ignoring debt capital which may have considerable impact on the size of a firm's operations. Share values are much influenced by profits and, where these are volatile, market values are likely to be so too. Thus there may be little consistency in measurement from year to year even when a firm's level of operations remains broadly constant.

TURNOVER (SALES)

This, perhaps, however, the most satisfactory method of all, is used in *The Times* 1000, a survey of the 1,000 largest industrial companies published each year. Turnover is possibly the ideal measure because, as we shall see later, one of the measures of gross national product is in terms of expenditure. Table 10.1 shows the top 12 U.K. industrial companies listed in terms of volume of sales. It also shows how they would be ranked if two other measures had been used.

While turnover is generally quite suitable in the majority of cases even this can sometimes be misleading. Czarnikow, a relatively small company in terms of capital, is highly placed on turnover. Perhaps the most

Table 10.1: Firm size – The 12 biggest U.K. industrial companies.

	TURNOVER (£m)	RANKING Turnover	RANKING Capital Employed*	Profits†
British Petroleum	34,932	1	1	1
"Shell" Transport & Trading	23,924	2	2	3
BAT Industries	11,255	3	6	5
ICI	11,123	4	7	4
British Telecommunications	10,185	5	5	2
British Gas	7,610	6	3	6
Hanson Trust	6,682	7	8	9
Shell UK	6,677	8	11	7
Grand Metropolitan	5,705	9	16	15
Unilever	5,428	10	17	17
Esso Petroleum	5,397	11	13	8
General Electric Co.	5,247	12	10	12

(*The Times* 1000: 1988/89)

* Tangible assets less current liabilities.
† Net profit before interest and tax.

Table 10.2: Firm size – Britain's two biggests banks.

	At 26.3.90 Market Capitalis'n (£m)	Deposits (£m)	At 31.12.89 Pre-tax Profits (£m) (a) (b)	Number of Employees	Total Assets (£m)
Barclays	6,474	103,806	2,089 692	116,500	127,616
National Westminster	5,339	101,251	1,839 404	113,000	116,189

(a) Before charge/provision for bad and doubtful debts. ⎱ See Chapter 39
(b) After charge/provision for bad and doubtful debts.   ⎰
Source: Annual Accounts and the *Financial Times*.

unsatisfactory aspect of turnover, however, is that it leaves out altogether firms in banking and insurance which do not make "sales" in the usually accepted sense of the word. In the case of banks the levels of deposits is one of several methods adopted for measuring relative size.

There is a growing view in the field of banking that sheer size is not as important as it was. The larger banks have been the least profitable since "Big Bang" of 1986. The importance of capital varies between the different branches of banking. Joseph Burnett-Stuart of Flemings, merchant bankers, was quoted in the *Financial Times*: "Some people say that you need lots of capital in this business. But I've always believed that the trick is to manage with as little capital as possible."

THE GROWTH OF FIRMS

Firms grow in size for several reasons:

1. Growth in the size of the market.
2. Increase in market share.
3. Production of new goods.
4. Acquisition of other businesses.

Of these the first is generally outside the control of the business although it (and the industry generally) may contribute to market growth by advertising. In some cases the market may not grow much, if at all – the market for basic foods for example. However, more efficient businesses may nonetheless expand by capturing a larger share of the existing market. In food retailing for example, Sainsbury's have done this at the expense of the co-operative societies; while in banking Barclays' resumption of Saturday opening after 13 years (since followed by the other Banks) had the same objective.

Another important reason for growth is by diversification – by producing a wider variety of goods or further services. In the last twenty years

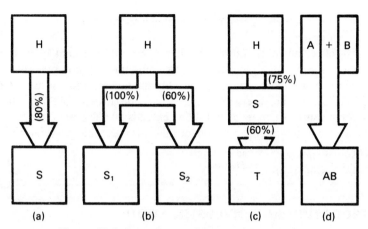

Figure 10.3: Some Forms of Business Combination.

the banks have all moved strongly in this direction – providing hire purchase finance, unit trusts, life assurance etc. – in addition to their traditional business.

Finally, a most important means of expansion is growth by combination: by the acquisition (take-over) of existing firms or by means of a merger which creates a new company out of two or more existing operations.

BUSINESS COMBINATION – TAKE-OVERS AND MERGERS

In a take-over situation one company acquires a majority (usually all) of the shares of another company. The company making the acquisition thus becomes what is known as a holding company while the company taken over is called a subsidiary company. The latter retains its identity but is controlled by the parent company. A number of different holding-subsidiary ownership patterns can be identified. These are illustrated in Figure 10.2.

In 10.2(a) we have the simplest situation. Here H Ltd's 80 per cent ownership of S Ltd. is in excess of the 75 per cent necessary to give it power to pass special and extraordinary resolutions. In (b) H has absolute ownership of S1 but only a 60 per cent stake in S2 while in (c) the subsidiary, S Ltd, has its own subsidiary, T Ltd, which is thus a sub-subsidiary of H Ltd. H's indirect interest in T is only 45 per cent – 75 per cent of 60 per cent – but it remains, in law, a subsidiary of H, the parent company being obliged to produce consolidated accounts showing the combined resources of all three companies. In (d) we have the kind of merger where a new company is formed in place of two (or more) existing companies.

In practice, however, most subsidiaries are 100 per cent owned. The Companies Act, 1985 enables bidding companies to compulsorily buy out minority shareholders in special circumstances; and the City Code on Take-overs and Mergers requires a company to bid for all the remaining shares when its own holding exceeds 30 per cent.

There are two principal reasons for take-over and merger activity:

1. Integration.
2. Diversification.

INTEGRATION AND DIVERSIFICATION

The general aim of integration is to achieve a greater degree of control or influence over markets or within the industry. Integration may take three forms:

(a) Horizontal (b) Lateral (c) Vertical

Horizontal integration occurs when two similar companies come together. They may be in precisely the same kind of business as when National Provincial Bank and Westminster Bank merged to become the National Westminster Bank. Frequently the subsidiary remains a well known name: Butlins, no longer a quoted company, is today a subsidiary of The Rank Organisation. Sometimes the holding company and its subsidiary trade in the same area in apparent competition with each other.

Lateral integration occurs when firms using similar techniques merge to produce different yet related products. A good example is Smiths Industries whose principal business was clocks but whose subsidiaries include companies making scientific instruments. In years to come we may see mergers between computer companies and manufacturers of word processors. Horizontal and lateral integration are concerned with mergers of firms engaged in parallel or related activities.

Vertical integration, on the other hand, involves firms at different stages of production. Thus, for example, Reed Paper Group has acquired interests in forestry (backwards integration) to ensure supplies of paper, its principal product. It also has interests in publishing (forwards integration) to secure markets for the same product.

Diversification, on the other hand, means the extension of a company's product lines. Dynamic companies seek to do this with their existing plant when demand patterns change and this is practicable: or they may

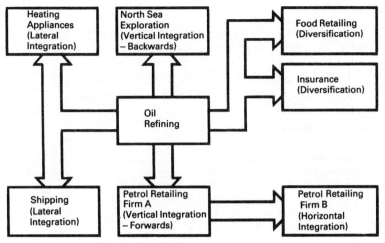

Figure 10.4: Take-overs and Mergers.

build the new plant necessary. Sometimes, however, this can be achieved more quickly and at less cost by take-over or merger. Many mergers of this kind occur. We may note in particular the interests the banks have taken recently in estate agents, travel bureaux and stock exchange firms. Diversification, like other forms of merger activity, may be aggressive or defensive – increasing market share or reacting to the expansionist plans of other firms. Tobacco firms have expanded into food manufacture while declining cinema audiences led Rank to join forces with office equipment manufacturers Xerox. Figure 10.4 shows in diagrammatic form the various types of take-over and mergers.

THE AIMS OF COMBINATION

It is a truism in business that to stand still is to fall back. Those firms which aim simply to maintain the status quo are likely to be overtaken by more vigorous newcomers to the industry. Firms, therefore, generally aim to expand their markets by one means or another.

In the case of horizontal integration the chief aim is to increase market share without actually setting up further plants: instead existing firms in the same industry get taken over. There is a tendency towards mono-poly. For this reason the Secretary of State for Tade and Industry may invoke powers under the Monopolies and Mergers Act of 1965 to refer proposed mergers to the statutory Monopolies Commission. With ver-tical integration, on the other hand, defensive considerations may some-times lie uppermost in the mind of the bidder.

QUESTIONS

1. Distinguish between internal and external economies of scale.
2. What are internal diseconomies of scale? Must they inevitably arise?
3. What factors have led to the decline in the small firm?
4. "The optimum firm is inevitably a large firm." Discuss.
5. Discuss various possible ways of measuring firm size.
6. What are the factors which lead to the growth of firms, and how are these reflected in their organisation?

CHAPTER 11

THE COSTS OF PRODUCTION

OPPORTUNITY COST AND NORMAL PROFIT

In Chapter 1 we encountered the important concept of *opportunity cost* – what a factor of production could earn in its best alternative form of production. Thus, if a civil servant, for example, gives up a safe job to form a business of his own he will aim to achieve at least the same financial benefits as he would enjoy by remaining in government employment.

If he earns £15,000 per annum while his capital provides a safe return of 10 per cent he will expect to at least match these returns in his business. If his business needs £10,000 capital he will require an overall return of £16,000 – (£15,000 salary plus £1,000) to remain no worse off. In fact, he will want to do much better than this because of the risks he is clearly taking. Indeed, he will not, except on non-economic grounds, venture on his own unless he believes he can obtain a substantially better return which would include what economists call *"normal profit"*. Thus his total costs might be made up as follows:

	£	£
1. Opportunity costs		
– salary forgone	15,000	
– interest forgone	1,000	16,000
2. Normal profit (say)		4,000
3. Other costs (say)		25,000
		45,000

If he actually achieves total revenue of £50,000 then he will earn additional profits – *super-normal profits* – of £5,000.

Opportunity cost and normal profit are important concepts but it is easy to lose sight of them. This is because they are implicit costs and not actual or explicit costs. They are, however, absolutely fundamental and unless they are covered a business cannot really be considered profitable.

Nevertheless there are probably thousands of businesses operating which do not cover these basic costs. These businesses may appear to prosper if we only look at their profit and loss accounts which do not take into account either opportunity cost or normal profit. Whilst no entrepreneur would enter an industry unless he thought he could achieve better than normal results firms do not necessarily leave the industry because they do not cover these costs. However, we must leave consideration of this and related matters until Chapters 13 and 15.

FIXED AND VARIABLE COSTS

The least complex division of explicit costs is between *variable* costs (i.e. broadly short run costs) and *fixed* costs (i.e. long run costs). Fixed costs do not vary with changes in output. Fixed costs are those costs which the firm must incur to do any businesses at all and which are not divisible into smaller units. Thus a florist might require a small delivery van no matter what the level of his sales. The capital cost of the van will be spread over the useful life of the asset – say five years – and he must also cover certain other fixed costs such as road tax and insurance. He will aim to maximise his sales so that the average fixed costs of using the van are minimised.

Variable costs, on the other hand, bear a direct relationship to output. The florist's major variable cost will be the flowers themselves but also some other costs such as the petrol to run the delivery van. In a manufacturing concern the major variable costs – often referred to as direct costs – are raw materials and direct labour because they are used in direct proportion to output.

Some costs may be a combination of both fixed and variable elements. Some prices, notably for public utilities, are based on a standing charge and a usage charge. Thus firms pay rent for the use of their telephone system in addition to charges for the calls they actually make. Such charges – sometimes called semi-variable costs – are usually grouped together with variable costs.

COST BEHAVIOUR IN THE SHORT RUN

The firm, it may be thought, aims to maximise production, and thus sales, but as we have seen there will come a point when the marginal product will be negligible if not negative. Before this point is reached the firm will normally have stopped taking on workers or using further units of capital because it is no longer profitable for it to do so. So we must now examine the way costs behave as production is increased.

Table 11.1 shows the total costs for a farmer analysed between fixed, variable and marginal costs.

Table 11.1: Fixed, variable and marginal costs (£).

Quantity of Variable Input	Total Fixed Costs (£)	Total Variable Costs (£)	Marginal Cost (£)	Total Cost (£)
0	30	0	15	30
1	30	15	5	45
2	30	20	2·5	50
3	30	22·5	5·5	52·5
4	30	28	9·5	58
5	30	37·5	22·5	67·5
6	30	60		90

Irrespective of the quantity produced fixed costs remain at £30 in the short run. The variable costs, however, increase as production is increased – at first quite steeply, then more gently, and finally fairly sharply again (Figure 11.1). Marginal cost, the increase in cost for each variable input added, on the other hand, falls steeply to begin with and then rises again ultimately quite sharply.

Although total costs are important for the purpose of analysis we are more interested in average costs and in particular marginal cost – the cost of producing one more unit. Marginal cost is, of course, closely related to the marginal product. Table 11.2 shows these costs:

We see that average fixed costs rapidly decline at first but thereafter fall much less steeply. Average variable costs also decline at first but will ultimately rise. Average total costs – which, of course, comprise both

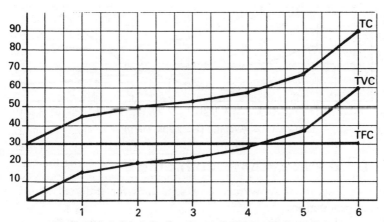

Figure 11.1: Total Costs – Fixed, Variable and Total Costs.

Table 11.2: Average costs and marginal costs (£).

Quantity of Variable Input	Average Fixed Costs (£)	Average Variable Costs (£)	Average Total Costs (£)	Marginal Cost (£)
1	30	15	45	15
2	15	10	25	5
3	10	7·5	17·5	2·5
4	7·5	7	14·5	5·5
5	6	7·5	13·5	9·5
6	5	10	15	22·5

costs fall steeply at first, then the curve flattens out somewhat before it, too, ultimately rises.

Of most interest, perhaps, is the behaviour of the marginal cost curve. This falls at first, then quite soon begins its steep rise and intersects each of the other three curves. The points at which the MC curve intersects the AVC and ATC curves are highly significant – the points at which average costs – variable and total – are lowest (see Figure 11.2).

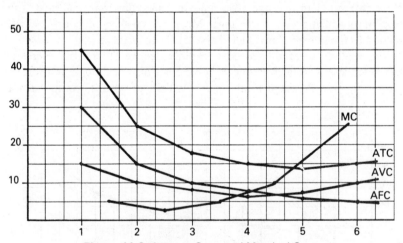

Figure 11.2: Average Costs and Marginal Cost.

THE LONG RUN AVERAGE COST CURVE

Table 11.3 shows four average cost schedules for different short run levels of production:

Figure 11.3 shows the equivalent short run cost curves. The first of

Table 11.3: Short run cost curves at different levels of production.

SAC1		SAC2		SAC3		SAC4	
Quantity	Average Cost (£)	Quantity	Average Cost (£)	Quantity	Average Cost (£)	Quantity	Average Cost (£)
5	30	15	20	25	12·5	35	10
10	22·5	20	12·5	30	8·5	40	8·5
15	19	25	11	35	6·5	45	7·5
20	17	30	10	40	5	50	7
25	19	35	12·5	45	6	55	10
30	24	40	17·5	50	8	60	13

these SAC1 shows the firms average costs at the initial stage of its development. At this level the firms costs are minimised when it produces 20 units. SAC2 and SAC3 represent average cost curves at higher levels of production with larger expenditure on fixed costs. SAC4 reflects a higher level of activity still but now higher average costs are encountered. The firm is no longer operating at optimum size. However, depending on the price at which it can sell its goods, it may be worth while to produce up to this level.

The long run average cost curve, in theory, consists of a virtually infinite number of short run cost curves. The LAC curve is therefore drawn so as to envelop the SACs so that it is tangent to each of them. Typically the LAC curve eventually turns upwards reflecting higher costs. In practice though it could be many years before this occurs. Indeed, it can be argued that given the rapidity of technological progress today, firms in some industries will continue to experience a long run reduction in their operating costs. Thus it could be said that the natural shape of the LAC is continuously downward sloping. In the long run the firm can vary all its inputs so that there are no fixed factors of production. Thus there are no true fixed costs and the firm can build plants of any size and scale.

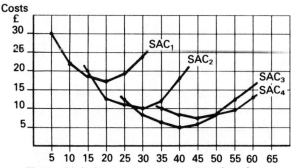

Figure 11.3: Short Run and Long Run Cost Curves.

QUESTIONS

1. "The economist's definition of profit is superior to the accountant's." Discuss.

2. Does the behaviour of costs in the short run inevitably dictate the optimum size of the firm?

3. Is there any limit to the reduction of costs in the long run?

CHAPTER 12

LOCATION OF INDUSTRY

THE PRINCIPLE OF LOCATION

In this chapter we are concerned with those factors which determine where a firm or an industry becomes established. The basic reason is economic: firms will be set up where the particular enterprise can be carried out as economically – i.e. at lowest cost – as possible.

Some costs within a region may be very high but firms will still be prepared to move there because these are more than compensated by the fact that other costs there are lower. Rents (indeed all costs) are very high in Central London but firms are still attracted to the capital. Although there may be some non-economic reasons for this, the main reason is that, despite the increased costs, the rewards of locating, at least part of its operations there, are still higher. West-end cinema prices, for example, are high not because the rents are high: rents are high because cinema owners can charge higher prices there than elsewhere.

FACTORS DETERMINING LOCATION

Traditionally a number of reasons have been given for locating an industry in a particular town or region. Many of these reasons arise from one natural advantage or another.

(a) Climate
(b) Raw materials
(c) Power
(d) Labour
(e) Transport
(f) Market access
(g) Communications
(h) Political stability
(i) Financial inducement
(j) Proximity to government
(k) Existing centre

The most basic reason of all is naturally *climate*: the climate of the U.K. rules out the growing of bananas and other tropical plants on an economic basic. Even within a country variations in climate can be important factors in determining where industries are based. The mild weather (and good soil) in the Worcester area is particularly suited to fruit growing, and further north the humid conditions around Manchester were an important reason for the establishment of the cotton industry in that region.

The land itself and the *raw materials* under it are historically a most important determinant of location of industry. When transport methods were relatively primitive and costly, industries were often based as close as possible to raw materials. Many of Britain's major industries – iron and steel production and electricity generation for example – are situated close to coal mines. Johannesburg, South Africa's largest city was a magnet for a large number of industries following the discovery of gold there in the 1880s; and in America cotton manufacturing is located close to the cotton growing regions of the south.

The source of *power* is a third important factor in decisions to locate industry. In earlier times the woollen industry was widely dispersed throughout Britain but with the development of water power in the Pennines and because of the abundance of coal close by, both the woollen and cotton industries found this region especially advantageous.

Another important reason is *labour* despite the fact that labour ought to be the most mobile of factors. Entrepreneurs will not normally establish factories in areas where labour is already in short supply but they may be tempted to move into areas of high unemployment. Quantity alone, however, is not enough. The workers must be suited to the needs of the firm. Thus a capital-intensive industry such as precision instruments will be established where there is a reserve of skilled labour. The electronics and computer industry is another case: it is centred around Cambridge where there are intellectual talents as well as a highly skilled labour force.

In earlier times the location of raw materials and of power was particularly important because of the difficulties of transport. The ease and cost of *transport* are still material factors for some industries although it will often pay a firm to establish operations a long way from its markets if the product is not too bulky, hence expensive to move. This is because in some remote areas – and in government assisted areas – rent and some other costs are very much lower. Many industries however are widely dispersed even today because of the impact of transport costs. Examples include breadmaking, brewing and brick manufacture.

If raw materials have to be imported then transport costs will not necessarily make much impact on the location of industry. An important exception is the case of oil refineries which are usually situated close to major ports. A more important consideration, in most cases, is the firm's *access to markets*. This is therefore a second reason why bakeries and breweries are to be found all over the country. The market is a most potent reason in making London the very important financial centre it is.

Sophisticated *communications* are another vital factor. The financial markets – not all of them tangible places – are very dependent on telephone, telex, fax and computer links as well as the excellent source of skilled labour to be found in and around the capital. London is in the forefront of the general advances in computer technology.

Another very important consideration in the modern world is the *political* situation. Multi-national companies often regard this as one of the most important factors in deciding whether to establish operations in another country. Financial inducements by the governments concerned may also be a determining factor.

Some firms will be attracted to the *capital of the country*. Thus Bonn – a comparatively small city – will have some special attractions not to be found in Hamburg or Munich. In the capital, being the seat of government, important contracts may be obtained if the firm is situated in the right place. It may also be a mark of status. Many companies whose operations are located in the provinces like to maintain a head office or a skeleton presence in the capital.

Finally we must mention the tendency of "birds of a feather to flock together". In many cases firms will establish operations close by their rivals. Sometimes this is because they are both seeking the same advantage – power or cheap labour for example – but more frequently this is because the *existing centre* is such an attraction for the consumer. The City of London's financial markets have already been mentioned but London itself is full of other examples: Bond Street for jewellery, Savile Row for tailors and Carnaby Street for trendy, modern fashions – to mention just three examples.

LOCATION – A COMBINATION OF FACTORS

Although it is sometimes a single factor, more often than not it is a combination of things which determines the location of firms and industries. The great historical reasons for the location of industry – raw materials, power and ease of transport – are less important today than they once were.

In deciding whether to locate a new plant in South Wales the great Japanese company, Mitsubishi, had in mind the cost of land (cheap because South Wales was an assisted area), an abundant labour supply due to redundancies in the coal and steel industries, close proximity to ports and, of course, the political stability found in the U.K.

Many historical cases of location of industry resulted because of a single over-riding factor. Today it is more likely to be a combination of factors which determine location. A single factor by itself is unlikely to be sufficiently important given today's methods of production and modern modes of communication and transport.

INDUSTRIAL INERTIA

If we look at some industries today it is sometimes difficult to understand why they are located where they are. The historic reasons, e.g. the abundance of cheap raw materials, proximity to water power and so on are no longer valid. The raw materials may have been exhausted and electricity has long since replaced the water wheel. Other locations offer much greater advantages in the latter part of the twentieth century but the individual firm and indeed the industry stay where they are. This tendency is known as *industrial inertia* and a number of reasons can be advanced to explain it.

1. Availability of external economies of scale (see Chapter 7) e.g. skilled labour, training facilities and ancillary services.
2. Difficulty of moving key personnel.
3. The high cost of closing down existing plant and setting up elsewhere.
4. Reputation of the region for the product.

LOCALISATION OF PRODUCTION

In some areas there has been a tendency for there to be a concentration of many inter-connected industries. This is true of the Birmingham area, of the West Yorkshire conurbation around Leeds and of the Ruhr in Germany. Each of these regions, originally the centre for one or more major industries, has spawned many ancillary industries and services which depend for their livelihood on the health of the major industry. When the dominant industry is sick – as was the case with the motor industry for many years – this seriously affects all the other industries in the region.

When an industry is in permanent decline this gives rise to what is known as *structural* unemployment – unemployment which arises from a permanent decline in the demand for a product. Two major cases in the U.K. are the Lancashire cotton industry and the more widely dispersed but uniformaly depressed shipbuilding industry. In a healthy economy the decline in the demand for the products of one area ought to be replaced by an increase in the demand for others as resources are shifted to new forms of production. But in the 1930s and more recently in the wake of various oil crises this did not always occur.

GOVERNMENT INTERVENTION

Today the cotton industry, now much slimmed-down, is relatively healthy, but shipbuilding, historically a victim of recession, is once again in decline. Steel and coal production, reflecting changing patterns of demand, have been much reduced in scale. Britain, of course, is not alone in all this: every industrialised country has been affected to some extent.

Very often the resulting unemployment is much more serious in some regions than in others. This is called *regional* unemployment. In the 1930s some regions experienced unemployment of more than 50 per cent.

Traditionally, the North of England, Scotland, Wales and Northern Ireland have been more seriously affected by severe *localisation* problems than the rest of the U.K. London and the south-east were for many years remarkably insulated from the problems of unemployment because of the wider variety of industrial and clerical employment and the lack of dependence on one or two major industries. As the figures in Table 12.1 show this situation has changed in recent times.

A number of methods have been tried to alleviate regional (often mainly structural) unemployment:

1. Development grants. Financial assistance towards capital expenditure on certain assets, e.g. industrial buildings and machinery.

Table 12.1: Annual Average Unemployment Rates by Regions.

	1960	1970	1977	1983‡	1986	1989§
South-east	1·0	1·6	4·5	9·3	8·7	3·6
Greater London*	–	–	4·3	9·5	9·5	4·7
East Anglia†	–	2·1	5·3	10·2	9·0	3·2
South-west	1·7	2·8	6·8	11·2	9·9	4·1
West Midlands	1·0	1·9	5·8	15·6	13·6	5·9
East Midlands	1·1	2·2	5·0	11·8	10·7	4·9
Yorkshire & Humberside†	–	2·8	5·8	14·1	13·5	6·9
North-west	1·9	2·7	7·4	15·8	14·6	7·8
North	2·9	4·6	8·3	17·7	16·4	8·9
Wales	2·7	3·8	8·0	15·9	14·4	6·9
Scotland	3·6	4·2	8·1	14·9	14·5	8·6
Great Britain	1·6	2·5	6·0	12·7	11·7	5·6
Northern Ireland	6·7	6·8	11·0	20·2	18·1	14·4
United Kingdom	1·7	2·6	6·2	12·9	11·8	5·8

* Greater London included in South-east – not available for 1960.

† Prior to 1965 East Anglia included in South-east and Yorks & Humberside in East Midlands regions.

‡ Relates to claimants. Figures before 1983 are for registrants.

§ Figures affected by withdrawal of income support from most of those under 18 years.

Source: Department of Employment.

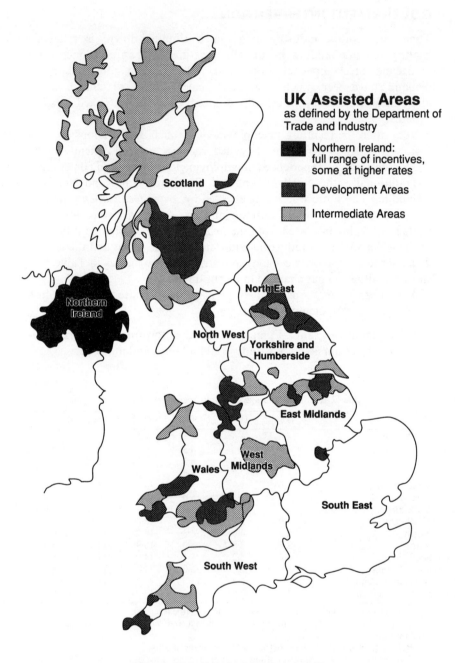

Figure 12.1: U.K. Assisted Areas 1989

2. Government factories. These may be rented or purchased on favourable terms. In certain circumstances they may be obtained rent-free for a limited period.
3. Development areas. Originally called special areas these were designated to receive special help according to the extent of their problems.
4. Contract preference schemes. Government contracts are made available to firms in development areas.
5. Decentralisation. A number of government departments have been based or relocated out of London or the South-East. The Royal Mint was moved to Cardiff and National Girobank was located in Bootle.
6. Training Allowances. These enable workers to train for work in new, "sunrise" industries such as electronics and computing.
7. Mobility Incentives. Help with fares, removal costs and lodging expenses have been given to encourage workers to move to different parts of the country.
8. Enterprise Zones. These are relatively small areas within cities such as Liverpool greatly affected by urban decay. A variety of incentives and subsidies may be provided under such schemes.

It can be argued that some of these schemes are mere palliatives and that they can make little or no difference to unemployment. Some economists indeed would argue that it is better to let a weak industry go to the wall so that new enterprises can be established, but governments have usually been unwilling to follow such a radical course of action in view of the serious social and political consequences. We undoubtedly live in difficult times. The computer and information technology seem certain to destroy more jobs than they can possibly create. Some radical new thinking may be needed to tackle this apparently intractable problem.

QUESTIONS

1. What factors determine the location of industry?
2. Why do some firms remain in areas where there are no obvious special advantages available?
3. Contrast the location of industry with the localisation of production.
4. What kinds of action have governments taken to deal with problems caused by the decline in our basic industries?

CHAPTER 13

PERFECT COMPETITION

INTRODUCTION

In this and succeeding chapters we seek to show how supply and
demand are determined under very different – and to a large extent
theoretical – conditions. In this chapter we will look at perfect competition and in the next at monopoly, the antithesis of perfect competition.
In the following chapter we consider some particular cases of imperfect
competition.

PERFECT COMPETITION – A DEFINITION

It must be stated at the outset that perfect competition does not exist in
the real world although conditions that approximate to it will be found
in some markets. A market is said to be perfectly competitive when all of
the following conditions exist:

1. There is a large number of buyers and sellers.
2. The commodity or good traded is homogenous – i.e. one item is
   identical with another.
3. There is complete freedom to enter or to leave the market.
4. All parties have perfect knowledge of present and expected future
   prices and costs.
5. There is perfect mobility of the factors of production.

THE FIRM'S DEMAND CURVE UNDER PERFECT COMPETITION

In the perfectly competitive market situation it is important to realise
that the following must also be true of the many buyers and sellers who
constitute the market:

(a) None of them must be dominant.
(b) There must be no preferential treatment on either side.
(c) All parties must be motivated only by consideration of price.

In these circumstances no individual buyer or seller will have any

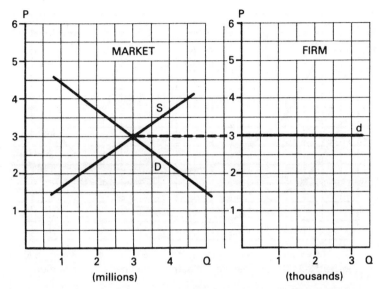

Figure 13.1: Market and Individual Firm Demand Curves under Perfect Competition.

influence on the price whatsoever. Price will be determined solely by the interaction of the market supply and demand curves for the good in question. Because of the existence of the various conditions enumerated above there can be *only one price*, and since each firm produces only a tiny part of the total, the individual firm can produce as much or as little of the commodity without affecting the price. In other words, the firm, in conditions of perfect competition:

(a) is a price taker and
(b) faces an infinitely elastic demand curve for its product.

This is explained in Figure 13.1. The market price, determined by the market supply and demand curves is £3. For the individual producer this is, at this point in time, the only price at which he can sell his product. If he raises his price, even slightly, he will make no sales whatever.

Similarly, individual buyers in the market have no influence on price. Their demand meets an infinitely elastic supply curve. The same is true for producers seeking labour or any of the other factors of production. The producer's demand is insignificant in relation to the market supply. He can therefore obtain all he requires at the prevailing market price.

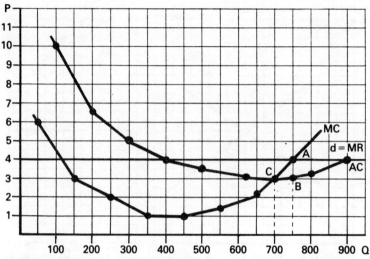

Figure 13.2: The optimal level of output under perfect competition.

MAXIMISING PROFITS UNDER PERFECT COMPETITION

It is a fundamental assumption of economics that the firm is a profit-maximiser. It will, therefore, given the nature of the infinitely elastic demand curve for its product, produce that quantity which will give it the largest overall profit. Study the data in Table 13.1.

The marginal cost, it will be recalled, is the additional cost of producing one more unit. In a case such as this where the quantity is increased by 100 units at a time the marginal cost is calculated as follows:

$$\frac{\text{Increase in total costs}}{\text{Increase in total units}}$$

Thus the marginal cost per unit between 600 and 700 units is £2·50 (£2,100–£1,850/100). As this is less than the marginal revenue production will be greater than 650 units at which level marginal cost is only £2·50 a unit. Production will, in fact, be 750 units since at this level of output marginal revenue and marginal cost are equal. The graphical presentation of the same data (Figure 13.2) confirms this.

Figure 13.2 shows that the rising marginal cost (MC) curve bisects the marginal revenue (MR) curve at an output of 750 units – point A. At this level the firm is in short run equilibrium. If it raises its price at all it will lose all its customers. If it lowers its price it will reduce total revenue, hence profits, unnecessarily since it can sell all of its output at the market price without difficulty. At this point the gap between the

Table 13.1: Perfect Competition: Costs, Revenue and Profit.

Quantity	Total Costs £	Total Revenue £	Total Profit £	Average Cost £	Marginal Cost £	Marginal Revenue = Price £
0	400	0	(400)	–	6·00	4·00
100	1,000	400	(600)	10·00	3·00	4·00
200	1,300	800	(500)	6·50	2·00	4·00
300	1,500	1,200	(300)	5·00	1·00	4·00
400	1,600	1,600	0	4·00	1·00	4·00
500	1,700	2,000	300	3·40	1·50	4·00
600	1,850	2,400	550	3·08	2·50	4·00
700	2,100	2,800	700	3·00	4·00	4·00
800	2,500	3,200	700	3·12	11·00	4·00
900	3,600	3,600	0	4·00		

MR curve and the AC curve is greatest, signifying the maximisation of profits – line AB. Note also point C, the point where the MC curve bisects the average (total) cost (AC) curve. The MC curve always does this at the point where average cost is at a minimum. However the equilibrium point always occurs at a higher level of output and when the MC curve is still rising.

THE FIRM'S SHORT RUN SUPPLY CURVE UNDER PERFECT COMPETITION

The relationship of the MC curve to the AC curve is very important. The MC curve is in fact the firm's supply curve in conditions of perfect competition. More precisely, it is that part of the MC curve that lies above the ATC curve which is the firm's true supply curve. This is because it will pay the firm to produce right up to the level of output at which the rising MC curve bisects the MR curve.

In Figure 13.3 we examine the MC curve in each of four different situations. This time, however, we separate the variable costs from the total costs because they only change with the level of output. The fixed costs, on the other hand, do not change in the short run.

1. At £15 (point A) the firm would produce and sell 5,000 units making a *profit* of £5 a unit (line AF).
2. At £9·00 (point B) the firm would obtain only sufficient revenue to *break even*.
3. At £6·00 (point C) the firm produces 3,400 units and makes an *overall loss* of £4 a unit (line GC) but because price exceeds its variable costs of £3·50 a unit it will also cover some of its fixed

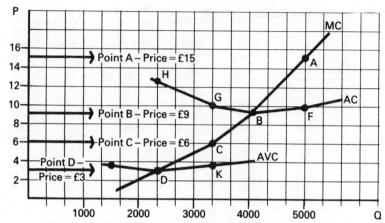

Figure 13.3: Output and Profit in Different Price Situations.

costs. It will receive a *contribution towards its fixed costs* of £2·50 a unit – line CK. Firms frequently get into this situation. They have incurred substantial capital investment expenditure, and selling up the plant and machinery is not a practicable solution. Costs such as these are known as "sunk" costs. The firm will remain in business in the short run because it is the better of the two options.

4. At the price of £3 (point D) the MC curve meets the average variable cost (AVC) curve. The firm is only just covering its variable costs and receives no contribution towards its fixed costs. This is known as the *"shut-down"* point. If prices fall below this level the firm cannot continue in operation unless the cost/price situation is considered to be of very short duration.

LONG RUN EQUILIBRIUM

The long run in economics, it will be remembered, is the period during which all costs, including fixed costs, can be varied. It is not a particular period of time. In the long run a firm will only remain in business if its total revenue is greater than its total costs. Its optimum level of output is achieved where both the short run marginal cost (SMC) curve and the long run marginal cost (LMC) curve intersect the MR curve, this point being, of course, above both the short run average cost (SAC) curve and the long run average cost (LAC) curve which are tangent to each other. In Figure 13.4 this occurs at point X where the price is £4 and output 7,000 units.

Of course, in this situation, other firms will be attracted by the

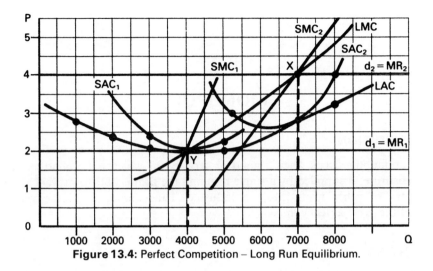

Figure 13.4: Perfect Competition – Long Run Equilibrium.

prospect of super-normal profits and will enter the industry. The increase in supply will result in a fall in price and this process will continue until all firms merely break even i.e. make normal profits only. This occurs at point Y where price and output are £2 and 4,000 units respectively. At this equilibrium level of operations:

$$\text{Price} = \text{MR} = \text{SMC} = \text{LMC} = \text{SAC} = \text{LAC} = £2.$$

New firms will no longer be attracted to the industry and existing firms will have no wish to leave it.

QUESTIONS

1. What are the conditions which underlie perfect competition?

2. Why in a perfectly competitive situation can there be only a single price for a particular product?

3. How do cost curves behave under conditions of perfect competition?

4. Why don't producers necessarily give up production when they cannot cover their fixed costs?

CHAPTER 14

MONOPOLY

DEFINITION

A monopoly exists when a good or service, for which there is no close substitute, is supplied by a single firm and the firm is able to prevent the entry of other firms into the industry. Thus monopoly is the very antithesis of perfect competition.

THE BASES OF MONOPOLY

There are a number of reasons why monopolies or near monopolies are found in the real world.

1. Scale of Operations
(a) Where the good or service can only be provided satisfactorily by a single firm, e.g. railways, electricity supply.
(b) Where the industry is a natural monopoly, e.g. oil or coal reserves.
(c) A monopoly may be created by one superior firm gradually benefiting from increased economies of scale. Eventually its market share is such that it becomes so dominant as to drive smaller firms out of business.

2. Exclusion of competition
(a) Legal prohibition, e.g. the Post Office which is given a monopoly of the postal service under an Act of Parliament, the Post Office Act.
(b) An already dominant firm may adopt certain tactics to deliberately undermine the trading capacity of other firms, e.g. temporary price cutting, collusive price arrangements with distributors. This is monopoly by stealth.

3. Patents, copyrights and trademarks
These are granted to individuals and firms to encourage invention and the development of new products.

LIMITS TO MONOPOLY POWER

Most economists from Adam Smith onwards have regarded monopoly as undesirable, and most governments – except in the case of natural monopolies and public utilities – have legislated against monopoly. In the United States the "anti-trust" laws are rigorously enforced, and in the United Kingdom the Monopolies and Mergers Act, 1965, can be invoked by the Secretary of State for Trade and Industry if, as a result of a proposed merger or a take-over, a single firm or group would then provide more than 25 per cent of the market supply.

Observation suggests that industries often move inexorably in the direction of monopoly. Therefore some degree of control certainly seems necessary in the public interest. Nevertheless it would be wrong to conclude that the monopolist has everything his own way. In fact the monopolist can control:

1. The quantity supplied OR
2. The price

but never both of them. Given the market demand curve for his product the greater the quantity he supplies the lower the price he can command and vice versa. Like the firm under conditions of perfect competition the monopolist endeavours to maximise profits. He achieves this to the extent that he achieves the optimum combination of price and quantity. This is a very different situation from the perfectly competitive one where price is established in the market and the firm can supply any quantity it can produce at the prevailing price.

MARGINAL REVENUE UNDER MONOPOLY

Under conditions of perfect competition, since there is only a single price at which the homogeneous product can be sold, marginal revenue is equal to price. This is not so in the monopoly situation. In this case, as we have seen, the more the monopolist sells the lower the price he can command.

Table 14.1: Monopoly – Total, marginal and average revenue.

Quantity Supplied	Price Received (£)	Total Revenue (£)	Marginal Revenue (£)	Average Revenue (£)
10	7	70	7	7
20	6	120	5	6
30	5	150	3	5
40	4	160	1	4
50	3	150	−1	3
60	2	120	−3	2
70	1	70	−5	1

Table 14.1 illustrates that for the monopolist his marginal revenue, as well as his price, declines as the quantity supplied increases. At each level of output average revenue is equal to price, and because the firm is a monopoly the average revenue curve is the market demand curve.

THE MR CURVE AND ELASTICITY

If demand is elastic a reduction in price will result in an increase in total revenue whilst if demand is inelastic reducing price will cut total revenue. This is made clearer if we look at the data of Table 14.1 in graphical form.

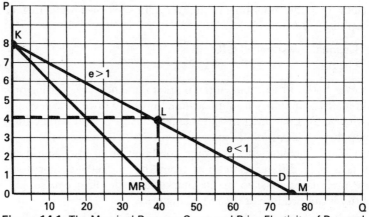

Figure 14.1: The Marginal Revenue Curve and Price Elasticity of Demand.

It will be recalled that on a straight line demand curve half of the curve will be elastic (KL in this case) and the other half (LM) inelastic. Only at the mid-point (L) is elasticity unitary. This is the point where total revenue will be greatest – where 40 items will be sold yielding £60. At this point the marginal revenue is zero. This might seem to suggest that the monopolist will always sell his product at such a point on the demand curve. This, however, ignores that other fundamental consideration – the monopolist's marginal cost.

SHORT-RUN EQUILIBRIUM UNDER MONOPOLY

In a theoretical zero-cost situation the optimal price and output situation would be £4 and 40 units respectively where elasticity is unitary. Suppose, however, that the firm's average total cost curve is such that average cost

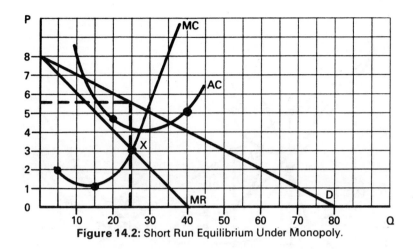

Figure 14.2: Short Run Equilibrium Under Monopoly.

is never less than £4 a unit. In such a case 40 units hardly seems likely to be optimal. In Figure 14.2 we have superimposed marginal and average cost curves on our original data.

The equilibrium level is found to be £5·50 at which price the firm will produce 25 units. As in the case of perfect competition it will be noted that this point is found by drawing a vertical line from the horizontal axis through the point at which the MR and MC curves intersect (Point X). The monopolist will normally find it most profitable to produce up to the level at which his rising MC curve meets his downward sloping MR curve.

A FURTHER CONSIDERATION OF ELASTICITY

In our example the equilibrium level of production is found to be 25 units at a price of £5·50. This actually occurs at a point in the demand curve where demand is elastic. This will always be the case in practice. Yet, paradoxically, the monopolist will always prefer a situation where demand is inelastic so that he can increase his price and thus his profitability. In short the monopolist operates more successfully in an industry where demand is relatively inelastic.

LONG RUN EQUILIBRIUM

Under perfect competition new firms attracted by the possibility of making super-normal profits enter the market and eventually all these profits are competed away. This will not happen under monopoly. The

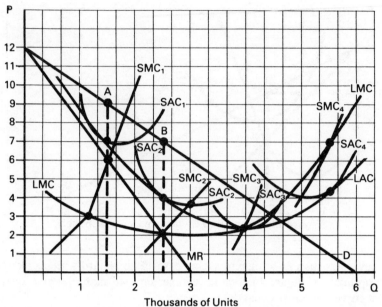

Figure 14.3: Monopoly – Long Run Equilibrium.

monopolist, like all profit maximisers, seeks lower costs and to the extent that he achieves these he should be able to push profits higher.

In Figure 14.3 we show a series of short run AC and MC curves linked together to form the long run average cost (LAC) and the long run marginal cost (LMC) curves. It will be noted that the LAC is drawn tangent to the various SACs and that each of the SMCs bisects the LMC.

1. The price and quantity determined by the intersection of SMC1 with the MR curve (point A) – £9 and 1,500 units – will provide a profit per unit of £2 and £3,000 in total. This, however, is not the equilibrium position because MR at this point is greater than the LMC.

2. Equilibrium price and output occurs at point B where 2,500 units are sold at £7 giving a profit per unit of £3 and £7,500 altogether. This is the equilibrium output because at this point all of the following conditions are satisfied:

   (i) MR = SMC = LMC
   (ii) SAC = LAC at the point of tangency
   (iii) Profit is maximised.

3. The third short run situation exhibits the case where costs have

been reduced further – plant size may now be optimal – but the firm is not in equilibrium.

4. Finally the short run cost curves turn upwards.

PRICE DISCRIMINATION

In some situations the monopolist may be able to both increase his price and maintain his output at the same level. This can occur where the monopolist can divide his market up into two or more segments each independent of the other. A well known case where such price discrimination occurs is that of electricity prices. Industrial users may be charged less on the grounds that their demand curve is more elastic because of their greater ability to switch to alternative fuels. In the days of widespread private medicine some doctors (monopolists in a limited area) would charge the wealthy more than was ordinarily justified while the poor whose demand curve was more elastic paid less. Price discrimination may thus also have some useful social welfare effect.

The essential requirements for successful price discrimination are:

1. Two or more separate markets – really sub-sections of the one market.

2. No arbitrage between markets – i.e. buying in one market and selling in the other.

3. Different elasticities in each market.

Figure 14.4 illustrates price discrimination in two markets. In addition to

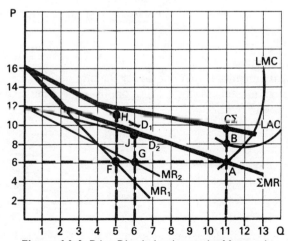

Figure 14.4: Price Discrimination under Monopoly.

the two sets of demand and MR curves we also show ΣD.* It will be noted that D2 is more elastic than D1 and the curve begins at £12 whereas that of D1 begins at £16.

The price and quantity for the monopolist without price discrimination is found as usual by drawing a vertical line through the intersection of the MC and ΣMR curve (point A) to the Point C on the ΣD curve. At this level of output (11 units) average cost is £8 and price £9.75 giving a profit per unit of £1.75 – a total profit of £19·25.

Now, if instead we draw vertical lines through MR1 (F) and MR2 (G) to points H and J we arrive at the prices and output appropriate in the two sub-markets:

	Quantity	Price (£)	Profit per Unit (£)	Total Profit (£)
D1	5	11	3	15
D2	6	9	1	6
	11			21

Thus although the monopolist has had to reduce his price in one market he more than makes up for it in the other.

QUESTIONS

1. How do monopolies arise?
2. "Monopolies are undesirable." Discuss
3. How much control does the monopolist have over output and price?
4. Show by means of a graph the position where a monopolist achieves short run equilibrium.
5. Is elasticity an important concept for the monopolist?
6. In what circumstances can the monopolist charge more to one set of people than he can to another?

* The sign Σ (pronounced sigma) is the eighteenth letter of the Greek alphabet. It is used in Economics to signify a total or aggregate figure.

CHAPTER 15

IMPERFECT COMPETITION

INTRODUCTION

Although the situations we have examined under perfect competition
and monopoly are largely theoretical there are firms in the real world
that approximate fairly close to these economic models. The commodity
markets and the Stock Exchange have many of the characteristics of
perfectly competitive markets. There are certainly some true monopolies;
but in the developed world they are invariably regulated either by law or
by government intervention, so that the full impact of their pricing and
production policies is not always felt by consumers.

In this chapter we consider some of the possible modes of competition
that lie in between the two extreme and largely theoretical models –
perfect competition and monopoly.

IMPERFECT COMPETITION

A vast amount of firm-consumer interaction is to be found in imperfect markets. The term imperfect competition describes a variety of
situations within the range from perfect competition to monopoly. We
shall look at three special cases, in each case using economic models to
illustrate in fairly simple terms some of the complexities of imperfect
markets:

    (i) Duopoly (two firms).
    (ii) Oligopoly (a few firms).
    (iii) Monopolistic competition (many firms).

DUOPOLY

We will look first at duopoly, simplifying our analysis by dealing with a
situation in which two firms both produce a homogeneous product at
zero cost. The important new consideration here is that each firm's
pricing and production policies will affect those of the other.

In a very simple example we can look at the case of two firms both
engaged in the distribution of spring water. At first the market comprises

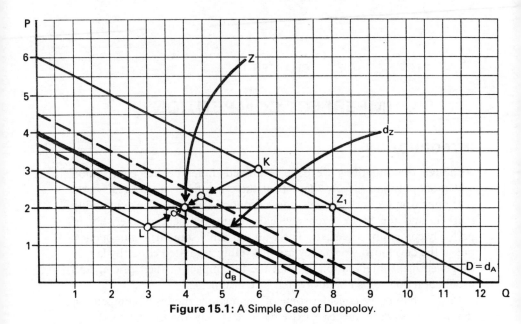

Figure 15.1: A Simple Case of Duopoloy.

only Firm A whose demand curve is shown on the extreme right of Figure 15.1.

With no competition Firm A's initial equilibrium position is at point K. At this point it will sell 600 units at the monopoly price of £3 to produce total income – in this zero-cost case a profit of £1,800. Now Firm B enters the market. Since total market demand is 1,200 units, but A is already supplying 600 of them, Firm B's demand curve (dB) will be dA–600 and its optimum position Point L at which it will sell 300 units at £1·50.

Firm A is now forced to reduce its price. Its demand curve now shifts to the left (the higher dotted line), its total possible market now becoming 1,200 − 300 − 900 units. B responds in like manner and this process continues until the two demand curves converge and each firm supplies one-third of the market at £2 (Point Z). The joint price and output position is shown at Point Z1 on the original (monopoly) demand curve.

Now while this simple model helps to explain why and how the monopolist's profits are reduced it is, in fact, fallacious. This is because the two firms could simply sit down together and agree to split the monopoly market 50–50 (Table 15.1). They would then each be better off! Collusion between firms does, in fact, take place in the real world and the forms it takes may be subtle and devious.

Table 15.1: Monopoly and Duopoly.

Output	A	B	Price (£)	Total Revenue (£)
Monopoly	600	–	3	1,800
Duopoly	400	400	2	1,600
Sharing Monopoly	300	300	3	1,800

OLIGOPOLY

The term oligopoly embraces the two-firm case but most typically is to be found where there are three or four large producers. There is no single oligopolistic model. Even in a three-firm situation we could find many variations. One well-known case is that of the U.K. detergent industry in which the two dominant firms account for over 90 per cent of the market. In such a case the Big Two could ignore any price cutting by their smaller rivals, but if one of the market leaders reduced its price that would be a different matter and would affect the responses of all the other firms.

Price fixing is not uncommon among oligopolists but often this will not be formally arranged or contracted. Frequently the smaller firms will react to prices set by the larger firms in the market. Although the major banks are a special case theirs is very much an oligopoly situation and it is not always Barclays or National Westminster (the two largest) who set the pace, with for example, interest rate changes.

Banks and other oligopolists are often more inclined to compete in non-price forms. Individual banks try to identify themselves strongly with particular kinds of business – personal, business, foreign etc., while trading companies use "free gifts", trading stamps, competitions and the like, rather than compete too fiercely on price, to enlarge or retain their market share.

The best known model of oligopoly is, perhaps, that devised by Sweezy. In his "kinked" demand curve Sweezy explains the price rigidity which is frequently to be found in oligopolistic situations. In Figure 15.2 we show the marginal revenue and demand curves facing the oligopolist. Note that these initially follow the same pattern as those of the monopolist in that marginal revenue falls as output is increased; and price is established by reference to the intersection of the marginal revenue and marginal cost curves – point E. Price and output will be £4 and 60 units respectively – point X.

Sweezy postulates that the oligopolist's competitors will be much more

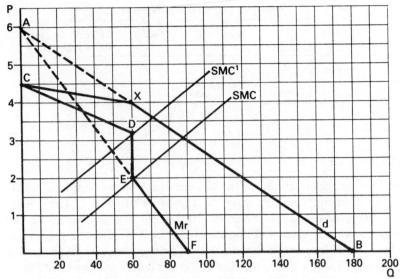

Figure 15.2: Oligopoly – the "Kinked" Demand Curve.

likely to respond to price cuts than to price increases. Hence he draws the conclusion that the demand curve facing the oligopolist is more elastic above X than below it. So in Figure 15.2 we show how the firm's demand curve AXB is transformed to CXB and its marginal revenue curve from AF to CDEF. The firm's MC curve can rise all the way from E to D without causing the firm to raise its price.

MONOPOLISTIC COMPETITION

Finally in our study of imperfect competition we look at the most typical situation of all – monopolistic competition. Under monopolistic competition there are many firms selling closely related but not identical products. A good example is the common aspirin. This product is sold in many different forms – Anadin, Aspro, Bufferin to mention only those at the beginning of the alphabet! Indeed some such products may be chemically the same but the name, the packaging and the price give them a degree of uniqueness which differentiates them, at least in the minds of consumers. Advertising and marketing have a very important part to play in monopolistic competition.

Because the seller is confronted with many close substitutes for his product he faces a highly elastic demand curve and this clearly sets substantial limits on his "monopoly" power. Figure 15.3 illustrates the

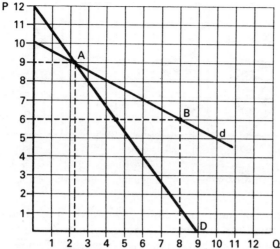

Figure 15.3: Monopolistic Competition – Industry and Firm Demand Curves.

difference between the relatively inelastic industry demand curve (D) and the highly elastic demand curve of the individual firm (d).

If the firm reduces its price to £6 its sales will increase almost fourfold to 8,000 units. If now the other firms in the industry follow suit, bringing their price down to £6 too, our firm's sales will only increase to 4,500 units. In practice, of course, all the firms in the industry will be selling differentiated products at different prices so it is not possible to derive a true industry demand curve. Thus in Figure 15.3 curve D only approximates to the industry demand.

SHORT RUN EQUILIBRIUM UNDER MONOPOLISTIC COMPETITION

In fact, the other firms will also reduce their prices but not just because one of many firms in the industry has done so. They will lower their prices because they too are not yet in equilibrium. Because they face similar cost curves they will also find it profitable to reduce their prices. In Figure 15.4 we extend our earlier example to take costs into account as well.

In Figure 15.4(a) starting at Point A, one firm decides to reduce its price to £4 in pursuit of equilibrium (X) – that point on its demand curve (d1) consonant with the intersection of its marginal revenue and marginal cost curves. Because other firms in the industry face similar cost curves, these other firms are likely to do the same with the result that there is a movement along the industry demand curve (D) to Point K. The

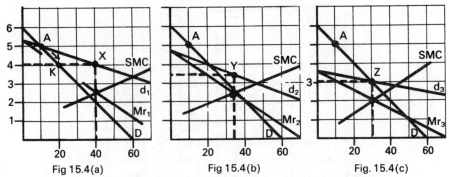

Fig 15.4(a)   Fig 15.4(b)   Fig. 15.4(c)

Figure 15.4: Monopolistic Competition – Short Run Equilibrium.

individual firm's demand curve shifts downwards to d2 (Figure 15.4(b)). Price and output for our firm are now at Point Y; and this process continues until the equilibrium point (Z) is reached (Figure 15.4(c)); the firm's price and output are now £3 and 30 units respectively. Note in particular that at Point Z the firm and industry demand curves intersect and there is therefore no incentive to reduce prices further.

LONG RUN EQUILIBRIUM AND INDUSTRY CAPACITY

As in the case of perfect competition the attraction of super-normal profits will bring new firms into the industry. This will have the effect of shifting each firm's demand curve downwards, and despite the possible attainment of reduced costs due to the economies of scale these super-normal profits will eventually be squeezed out and firms will only earn normal profits.

Under perfect competition, since each firm produces but an insignificant part of the total output and can sell everything it can produce at the prevailing price, it will produce as much as possible subject only to capacity and cost considerations.

In the case of monopoly and oligopoly output is usually restricted to the level at which the firm achieves the right price/output mix and hence maximises its profits. As we have seen the individual firm under monopolistic competition also restricts output. It does this because in the long run its demand curve must shift to the left and its optimum level of production must also be reduced.

A feature therefore of monopolistic competition is that firms are normally operating at less than full capacity. Individual firms, however, will continue to strive to maximise their profits and indeed to earn super-normal profits. The better ones among them will continue to do so while the weaker ones will collapse.

MONOPSONY

An important development of recent decades has been the growth of buying power. Where there is one buying firm only in a particular market this will be termed "monopsony": instances would be highly specialised equipment for the armed forces bought by the Department of Defence (with, as yet, no overseas market), and some much specialised categories of labour.

Often the situation is one of a high concentration of buying power with a few buyers – oligopsonists – dominating the market. The concept of "countervailing power" has been developed by Professor J. K. Galbraith to show the weakened power of sellers in many markets; indeed, in some instances, the buyer is now the dominant force. The growth of large-scale, concentrated retailing (e.g. Tesco, Sainsbury) has led to a diminution in the selling power of many manufacturing enterprises.

MARKET STRUCTURES – in summary.

	Perfect Competition	Monopolistic Competition	Oligopoly	Monopoly
Number of sellers	Many sellers and many buyers	Several sellers	Few sellers	One seller
Entry/exit	Free entry and exit	Free entry and exit	Constrained by scale of activity and/or product differentiation	Entry likely in longer run only
Product	Homogeneous	Differentiated	Homogeneous or differentiated	One product only in given market
Knowledge	Full knowledge of market situation	Full knowledge	Need for high level of awareness of likely action of competitors	Information network within the single supplier firm
Slope of demand curve	Horizontal	Downward sloping	Downward sloping	Downward sloping
Power to determine selling price	Price acceptor	Substantially a price acceptor though some price determining power arising from product differentiation	Governed by extent of competition and effectiveness of product differentiation. Tendency to avoid price competition	In short–medium term constrained only by overall economic effectiveness ($mc = mr$)
Long-run equilibrium output	Where Average Total Cost at minimum	Below capacity level	Below capacity level	Below capacity level
Long-run equilibrium profit	Normal profit	Tendency to normal profit	Some monopoly profit	Super monopoly profits

MULTIPLE CHOICE Test No. 1

There is only one correct answer to each of the following. Answers are given on page 370.

1. Opportunity cost:
    (a) is always measurable in money terms
    (b) is an indicator of productivity performance
    (c) relates peculiarly to business affairs alone
    (d) measures the cost of doing "x" in terms of what else might be done.

2. The normal downward slope of demand curves is necessarily explained by:
    (a) growth in the size of the population
    (b) the adroitness of advertisers
    (c) limited spending power
    (d) technological advance.

3. The change of output from $0q$ to $0q_1$

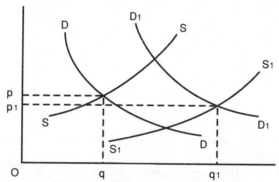

    (a) is the result of demand-led supply
    (b) represents a combination of supply improvement and demand increase
    (c) will mean higher fixed costs per unit of output
    (d) will of necessity take much time to achieve.

4. The law of diminishing returns:
    (a) assumes that there are changes taking place in production techniques

  (b) will always result in a positive figure
  (c) results in average product equalling marginal product when the average product is at its maximum
  (d) shows that the average product rises more rapidly than the marginal product.

5. In conditions of perfect competition:
  (a) the firm's supply curve lies above the average total cost curve
  (b) the participants' knowledge of market conditions is incomplete
  (c) sub-normal profits indicate a position of long-run equilibrium
  (d) the firm faces an infinitely inelastic demand curve for its product.

6. Income elasticity of demand for a particular product:
  (a) will always have a positive measurement
  (b) will be of value to the Government in setting the coming year's direct tax rates
  (c) will be unrelated to the possibility of changes in design of the product
  (d) could be affected by changes in levels of discretionary spending power.

7. The monopolist:
  (a) is able to control both price and quantity supplied
  (b) is concerned primarily with maximising selling price
  (c) favours elastic demand and therefore will always produce at a point in the demand curve where demand is elastic
  (d) who attempts price discrimination requires different demand elasticities in each market.

8. Giffen goods:
  (a) exemplify diminishing utility
  (b) illustrate the predominance of the substitution effect over the income effect
  (c) result in an upward sloping demand curve
  (d) are an example of the income effect reinforcing the substitution effect.

9. In the diagram, below, of a perfectly competitive industry, at what price–output combination would you expect the firms to operate?
  (a) wk
  (b) xk
  (c) yl
  (d) zk

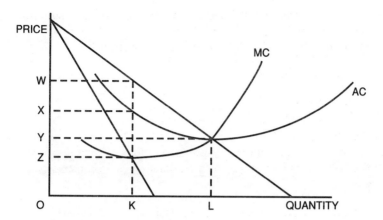

10. Oligopolists will:
    (a) always avoid price competition
    (b) be likely to be operating at capacity level in a situation of long-
        run equilibrium
    (c) have no significant differences from firms operating in monopolis-
        tic competition
    (d) be concerned about competitor strategy.

11. In the case of two related products, x and y, an increase in the price
    of x would:
    (a) result in an increased demand for y
    (b) lead to a proportionate fall in the demand for x
    (c) immediately affect the cross elasticity of demand of y for x
    (d) on the information given, have an indeterminate effect on the
        demand for y.

12. Monopolistic competition is a situation of:
    (a) many firms selling related yet differentiated products
    (b) a few firms operating in conditions of only limited competition
    (c) many firms selling the same product(s)
    (d) a few firms operating in a market where demand is essentially
        price inelastic.

Answers on page 370.

QUESTIONS

1. "Imperfect competition covers all the real world situations. Monopolies and perfectly competitive firms simply don't exist in the real world."
Comment.

2. To what extent is non-price competition a factor in situations of imperfect competition?

3. What does the kinked demand curve demonstrate?

CHAPTER 16

DISTRIBUTION THEORY

As we have noted earlier, the production of a given commodity requires the use of the various factors of production, land, labour, capital and enterprise. It follows that the total proceeds from the sale of any given commodity must equal the total payment to these factors of production. Part of the proceeds will go to labour in the form of wages, part to land in the form of rent, part to capital in the form of interest, and any proceeds remaining will constitute profit for the entrepreneur. As this must be true for all the goods and services which society produces, we can see that the total output of the economy will be distributed as rewards to the factors of production. Table 16.1 shows how the national output was distributed in 1988.

Table 16.1: The Distribution of National Output1988.

	% share
Income from employment	63
Income from self-employment	9
Gross trading profits of companies	18
Gross trading profits of public corporations	2
Rent	8
Total domestic income	100

Source: National Income and Expenditure Accounts 1989.

Distribution theory is the name given to that branch of economics which examines how these relative shares are determined, and in this, and succeeding chapters, we shall discuss the factors which have been put forward to explain the distribution of the national output.

MARGINAL PRODUCTIVITY THEORY

One approach to the problem of relative factor shares is to treat each factor of production as just another commodity, with its price being determined by the interaction of demand and supply. If the demand for a factor (say labour) rises in relation to supply, the price of labour, and hence its total earnings, will rise. Similarly, an increase in the supply of a particular factor will cause a fall in that factor's price. Therefore, we must examine what determines the demand and supply of each factor if we wish to understand the distribution of total income between them. We will begin by looking at the demand for a factor in general (using labour as an example) before turning to a more detailed study of land, labour, capital and enterprise.

Let us assume that a farmer has a fixed area of land on which he grows wheat, and that he is deciding how many labourers he should hire to harvest this year's crop. The price of wheat is currently £10 per tonne, and he can sell any amount he produces at this price. In addition, we assume that each labourer is equally efficient and that each will ask for the same wage. Table 16.2 illustrates the effect on total production as additional workers are employed.

Table 16.2: Total Production of Wheat (tonnes).

Labour	Total Product	Marginal Physical Product	Marginal Revenue Product (£)
1	30	30	300
2	70	40	400
3	100	30	300
4	125	25	250
5	145	20	200
6	155	10	100

It is clear that total output increases with each additional worker, as one would expect, but that the third worker adds less than the second, the fourth less than the third, and so on. The amount that each worker adds to production is called the Marginal Physical Product and we can see from the table that this begins to decline after the second worker. This illustrates a general condition of production which is known as the Law of Diminishing Returns (see also Chapter 9). This states that if additional quantities of a variable factor are added to a fixed factor the marginal physical product will eventually decline. Labour is obviously the variable factor in our example, with land as the fixed factor.

Our farmer will not be interested in the total amount each labourer adds to production, but rather the total value of this extra production. If we multiply the marginal phusical product by the price of wheat (£10 in this case), we obtain what is termed the Marginal Revenue Product, and

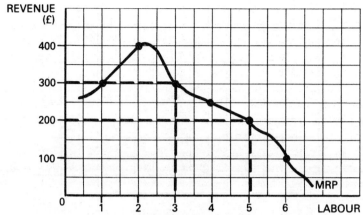

Figure 16.1: The Marginal Revenue Product Curve.

this tells the farmer how much each worker adds to total revenue. If we now plot this marginal revenue product on a diagram we can see that it is, in fact, the farmer's demand curve for labour.

How many workers would the farmer employ if the wage was £200 per man? From Figure 16.1 we can see that the sixth worker adds less than this to revenue, so if the farmer wishes to maximise profits he would only employ five labourers. Just as firms maximise profits by producing where marginal revenue equals marginal cost, so they will maximise returns from using the factors of production if they employ factors up to the point where their marginal revenue product is just equal to their cost. This is known as the Marginal Productivity Theory and we can use it to explain the demand for any factor of production.

To return to our farmer, what would happen to his demand for labour if the wage rate rose to £300 per man? It would no longer be profitable for him to hire the fifth labourer, or indeed the fourth, as they add more to cost than to revenue. To maximise profits he would reduce his demand for labour to three workers. In other words, the marginal revenue products curve is the demand curve for the particular factor of production, as it shows the demand for the factor at various prices of the factor.

THE DEMAND CURVE FOR A FACTOR OF PRODUCTION

In Figure 16.2 the relevant area of the marginal revenue product curve has been reproduced as the demand curve for labour in our agricultural example. The curve will always be downwards sloping from left to right

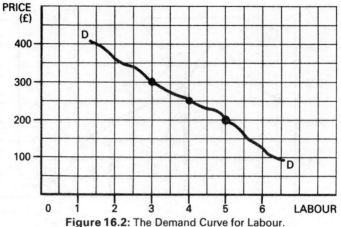

Figure 16.2: The Demand Curve for Labour.

as long as diminishing returns operate, but the *position* and *slope* of the curve are dependent on a variety of factors.

When examining the position of the demand curve it should be remembered that a *demand for any factor of production* will only occur if there is a *demand for the product* it is helping to produce. A farmer would not require any labourers to harvest his wheat if there was no demand for wheat. So the demand for any factor of production is a *derived demand,* in that it is derived from the existence of a demand for the final product. Therefore, a rise in demand for the final product will cause a rise in demand for the factor of production i.e. the demand curve for the factor will shift rightwards. The other main determinant of the position of the curve is the *productivity of the factor* itself. If each labourer in our farming example produced more units of wheat, the whole marginal revenue product curve, and hence the demand curve, would shift rightwards. Similarly, if each unit of the factor is less productive the demand curve for the factor would shift leftwards.

The *slope of the demand curve* has important implications for the total earnings of a factor of production. In Figure 16.3 we have two demand curves, both downwards sloping, as marginal productivity theory suggests. In each case more of the factor would be employed following a fall in the factor price, but in case (A) the total spent on the factor (and hence its total earnings) has actually fallen. In case (A) demand for the factor is very unresponsive to a change in its price, but in case (B) a small change in price leads to a large change in demand. We saw in chapter 5 that this responsiveness of demand to a change in price is known as price elasticity of demand, and it is clear that demand in case (A) is inelastic, and elastic in case (B).

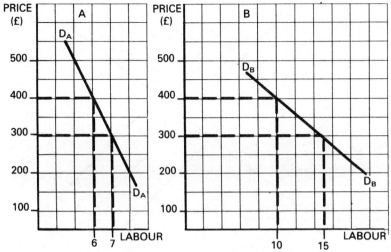

Figure 16.3: Changes in the Slope of the Demand Curve for a Factor.

The following factors will affect the price elasticity of demand for a factor of production:

1. The ease of *substitution* of other factors – If a factor is highly specialised and it has no close substitutes, a given rise in price will not have a large impact on demand, as other factors cannot be used in its place. Therefore the demand for skilled labour is likely to be more inelastic than the demand for unskilled labour.

2. The *importance of the factor in total costs* – If the total spent on the factor is only a small part of total costs, a given percentage change in the factor's price will only be a small amount in money terms, and so the firm will not reduce demand for the factor by as much as it would if total spending on the factor were a high proportion of costs.

3. The *price elasticity of demand for the final product* – If the demand for the final product is unresponsive to a change in price, the demand for the factor is likely to be inelastic as well. This is due to the fact that a rise in the factor's price will obviously increase costs, but that this can more easily be passed on to the final consumer if the demand for the final product is inelastic.

THE TOTAL EARNINGS OF A FACTOR OF PRODUCTION

As we have seen, marginal productivity analysis allows us to derive the demand curve for any factor of production, and this demand curve will

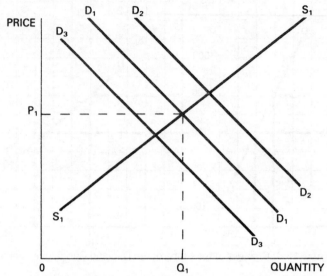

Figure 16.4: The Demand and Supply Curves for a Factor of Production.

be downwards sloping from left to right (although its position and slope can be affected by the factors outlined above). We will assume for the moment that the supply curve for a factor of production will also have the conventional shape i.e. upward sloping from left to right. If we now bring the two curves together, as in Figure 16.4, we can examine factor earnings.

The original demand and supply curves are D_1D_1 and S_1S_1, with the price of the factor being P_1. Total factor earnings are given by the area $OP_1\ OQ_1$. If demand for the factor rises (perhaps due to a rise in its productivity) the demand curve shifts to D_2D_2, giving rise to increased employment of the factor and to an increase in its earnings. If demand for the factor of production falls (perhaps due to a fall in the price of a substitute) the demand curve shifts to D_3D_3, with a corresponding fall in earnings and employment.

We can use demand and supply analysis in this manner to explain changes in the distribution of national output. For example, if labour's share falls at the expense of capital's, it may be that the cost of labour has risen relative to the cost of capital, leading to a movement up the demand curve for labour and to a rightward shift in the demand curve for capital.

CRITICISMS OF MARGINAL PRODUCTIVITY THEORY

A major difficulty with marginal productivity analysis is that it requires the separation of each factor's contribution to production. This may not be possible if two or more factors have to be combined in fixed proportions. For example, a particular process may require each worker to use a specific machine, making it impossible for the entrepreneur to distinguish between labour's contribution to production and the contribution of capital.

A second problem arises from the fact that it may be impossible to measure the productivity of a particular factor. This is true in many service industries where it would be difficult, for example, to compare the output of a teacher with that of a nurse.

A third criticism of marginal productivity analysis concerns its neglect of the supply of the factors of production. It is purely a theory of the demand for factors of production, but, as we have seen, the earnings of a factor can be affected by a change in the amount supplied although marginal productivity analysis has nothing to say on this matter.

A final criticism concerns some of the implicit assumptions we have made in deriving the theory. It was assumed that each worker was identical and that each one was willing to work for the same wage. In practice the labour market, or indeed any factor market, is likely to contain many imperfections and institutional constraints, making the simple application of marginal productivity analysis inappropriate.

A BARGAINING THEORY OF DISTRIBUTION

Some economists reject the traditional marginal productivity approach for the above reasons, and instead emphasise that the distribution of national income depends upon the outcome of a bargaining process between management and workers. The outcome of this process depends upon a host of complex institutional and sociological factors, including the power of trade unions, the legal framework of union action, the profitability of the firm, the cost of a strike, the respective leadership of management and workforce, the importance in the economy of the industry concerned, and the government's attitude to wage bargaining.

Nevertheless, demand and supply analysis is still a useful starting point for any examination of distribution theory, and we can now examine each factor of production in more detail within the framework of marginal productivity analysis. Where such a framework is inappropriate, however, additional political and sociological factors will be emphasised.

QUESTIONS

1. Examine the total production figures given in Table 16.2. By calculating the total cost and revenue figures, show that the farmer would maximise profits by employing 5 workers when the wage rate is £200 per man. (Assume that land costs £100.)

2. What would happen to the marginal revenue product curve if the price of the final product rose?

3. Examine Figure 16.3 showing the different sloped demand curves. What happens to the total earnings of each factor if price rises from £300 to £400?

4. Is the demand for the following likely to be elastic or inelastic:

  (a) A heart transplant specialist. (b) A door-to-door salesman. (c)
    A space satellite. (d) Rail transport?

5. How might one try to measure the output of a teacher? In the middle of the nineteenth century teachers pay was linked to the results of their pupils. Is this a good way to measure productivity?

CHAPTER 17

LABOUR AND WAGES

Labour is defined as the mental and physical effort made by human beings in the production of goods and services. As a factor of production, labour differs fundamentally from land and capital. If a machine lies idle there is an obvious economic cost in terms of the output which could be produced. If labour lies idle, however, the economic cost must be measured alongside the social and personal cost to the individual involved. People, unlike machines, have feelings and emotions and long term unemployment can seriously damage a person's mental and physical well-being.

There are a number of other differences making labour unique as a factor of production. Workers often take non-monetary rewards into consideration when seeking employment, including status, "job satisfaction" and the companionship of fellow workers. Again, unlike machines, workers can combine together to influence their earnings by restricting the amount of labour offered at a given wage or by threatening to withdraw labour altogether. Finally, as we shall see, labour tends to be less mobile than some other factors of production.

WAGES AND THE REWARDS TO LABOUR

Wages is the general name given to the payments made to secure the services of labour. This is a broad term, however, covering a variety of methods used to reward labour. Some workers are self-employed, and as such bear an element of risk, in that earnings can fluctuate from week to week. So in one sense they can be viewed as entrepreneurs, making their reward profit rather than wages. Others, particularly those with a professional skill, receive a fee in return for services to a client. The term "wage" is not used here because a regular contractual payment is absent. Many clerical and administrative staff receive their payments on a monthly basis, often by cheque, and the term "salary" is used to describe this particular method of rewarding labour for its services to production. There are also distinct methods of calculating the wages paid to labour. Piece-rates are often used where the output of the worker is measurable and where his effort can be directly related to the number of units produced. Time-rates are paid when the employee is contracted to work a set number of hours per day or per week.

Piece-rates have a number of advantages. Higher productivity is encouraged (the more a worker produces, the more he earns), and dull work is made more interesting for the workforce. The management will also benefit as less supervision is required, and capital equipment is likely to be used more intensively. A number of disadvantages are also apparent with this type of payment. The quality of work may deteriorate as each worker strives to increase his total output. Obtaining nationally agreed rates of pay may be difficult, as the efficiency of capital used by the workforce may differ from area to area. This type of payment may also lead to bad feeling and industrial unrest amongst the workers, if certain individuals sustain a level of production which is significantly higher than the average.

Time-rates are used when it is not possible to measure the output of individual workers, or when the quality of the work requires lengthy application. In addition, many jobs require the worker to undertake a variety of different tasks, and piece-rates, as a method of payment, would be inappropriate. The disadvantages of using time-rates are that there is no incentive for the individual worker to improve his productivity, and the management may be required to supervise the workforce.

A final word on terminology is necessary here. The terms "wages" and "earnings" are often used synonymously in reference to the rewards to labour. However, there is an important distinction. Wages are the contractual sum paid to the worker in return for services rendered, and the wage-rate is often nationally negotiated. Earnings are often higher than these stipulated wage rates, because overtime and bonuses are included in the worker's pay-packet. *Wage-Drift* is the name given to the fact that earnings exceed wages, and the level of such wage-drift is a good indicator of the pressure of demand for labour. If a particular firm wishes to increase output, it is likely to be willing to pay workers more than any nationally agreed wage-rate.

THE SUPPLY OF LABOUR

The supply of labour is measured in terms of the number of hours of work offered by the population. The supply available to a particular industry will depend upon the following factors.

1. THE TOTAL POPULATION

The overall size of the population sets an upper limit to the labour supply. The growth of population is affected by the number of births, the number of deaths, and the level of net migration. In most western countries the number of deaths does not vary greatly from year to year, and the main cause of changes in the rate of population growth is changes in the number of births. In fact it has proved very difficult to predict future population trends with any degree of accuracy, given these unexpected swings in the birth rate. For this reason all such forecasts are constantly revised in the light of changing circumstances.

2. LABOUR FORCE PARTICIPATION

The working population in the U.K. is much smaller than the total population, because many people do not participate in the labour force. Children under 16 are legally excluded from full-time work, and there is also an official retirement age – currently 60 for women and 65 for men. Some people of working age choose not to participate. Many young adults decide to postpone seeking employment in order to undertake courses in further and higher education. In addition, a large number of married women withdraw from the labour force, although they may return when the demand for labour is high. Therefore, as we can see in Table 17.1, the total supply of labour differs substantially from the total population.

Table 17.1: The U.K. Working Population 1983–1988.

	millions	
	1983	1988
Total population	56·3	57·1
Total working population	26·7	28·2
Of which:		
Total employees	21·2	22·2
Total unemployed	3·0	2·3
Total employers, self-employed and armed forces	2·5	3·3
In work-related Government training programmes	—	0·3

Source: Annual Abstract of Statistics.

3. THE NUMBER OF HOURS WORKED BY THE INDIVIDUAL

Certain institutional and legal forces may set limits to the number of hours a week the worker can supply, but the main influence within these limits is likely to be the wage rate. The individual worker faces a choice between work and leisure, with the opportunity cost of an hour's work being the leisure forgone. Therefore, in order to compensate the worker for losing this leisure time the employer has to offer a monetary reward. Following this line of reasoning it would appear that higher rates of pay

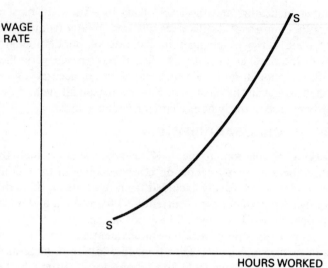

Figure 17.1: The Supply Curve of Labour.

per hour may encourage the individual worker to sacrifice more of his leisure time. This would give rise to the upward sloping supply curve in Figure 17.1.

In Table 17.2 we can see that the average number of hours worked in the U.K. has actually fallen over time (although there has been a slight rise in recent years). This casts some doubt on the shape of the supply curve as drawn above.

Table 17.2: Average number of hours worked by male manual workers.

Year	Hours
1955	48·6
1960	47·4
1965	46·7
1970	45·7
1978	43·5
1983	42·6
1987	43·5

Source: Annual Abstract of Statistics.

It may be that at higher wage rates the individual may prefer to take increased leisure rather than work longer hours. Consider the following

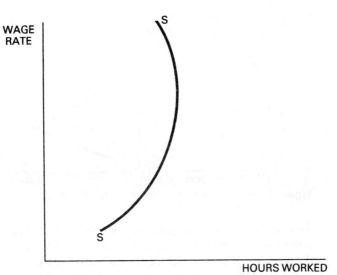

Figure 17.2: An Alternative Supply Curve of Labour.

example. A man works 40 hours per week at a wage rate of £10 per hour, thereby earning £400. Following a rise in his wage rate to £11, he could work for 39 hours and still have a higher income than the previous figure. Therefore higher wage rates may encourage some workers to substitute leisure for work, in that they can maintain their existing standard of living by working fewer hours. This gives rise to the backward sloping supply curve illustrated in Figure 17.2. Note that this curve implies that a rise in income tax (a cut in net pay) may encourage people to work harder!

WAGE DIFFERENTIALS

Skilled workers usually earn more than unskilled workers, and this wage differential persists over time. We can use the marginal productivity theory developed in the previous chapter to explain this. For the moment we shall assume that wages are determined, in a market free from imperfections, by the interaction of demand and supply. Remember that the demand for labour is determined by its marginal revenue product, and that the supply of labour will be positively related to the wage rate (we ignore the possibility of a backward sloping supply curve). In Figure 17.3 we see the relevant demand and supply curves.

In each market the wage rate is determined by the intersection of the respective demand and supply curves. The wage paid to skilled

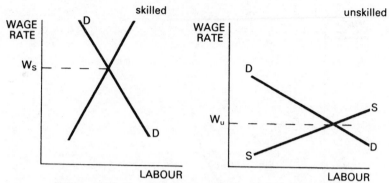

Figure 17.3: The Wages of Skilled and Unskilled Workers.

labour (Ws) is higher than that paid to the unskilled (Wu), because demand for the former is higher in relation to the available supply. Note the slope of the curves. The demand for skilled labour is less elastic than the demand for unskilled workers, as capital can be substituted more readily for the latter. The supply of skilled workers is also more inelastic, due to the fact that it would take time for labour to acquire the relevant skills.

Why should this wage differential persist? Surely the unskilled workers would perceive the gap in earnings and so take steps to learn the necessary skills? This would eventually lead to a rightward shift in the supply curve of skilled labour, and a subsequent fall in wages, until the differential had been eroded. In fact, there are many factors in the labour market which prevent workers moving, either occupationally or geographically. It is to these factors that we now turn.

THE MOBILITY OF LABOUR

The mobility of a factor of production is the ease with which it moves between uses and locations. An electrician living in Manchester could move to London to practise his trade, or he could re-train as a computer programmer. In reality, either change would be difficult, as there are certain barriers to mobility.

The following obstacles prevent workers changing occupations easily:

(a) An individual may lack the natural ability required to enter an industry.

(b) A high level of intellectual ability may be necessary for certain occupations.

(c) Some workers may be too old to train for a new skill.

(d) Acquiring a skill involves giving up time as well as incurring financial costs. Many people are unwilling to sacrifice the former, and cannot afford the latter.

(e) Trade unions and professional associations restrict entry to certain occupations, in order to maintain high rewards for the existing workforce in those occupations. (We shall examine this more closely later in this chapter.)

(f) Discrimination may exist on grounds of sex, race, social class and religion.

Workers also face difficulties in moving from one part of the country to another. These include:

(a) The cost of moving. This can be high, especially if the whole family is involved.

(b) House prices. These vary greatly from area to area, and it may be difficult to secure comparable accommodation. In the case of council tenants, a move to a new locality might entail the giving up of one's home, with no guarantee of being offered council property in the new area.

(c) Educational factors. Many families would be reluctant to move if it meant the disruption of the children's education.

(d) Family and social ties. Moving away from a particular area means breaking these ties, and many people are unwilling to suffer the psychological upheaval which this implies.

(e) Lack of knowledge of opportunities elsewhere. It may be that most workers are simply unaware of wage and employment conditions in other parts of the country.

The existence of these barriers to mobility means that the labour market is largely made up of "non-competing groups", and that wage differentials are maintained. Of course some workers do change occupations, but this move is more likely to be to a job with similar conditions and pay. For example, a docker may become a factory worker, but he is unlikely to become a solicitor. Similarly, labour does move geographically, but such movement, particularly among the unskilled, is often confined to the young and single.

THE PUBLIC SECTOR AND THE LABOUR MARKET

About 25 per cent of those in employment work in the public sector, either directly for the state or in the nationalised industries. Many of these workers produce services, or goods which are provided free of charge to the user. In each case it is difficult to quantify a marginal product e.g. how do you measure the productivity of a civil servant? It is therefore impossible to determine a demand curve for labour in the manner used in our agricultural example, in the previous chapter. One could argue that workers in the public sector should receive the same wage as similar workers in the private sector, where the final product is presumably sold at a profit maximising price. However, this often proves difficult in practice, as the private sector equivalent is either too small to influence the public sector, or does not exist at all.

For this reason the wages of many groups in the public sector owe more to historical factors, and trade union pressure, than to any economic considerations. However, demand and supply factors do have a role to play in the long run, in that if the rewards to labour in a particular occupation fall, relative to other occupations, workers may simply leave. In economic terminology each worker is said to have certain *transfer earnings* which is defined as the minimum payment required to keep that worker in his present occupation. So if the wages of, say, policemen, fall below their transfer earnings, the authorities will have to raise the wage rate if they wish to prevent a substantial exodus from the Force.

EMPLOYMENT LEGISLATION AND THE LABOUR MARKET

The marginal productivity theory of wage determination implies that if demand for the final product falls, or if wages rise faster than productivity, the firm will reduce its demand for labour. This may be difficult to achieve in practice. Various statutes exist which make it difficult for a firm to make workers redundant. Similarly, equal pay legislation prohibits firms paying women less than men for the same type of work, even though the firm may consider the men to be more productive.

Employers are also legally obliged to pay National Insurance contributions for all but the lowest paid workers, and this obviously raises the cost of hiring labour. On the supply side, the employee does not receive the wage paid by the firm, as he must also pay national insurance, and, in most cases, income tax.

INCOMES POLICIES

The labour market in the 1960s and 1970s was characterised by the successive attempts of various governments to impose ceilings on the level of wage increases. Such measures distorted the labour market as they prevented wages responding to movements in demand and supply. A flat rate incomes policy will reduce the wage differential between the skilled and unskilled, and it is the former who usually break such policies. In addition, firms wishing to increase their workers pay above the permitted limits may resort to providing "perks", such as subsidised meals, longer holidays or profit-sharing schemes. Even when a formal incomes policy does not exist, the public sector is often subject to government imposed spending limits, and this amounts to a *de facto* incomes policy.

TRADE UNIONS AND COLLECTIVE BARGAINING

About half of those employed in the U.K. belong to trade unions, and such organisations have an important impact on the labour market. It is possible to distinguish four types of union.

1. **Craft unions**, which consist of skilled workers such as engineers or boilermakers. These unions recruit their members across industries.

2. **General unions**, who are willing to accept members from all occupations and industries, although the bulk of the membership is unskilled. Many of the largest unions in the U.K. are of this type, such as the Transport and General Workers Union.

3. **Industrial unions**, who try to persuade all workers in a particular industry to join. The National Union of Mineworkers is an example of such a union.

4. **"White-collar" unions**. These unions consist of non-manual workers such as clerical and administrative staff and other salaried employees. They can be organised on an industry basis, or attempt to recruit members across the industrial structure.

In many European countries single industries are often represented by one union, unlike the above situation which exists in the U.K. This makes it more difficult for British management to negotiate with its workforce, as numerous unions might be involved. Demarcation disputes also occur, when different unions argue about which particular trade should be responsible for a particular task.

Specific trade unions have a number of objectives, but all unions desire to improve the living standards of their members. This means improving their wages and conditions of work, and to achieve this, the unions conduct negotiations with employers or employers' associations. This process is known as *collective bargaining*. As well as the general wage rate, a variety of additional considerations may enter the negotiations. These might include the number of hours to worked, the rate for overtime pay, holiday entitlement, and wage differentials. The union's main weapon in these negotiations is its ability to withdraw the labour

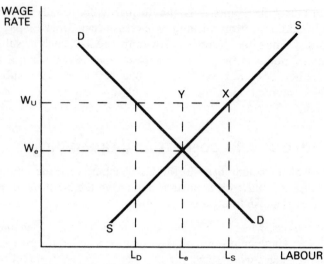

Figure 17.4: Trade Unions and Wage Determination.

force from employment if the outcome is not to its satisfaction. On the employer side, the level of profits in the industry and the ability to withstand a strike are the prime considerations. The power of the unions in collective bargaining will be greatly increased if a *"closed shop"* exists. This means that all the workers in question must belong to the union to gain employment in the industry. Such an arrangement obviously reduces individual liberty at the expense of increasing the power of collective action. The present legal position on closed shops attempts to safeguard the rights of the individual, by providing for a ballot of the workforce where such a system exists.

WAGE DETERMINATION AND COLLECTIVE BARGAINING

We can now extend our simple demand and supply analysis of wage determination to take account of the existence of trade unions. In Figure 17.4 the demand and supply curves intersect at an equilibrium wage of W_e, and an equilibrium employment level of L_e. If a trade union were to impose the higher wage, Wu, no worker could offer himself for employment at any wage below this, making the new supply curve of labour $W_U YXS$. Therefore, the new equilibrium wage is W_U, with total employment now reduced to L_S–L_D, as the higher wage rate gives rise to an excess supply of labour. So the union has secured an increase in the earnings of its members, but at the expense of unemployment.

Can the union secure the higher wage rate *and* maintain the original level of employment? The answer is yes, but only if one of the following occurs:

(a) Productivity increases, shifting the demand curve for labour right-ward until it cuts point Y in the diagram.
(b) The firm raises the price of the product, again shifting the demand curve rightward.
(c) The firm agrees to pay the new wage without reducing its demand for labour i.e. it moves off the demand curve to point Y. This implies that the firm would not be maximising profits, as some workers are being paid more than their contributions to output.

So, in summary, we can see that if trade unions secure wage rises in excess of productivity, it must lead to either a rise in the price of the final product, or to a reduction in the firm's profits. This is a useful point to remember when we come to consider economic management of the economy as a whole viz. if the growth in wages exceeds the growth in productivity, prices must rise, unless profits fall at the expense of wages.

QUESTIONS

1. What factors might influence a married woman's decision to enter the labour force? What type of jobs would be most suitable?

2. Some economists claim that a cut in income tax would encourage workers to work longer hours. Is this necessarily true? (check the different shapes of the supply curves of labour).

3. Examine Figure 17.3, which shows the wages of skilled and unskilled workers. In which market would wages fluctuate most if demand changed?

4. How might the government improve the mobility of labour?

5. How might a trade union restrict the supply of labour to a particular industry in order to raise wages?

CHAPTER 18

CAPITAL AND INTEREST

Capital can be defined as a stock of goods made by man for the production of further goods. A distinction is usually made between *fixed capital*, such as buildings, plant and machinery, and *circulating capital*, such as raw materials and semi-finished goods. Capital enhances the productivity of land and labour, and is therefore demanded as a factor of production. Additions to the capital stock are known as *investment*, and we must be careful here to distinguish between the conventional use of this term and its specific economic use. Many people speak of "investing" their money in stocks and shares, or in building society accounts. Investment in economics, however, is only used to describe the creation of real capital, such as the building of a house or the manufacture of a machine.

THE DEMAND FOR CAPITAL

If a firm decides to increase its capital stock, by, say, adding to its machinery, it must first obtain the money to purchase such machinery. We call this money *liquid capital*. The purchase of each machine will add to total costs, but will also result in increased output. However, remembering the law of diminishing returns, we would expect that beyond a certain point, each additional machine would add less and less to revenues, giving rise to the familiar marginal revenue product curve illustrated in Figure 18.1.

In deciding how many machines to purchase, the firm will obviously compare the revenue from each machine with the cost of that machine. We can express the cost of capital as a rate of interest, in that it is the price a firm would have to pay for the use of liquid capital. Similarly, we can measure the revenue generated from additional units of capital as a rate of return. So, in Figure 18.2, the marginal revenue product curve has been reproduced, but the revenue axis is now expressed in percentage terms. If the cost of liquid is R_1, the firm will demand Q_1 units of capital, as any additional units would produce a rate of return lower than the prevailing rate of interest. A rise in the rate of interest above R_1 would result in a fall in demand for capital, and a fall in the rate of interest would result in a rise in the demand for capital.

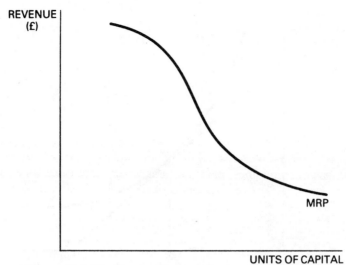

Figure 18.1: The Marginal Revenue Product Curve for Capital.

Therefore, the demand curve for capital by any one firm will be the marginal revenue product curve of that capital. It follows that the industry's demand curve for capital will be the sum of the individual firms' curves, and that the total demand for capital in the economy will be the sum total of each industry's demand.

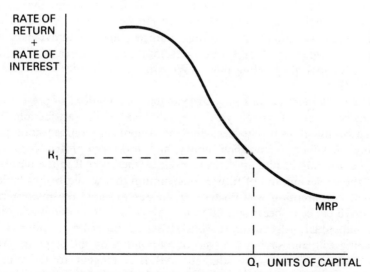

Figure 18.2: The Demand for Capital and the Rate of Interest.

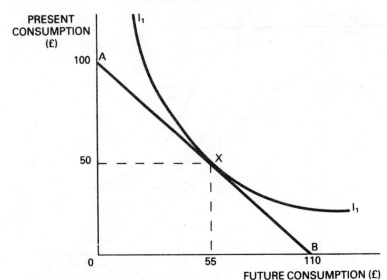

Figure 18.3: An Indifference Curve Approach to Saving.

THE SUPPLY OF LIQUID CAPITAL

The supply of liquid capital for investment comes from the total level of funds which individuals, or firms, are prepared to lend for this purpose. What is the likely relationship between these funds and the rate of interest? To answer this question we must first examine the choice between spending and saving which each individual faces. Saving means that present consumption is being sacrificed, and so individuals will require a higher level of future consumption to compensate for the immediate loss of spending power. We can see this choice illustrated in Figure 18.3.

The indifference curve I_1I_1 represents the combinations of present and future consumption which yield the individual equal satisfaction. The actual combination he chooses will depend upon the compensation paid to anyone willing to lend their money, and thus forgo present consumption i.e. the rate of interest. This is given by the line AB in the diagram, as it shows the amount of future consumption that would be available if present consumption was postponed. In our example the interest rate equals 10 per cent, because £100 today will yield £110 in one year's time. The individual will maximise satisfaction at this rate of interest by spending £50, and saving £55 (shown by point X on the diagram). This combination occurs where the line AB is a tangent to the highest available indifference curve. He has insufficient income to reach any

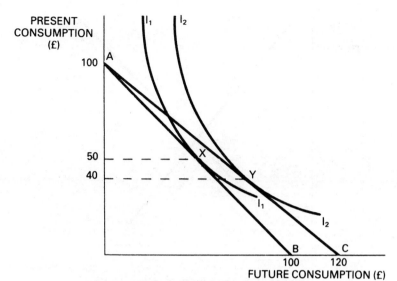

Figure 18.4: Change in the Rate of Interest.

combinations to the right of X, and any point to the left would reduce total satisfaction.

What would the individual do if the rate of interest rose, say to 20 per cent? Figure 18.4 illustrates the outcome.

The rise in the rate of interest has changed the slope of AB, as £100

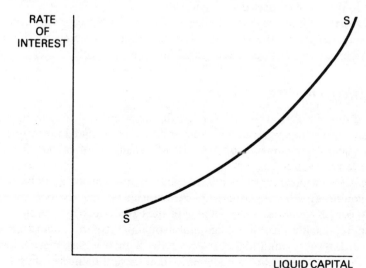

Figure 18.5: The Supply Curve of Liquid Capital.

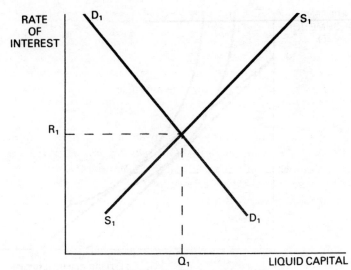

Figure 18.6: The Equilibrium Interest Rate.

today will now yield £120 in one year's time. So we have a new line, AC. This means that the individual can now reach a higher indifference curve I_2I_2, and we can see on the diagram that his new equilibrium position is at point Y. The end result is that he has reduced present consumption to £40, and therefore increased saving to £60.

This analysis indicates that the level of saving in the economy will be positively related to the rate of interest, yielding the upward sloping supply curve of liquid capital illustrated in Figure 18.5.

THE RATE OF INTEREST

We are now in a position to examine the determination of the rate of interest. In a competitive market this will simply be that rate of return which equates the demand for capital and the supply of capital. This is illustrated in Figure 18.6.

The equilibrium interest rate is R_1, and the amount of liquid capital forthcoming at this rate equals Q_1. A change in either the demand or supply curves would lead to a change in the equilibrium rate of interest. A rise in demand for liquid capital would shift the demand curve rightward, resulting in a higher interest rate. Similarly, a rise in the level of savings would shift the supply curve rightward, this time leading to a fall in the rate of interest.

OTHER INFLUENCES ON THE LEVEL OF SAVINGS

The above analysis of the rate of interest is known as the *Loanable Funds* theory, and it was an integral part of the classical tradition in nineteenth century economics. However, modern economists point out that the rate of interest may not longer be the main determinant of the level of savings. A variety of other influences exist, including:

1. Income. The ability to save depends upon the level of an individual's income. At low levels of income saving may be zero whatever the rate of interest, as all income is necessary for consumption. In fact, empirical evidence suggests that saving is positively related to income, and that the *proportion* of income saved tends to rise with the level of income.

2. Contractual elements. A proportion of saving is carried out through insurance companies and pension funds, where the individual is contracted to pay a fixed sum at regular intervals. The level of such savings will therefore be unaffected by changes in interest rates, at least in the short term.

3. Inflation. High levels of inflation, which the U.K. experienced in the 1970s, increase the proportion of income saved. This is due to the fact that rising prices reduce the real value of nominal assets, and so more income has to be devoted to saving in order to maintain their value in real terms.

4. Habit. Many people save a certain part of their income through habit, and small changes in the rate of interest will not affect their consumption decisions.

For the above reasons one should be wary of relating the rate of interest to the level of saving in any simple manner. Very high or very low interest rates may affect savings significantly, but small changes around the average level are unlikely to have anything other than a minor effect.

A MONETARY APPROACH TO THE INTEREST RATE

An alternative approach to the determination of the rate of interest was put forward in the 1930s by Lord Keynes. He stressed the fact that the rate of interest was a monetary phenomenon, and that conditions in the money markets are likely to be the major influence. For this reason we shall postpone our examination of this approach until chapter 22, where we will look at the demand and supply of money in detail.

THE STRUCTURE OF INTEREST RATES

So far we have discussed the rate of interest as if there was only one single rate for all loans. A cursory glance at the financial press reveals that this is far from the truth. Interest rates differ for a number of reasons.

1. The risk involved. Loans to the government carry a lower rate of interest than equivalent loans to industry. This is because the risk of default is higher with the latter, and so borrowers have to compensate lenders for this. Generally, the riskier the loan, the higher the interest rate.

2. The time period involved. In any loan transaction the lender is sacrificing liquidity. This means that he cannot spend the money involved until the end of the loan period. Therefore, the longer the loan period, the greater sacrifice the lender is making, and the greater the compensation required. Consider the interest rates offered by building societies to their account holders. Higher rates are offered to those willing to accept restrictions on the notice required to make a withdrawal.

3. The differential charged by financial institutions. A variety of financial institutions exist to bring borrowers and lenders together. So, for example, building societies pay savers a given rate of interest, and in turn lend this money to borrowers on the security of property. The rate of interest which the latter pay is higher, in order to cover the cost of administration involved. This differential varies from market to market, and is likely to be affected by the degree of competition among financial institutions.

4. Expected inflation. The rate of interest is usually fixed in nominal terms, and its real value may therefore change if prices change. Let us take the following example to illustrate the consequences of this. A lends B £100 for one year, at an interest rate of 10 per cent. This means that A will receive £110 payment for the loan. If prices rose during the year, however, this sum would buy less than A thought it would, when he agreed to make the loan. Therefore, if A expected prices to rise he would raise the interest rate, to protect the purchasing power of his money. We can witness this principle at work in the economy in general, with interest rates drifting upward if inflation is expected to increase.

INVESTMENT APPRAISAL

The marginal productivity theory of investment, as developed earlier in this chapter, led to the conclusion that the level of investment spending would be inversely related to the rate of interest. In deriving this result, we assumed that a firm could compare the revenue generated by successive units of capital, with the cost of obtaining that capital. The term "investment appraisal" is used to describe this analysis of the prospective costs and benefits associated with capital investment.

In practice, such investment appraisal involves a difficulty which we have ignored for the sake of simplicity. This is the fact that in making an investment decision, the firm has to compare the cost of a machine today with a flow of revenue from the machine in the future. A problem arises here, in that money now is worth more than money in the future, because it can be invested today to produce a greater sum tomorrow. How then do we compare the *present value* (PV) of a flow of future receipts? The answer is that we *discount* it, using the rate of interest that it would obtain if invested. So £110 in a year's time has a present value of £100 if the current interest rate is 10 per cent. Note that a rise in the rate of interest reduces the present value of future income, in that less than £100 would have to be invested today to yield £110 next year.

Let us take an example to explain how this approach to investment would be utilised by a firm. Assume that a company can purchase a machine for £200, and that it will last for three years, yielding revenue of £130 in the first year, £120 in the second, and £110 in the third. What is the present value of this flow of income? The following formula can be used to calculate it.

$$PV = \frac{R_1}{1 + r} + \frac{R_2}{(1 + r)^2} + \frac{R_3}{(1 + r)^3}$$

where R = the receipts in each year and r = the rate of interest. If we assume that the current interest rate is 10 per cent, we can insert our figures into the above equation. This yields

$$PV = \frac{£130}{1 + 0·1} + \frac{£120}{(1 + 0·1)^2} + \frac{£110}{(1 + 0·1)^3} = £300$$

So the present value of the future stream of income exceeds the present cost of the machine, and the firm would therefore undertake the investment. A rise in the cost of the machine to a figure above £300 would obviously cause the firm to reconsider, as would a rise in the interest rate (remember that this reduces the present value of future income).

We have reached the same conclusion here as we did with marginal productivity analysis, namely that a rise in the cost of capital, or a rise in the rate of interest, will reduce the amount of capital investment in the economy. As we shall see in Chapter 34, this has important policy implications for the government, if it wishes to influence the level of unemployment and the rate of economic growth.

QUESTIONS

1. How would the marginal revenue product curve be affected by a fall in the productivity of capital? How would this affect the demand for capital at a given interest rate?

2. Some economists argue that social factors have an important influence on the level of saving, in that thrift is more acceptable in some societies than in others. Is this true?

3. Why is borrowing money to pay for a car more expensive with Hire Purchase than with a bank loan?

4. Consider the example of the present value calculation used in the text. Find the present value of the same income stream if the rate of interest was 20 per cent. Does this change affect the firm's decision to purchase the machine?

CHAPTER 19

LAND AND RENT

Land, as a factor of production, is defined as all "free gifts of nature" including, therefore, minerals and the resources of the sea. Rent is the payment for the use of this "land". A problem of terminology arises here, as rent means something more in everyday speech. People talk of renting a house, or renting a television set, and they are obviously using the term to refer to the periodic payment for the use of an asset. An economist would explain that such a payment includes an element of interest for the use of capital, and a measure of profit. In the remainder of this text the term "rent" will be used solely in its economic sense.

RICARDO'S THEORY OF RENT

One of the first economists to systematically examine the nature of land and rent was David Ricardo (1772–1823), who published his work in the early nineteenth century. To Ricardo, land was unique as a factor of production. Unlike capital or labour, it had no supply price. He argued that if the reward paid to either capital or labour fell, the supply of each factor would also contract. Indeed, if the price paid fell to zero, supply would also fall to zero. Land was different. Its total supply was fixed, regardless of price. Supply could not be expanded if price rose, nor contracted if price fell. Even if price fell to zero, total supply would be unchanged.

Ricardo used this line of reasoning to answer a political question which captured the imagination of the other economists of his day – was the price of corn high because the price of land was high, or vice versa? IIis theory of rent, developed from the above definition of land, led to the conclusion that high rents were a result of high corn prices, and not the reverse. We can see how Ricardo reached this conclusion by examining Figure 19.1.

The diagram illustrates that the supply of land is totally inelastic with regard to price. This means that the rent payable for its use is demand determined. If demand rises from D_1D_1 to D_2D_2 the equilibrium value of rent also rises. Ricardo was therefore able to argue that rents were high because the demand for land was high, and that the latter existed

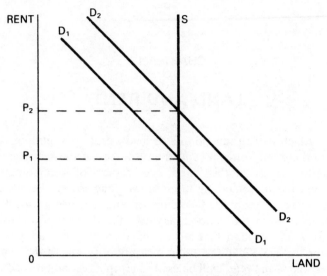

Figure 19.1: Rent for the Use of Land.

because it was very profitable to grow corn. Landlords could only charge high rents because the price of corn was high, making possible the high return on corn growing. If the price of corn fell, landlords would have to reduce rents as the demand for land would fall. Ricardo believed that the latter event was unlikely. He imagined a steadily increasing population, leading to an increasing demand for food, and therefore to the inevitable high rents for land. He spoke of landlords as having "reaped where they never sowed", and considered rent as a surplus, in that it could be removed without having any affect on the total supply of land.

CRITICISM OF RICARDO

There are several criticisms which can be made of Ricardo's theory of rent. First, the total supply of land may be fixed in the short run, but in the long run the supply can change. In many areas of the world land has been reclaimed for agricultural and industrial use. Conversely, man can abuse the land, rendering it unfit for economic use. So the total amount of land available is by no means fixed. Secondly, the owners of land have to devote capital resources to the upkeep of their property. If the rent of land fell below a certain level, it would be uneconomic for landlords to maintain their property, and the supply of usable land would contract. Thirdly, land as a whole may be fixed in the short run, but the supply for

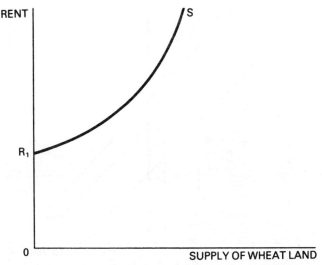

Figure 19.2: The Supply Curve for Land in a Particular Use.

any particular use is variable. Farmland can be used to grow a variety of crops, and urban land can be used for industrial or residential building. In order to secure its use for a particular purpose, the person renting the land must pay a sufficient price to prevent it being transferred to an alternative use. This means that the supply curve of land available for growing (say) wheat is as illustrated in Figure 19.2. If the return to the landlord falls below OR_1, he will transfer the land to an alternative use, perhaps for growing barley.

ECONOMIC RENT AND TRANSFER EARNINGS

Ricardo had used the concept of economic rent to apply solely to land, but the term is now used to describe the returns to any factor fixed in supply. It was recognised that particular types of labour can be totally unresponsive to changes in wages, and that capital too can be completely inelastic in supply. So the return payable to any factor of production which is fixed in supply is termed economic rent. This is illustrated in Figure 19.3.

The above supply curve indicates that the factor has no supply price i.e. if price fell to zero the factor would still be available for that particular use. We can therefore consider economic rent, more generally, as the payment over and above that required to keep a factor in its present use. This latter sum is often called the factor's transfer earnings, as we have already noted in our discussion on labour and wages. In

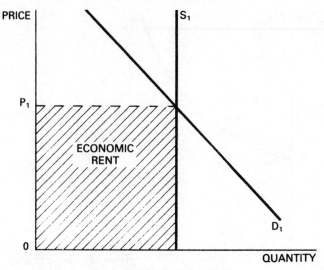

Figure 19.3: Economic Rent.

Figure 19.4 we can see a situation where all the returns to the factor are transfer earnings, in that if price falls below OP_1, the total supply of the factor in that particular use would fall to zero.

The supply of most factors of production is unlikely to be either completely elastic or completely inelastic. However, we can still apply

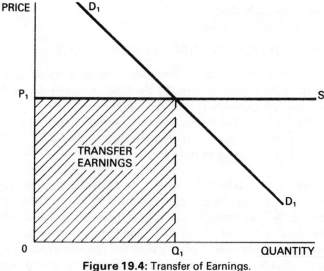

Figure 19.4: Transfer of Earnings.

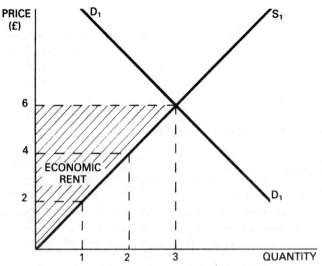

Figure 19.5: Economic Rent and Transfer Earnings.

the concepts of economic rent and transfer payments to any supply curve. Figure 19.5 illustrates this. The equilibrium price of the factor is £6, and 3 units are supplied at this price. This price was actually only necessary to secure the third unit, as the first would be supplied at £2 and the second at £4. So the first unit is earning £4 over and above that required to keep it in the industry i.e. it is earning £4 economic rent. Similarly, the second unit is earning £2 economic rent. Therefore, any payments above the supply curve can be considered economic rent, and any below it, transfer earnings.

Thus if a professional footballer can earn £60,000 in his present occupation, but only £20,000 in his best alternative, we say that he is receiving an economic rent of £40,000. Similarly, many office blocks in the City of London earn rents far in excess of what they would earn as residential accommodation, and we can classify a large part of these earnings as economic rent.

ECONOMIC RENT AND TAXATION

Economic rent, by definition, is a surplus over and above the factor's supply price. Therefore, it could be removed without having any affect on the supply of the factor. This makes economic rent eminently suitable for taxation, a fact not lost on Ricardo's contemporaries. Many proposals were made for taxes on rent, using his contention that the supply of land would be unaffected as support. Indeed, one Henry George started the "single tax" movement in the United States, many years after Ricardo's death, claiming that all other taxes could be abolished in favour of one tax on land. Unfortunately, as we have already noted, the supply of land is not completely inelastic, and taxes on land would have an economic effect. Nevertheless, it is true that taxing the economic rent payable to any factor of production should not affect the supply of that factor. The footballer, in our example above, could lose up to £40,000 and he would still remain in that profession.

QUASI-RENT

Many factors of production may be fixed in supply in the short run but have an elastic supply in the long run. Therefore, any economic rent earned will be only temporary. The term "quasi-rent" is used to differentiate this short run payment from economic rent which persists in the long run.

As an example, consider a shop subject to a seven year lease. Two years after starting business, a large office block is built nearby and this results in greatly increased business which the owner enjoys, in the form of increased profits, during the remaining years of the lease. When the term of the lease is renegotiated this factor will be taken into account: in the short run such extra profits are known as quasi-rents.

RENT AS A PAYMENT FOR A PARTICULAR SITE

Finally, we can now examine the determination of the rent for a particular site. Land has another unique quality here, in that specific sites are completely immobile. So if an area of land has a particularly favourable geographical position, it may earn a substantially higher rent than comparable land elsewhere.

Let us take city-centre sites as an example. The number of sites in the high street is strictly limited, whatever the price offered. However, the demand for such sites will be high, and it will come from a variety of sources. Banks, building societies, supermarkets and restaurants may all consider the land as suitable for their location. In a competitive market the site would go to the highest bidder, as illustrated in Figure 19.6.

The demand for the site from a building society is represented by the curve D_3, with D_2 representing the demand from a bank, and D_1 from a supermarket. In this case the site will be used to locate a building society, as the marginal productivity of the site is highest in that use. Note that the distance R_3 minus R_2 is the economic rent earned by the site, and that R_2 represents the site's transfer earnings as a location for its present use.

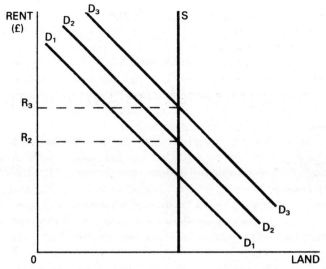

Figure 19.6: The Demand for a City-Centre Site.

QUESTIONS

1. Is the total supply of land available to the whole planet fixed?

2. Why can the earnings of top film stars be considered as mainly economic rent?

3. What happens to such economic rent if the demand for a particular film star falls?

4. The "brain drain" was a phrase used to describe the exodus of top scientists and businessmen from the U.K. High levels of taxation were often blamed. Does this refute the argument that economic rent can be taxed without affecting the supply of a factor?

CHAPTER 20

THE ENTREPRENEUR AND PROFIT

Production involves the use of land, labour and capital. These factors of production have to be brought together and organised, and the entrepreneur is responsible for undertaking this task. He decides on the quantity of each factor to be used, and the nature of the product to be produced. If the venture is successful the entrepreneur is rewarded with profit. If it fails he alone must face the loss. Profit is essential if the capitalist system of production is to function efficiently.

PROFIT IN A PRIVATE-ENTERPRISE SYSTEM

Profits fulfil a number of important functions within the private-enterprise system.

1. A reward for risk-taking. The production of any good or service involves certain risks. The raw materials might be damaged or stolen, the factory might catch fire, the employees might be injured. Any, or all, of these eventualities would involve costs which the entrepreneur would have to meet. However, all of these risks are known as "insurable", as an insurance company would be prepared to offer cover against the possibility of their occurrence. Because statistics exist detailing how often such events have happened in the past insurance companies can calculate the probability of a similar event occurring, and such knowledge assists in the setting of the premium i.e. the sum paid by the person requiring insurance cover.

There are certain risks, however, which cannot be calculated in this way. These are known as "non-insurable". The most important, in production, is the risk that the final product will not sell. Consider the case of an entrepreneur who decides that during the next two years home computer sales will be particularly strong. Consequently, he hires the factors of production in order to expand production. Other manufacturers take the same view and competition is so intense that his sales fall rather than rise. The problem is that there is no way he can insure against competition, or that his particular brand will not sell. He must face these risks himself, and suffer losses if the above events occur. Profit is his reward if such events do not occur. In other words, if his prediction is right and his product is a success, the entrepreneur will be compensated for undertaking these non-insurable risks.

Demand for any product in a dynamic economy can never be predicted with any degree of certainty. Firms can do something to reduce the uncertainty by market research, and advertising, but consumer tastes are constantly changing. Given these circumstances, the possibility of profits is essential if firms are to undertake the production of goods and services.

2. A signal for the movement of resources. Why do resources move from one use to another in the capitalist system? No single person, or institution, exists to transfer factors of production away from goods which consumers do not wish to purchase, and yet land, labour and capital seem to switch to those goods which consumers do wish to purchase. The answer is that profit acts as a signal, directing resources to where society wishes them to go. The following example will make this clear.

Let us imagine that consumers tire of eating white bread, and desire more brown bread. Sales of white bread will therefore fall, and bakers will find that orders for brown bread will increase. Profits are likely to fall for those making white bread, and are likely to rise for those baking brown bread. The latter will increase production to take advantage of the possibility of more profits, and the former will switch production from white to brown bread. So some resources will now be moved away from an activity to which consumers no longer value, and towards an activity which consumers wish more resources to be devoted. This result has occurred because entrepreneurs reacted to changes in profits in the relevant industries. Each one acted out of self-interest, but the outcome was beneficial to society as a whole, in that the demands of the consumer were met. So profits are essential if resources are to be allocated efficiently.

3. A source of funds for investment. If a firm wishes to expand it must obtain the services of more factors of production. In order to achieve this, the firm must possess or acquire sufficient finance to pay for these factors. There are three main options open to most large firms in this case.

(a) The firm can borrow the money from a financial institution, such as a bank.
(b) It could raise finance by issuing shares.
(c) The firm could use past profits.

In practice, method (c) is the most popular, and most investment spending by companies is financed internally. This is known as "ploughing back" profits, and without a healthy level of profits in the economy the level of capital investment would be low.

DIFFERENT USES OF THE TERM "PROFIT"

We can distinguish four different uses of the term "profit".

1. Popular usage. Profit, as used in everyday speech, is simply the difference between the total receipts of a firm and its total costs. This is the concept of profit used by statisticians in calculating total profit shares in national income.

2. Normal profit. The economist uses a slightly different concept, one which involves the notion of profit as cost. Each factor must receive a certain sum to keep it in its present use, its transfer earnings or opportunity cost. We already know that this applies to land, labour and capital, and so, to be consistent, it should apply to the entrepreneur. Therefore, the entrepreneur in any industry is considered to require a "normal profit" to remain in the industry, this normal profit being his opportunity cost.

The following example brings out the distinction between the two concepts of profit. A shopkeeper turns down the offer of a job as the manager of a local supermarket. He prefers to work for himself, even though the salary mentioned was £18,000. At the end of the year an accountant completes the shopkeeper's records, and declares that total profits for the year amount to £23,000. An economist could now point out that this includes £18,000 of *normal profit*, the sum the shopkeeper could have earned in his alternative occupation.

3. Super-normal profits. This is the name given to any profit over and above normal profit. So, in terms of the above example, £5,000 would be called *super-normal profit*. Such profits act as a signal to other entrepreneurs, attracting new firms into the industry in order to take advantage of them. In a competitive market economy, with no barriers to entry, such profits would be reduced by an increase in the number of firms in a particular industry, and eventually eliminated.

4. Monopoly profits. This term is used to describe those super-normal profits which exist in the long run. In order for such profits to persist, barriers to entry must be present in an industry, preventing direct competition. Monopolies are a case in point, and so the term "monopoly profits" is used.

MEASURING PROFIT

Profit can be measured in a variety of ways, and we shall consider three of these here.

(a) **The gross profit margin.** This refers to the difference between the cost price of a given unit and its selling price. It is usually expressed as a percentage. So if the product costs the firm £8 to produce, and the selling price is fixed at £10, we can see that the profit margin is 20 per cent i.e. $\frac{2}{10} \times 100$.

(b) **The rate of return on capital.** The economist will usually be more interested in total profits, rather than the profit made on individual items, A common measure here is to express the total profits made by a company as a percentage of the value of capital employed. This allows us to make meaningful comparisons between companies, because we are relating profits to the size of the firm. For example, company A makes £100,000 profit, and company B earns £50,000. However, firm A employs capital to the value of £500,000, whereas B's capital is only valued at £200,000. So the rate of return on capital for B is higher than it is for A.*

(c) **The rate of return on capital, net of stock appreciation.** One problem with the above measure is that it takes no account of the distorting effect that inflation can have on profits. Gross profits include any increase in the value of stocks which the firm is holding, and if prices are generally rising, the value of such stocks will also rise. However, this increase can be regarded as mere "book" profits, as the firm would have to pay the higher prices to replace the stocks. For this reason an adjustment known as "stock appreciation" is made to total profits, in order to remove the effect of inflation.

PROFITS AND ECONOMIC GROWTH

We have already noted that profits fulfil a number of important functions in the economy. It can be argued, moreover, that a healthy level of profits is essential if the economy is going to grow at a desirable rate. On the one hand, a high level of profits provides the incentive for firms to increase output further, and to invest in the capital equipment necessary to increase productive capacity in the future. On the other hand, profits are also the major source of these investment funds, and so high profits provide the means for high investment. We can see in Figure 20.1 that

* For A it is $\frac{100,000}{500,000} \times 100 = 20$ per cent and for B it is $\frac{50,000}{200,000} \times 100 = 25$ per cent.

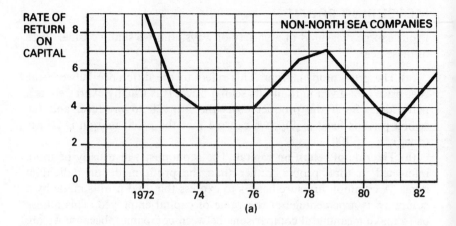

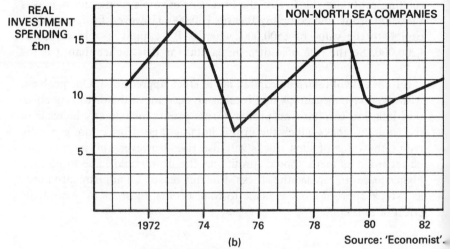

Figure 20.1: Profits and Investment.

there does seem to be a broad relationship between the level of profits and the level of investment spending.

Some further evidence on this relationship between profits and economic growth is provided in Table 20.1. This compares the level of profits in the U.K. over time, with that of West Germany. All international comparisons involving economic data should be treated with some caution, but two facts are apparent. First, the level of profits in both countries for the period concerned was on a downward trend. Secondly, the rate of return on capital appears to have been significantly higher in West Germany than in the U.K. This is interesting in the light

Table 20.1: An international comparison of profits. Pre-tax rate of return on fixed capital in manufacturing industry.

Average for years	U.K.	West Germany
1955–58	17	39
1959–62	16	31
1963–67	14	22
1968–71	11	23
1972–75	8	17
1976–80	6	16

Source: Economic Progress Report. Sept. 1983.

of our discussion about profits and economic performance, in that the German economy has consistently grown at a faster rate than that experienced in the U.K. Of course there is a host of other factors which affect the growth of national income, but it seems plausible to suggest that low company profits may have a dampening effect on economic growth.

The 1980s undoubtedly saw a rise in the return on capital employed in U.K. companies, as shown in Figure 20.2; although the rise has not been sufficient to push profit margins above the levels recorded in the early 1970s. Nevertheless, the rise in company profits has been sufficient to encourage markedly higher levels of capital investment.

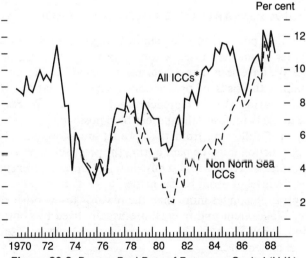

Figure 20.2: Pre-tax Real Rate of Return on Capital (U.K.).
* ICCs: Industrial and Commercial companies.
Source: Bank of England Quarterly Bulletin, May 1989.

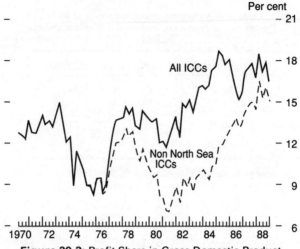

Figure 20.3: Profit Share in Gross Domestic Product.

Source: Bank of England Quarterly Bulletin, May 1989.

In 1990, despite the enhanced return on capital employed, the company sector as a whole is experiencing a financial deficit. This appears to have resulted from a markedly higher level of company dividend payments to shareholders (a 48 per cent increase was recorded for 1988) as well as from the raised level of capital investment.

PROFIT AS A REWARD TO A FACTOR OF PRODUCTION

We are now in a position to understand how profit differs in character from the other payments to the factors of production. First, profits can be negative. We have seen that profits are the reward to the entrepreneur for undertaking the risks of production. It may be that the venture is unsuccessful, leaving the entrepreneur to face losses. Wages, rent or interest are unlikely to be anything other than positive.

Secondly, and following from this, profits are a residual. The other factors of production must be paid during the production process, before the final product is actually sold. Only then will the entrepreneur be able to calculate the level of profit he has made.

Finally, profit fluctuates more than the rewards to the other factors of production. Wages, rent and interest are usually fixed by contract for a given period, whereas profit, by its very nature, tends to rise and fall with the level of demand.

THE ROLE OF THE ENTREPRENEUR TODAY

It was very easy to recognise the entrepreneur in the nineteenth century, as many firms were built up by one man, bringing together the factors of production and risking all in producing a new product. Such "captains of industry" are few and far between in our modern mixed economy, where production is often dominated by large limited companies and public corporations. There is now more frequently a divorce between ownership and control, with salaried managers organising production, and shareholders, or taxpayers, taking the risks. Most shares are now owned by financial institutions, rather than individuals, but the traditional entrepreneur is still to be found in many small undertakings. Nevertheless, in any enterprise there are always risk-takers, however remote, and it is these risk-takers who will be rewarded with profit, or will suffer the losses.

QUESTIONS

1. What factors would a firm take into account when deciding where to obtain finance for investment?

2. Consider the example of the shopkeeper. If profits fell to £16,000, and he still preferred to keep the shop, what can we infer about the money value he places on his independence?

3. The rate of profit is a measure of profit per unit. If the rate of profit is low, therefore, a high total profit implies that a large number of units are sold. What does this tell us about the rate of profit charged in (a) a high quality jewellers, and (b) a supermarket?

4. Why do the figures on rates of return quoted in the text refer to companies excluding those connected with North Sea oil?

CHAPTER 21

MONEY

WHAT IS MONEY?

There is a saying "Money is as money does". In other words whatever carries out the functions of money can be regarded as money. In times past – in some cases comparatively recently – many things have been treated as money – cowrie shells, salt and, in post-war Germany, cigarettes. Our word "pecuniary" is derived from the Latin "pecunia" (money) which is in turn derived from the Greek word for cattle, "pecus". In parts of the world today, in fact, cattle still carry out one of the functions of money – as a store of value. To the primitive African tribesman the quantity of cattle owned is so important his land may become over-grazed and his cattle emaciated – hardly the evidence of wealth they are intended to be.

IS MONEY NECESSARY?

Without money we would have to resort to barter – exchanging some things for other things – and this still occurs from time to time even in the modern world – in newspaper advertisements and by mutual arrangement. In the form of bi-lateral trade agreements between countries – "We will buy your shoes if you will buy our agricultural machinery" – barter is still taking place albeit in a more sophisticated form.

Money, a common denominator for goods of all kinds, is necessary because of the problems inherent in barter:

1. Wants cannot often be precisely matched.
2. The indivisibility of large items.
3. The problem of value determination.

The use of money gets over all of these problems. It is, in fact, a prime example of economic specialisation and is essential to the smooth running of the modern economy. We shall return to a consideration of the problems of barter when we look at the functions of money later in this chapter.

THE CHARACTERISTICS OF MONEY

Before we consider each of the various functions that money performs, or ought to perform, it is useful to examine the qualities which tend to be associated with money. Money should be:

1. Acceptable.
2. Durable.
3. Portable.
4. Divisible.
5. Uniform.
6. Counterfeit proof.
7. Stable in value.

Primitive forms of money had, and precious metals still have, intrinsic value; and it was this quality that originally made money generally acceptable. Over a period of time we have gradually become more accustomed to the idea that acceptability is more important than intrinsic value – gold after all is measured in terms of money, not money in terms of gold. Acceptability is, therefore, of primary importance.

Money also needs to be durable. Modern money in the form of banknotes does not last particularly well but is readily replaced as it becomes worn out. Some earlier note issues – the 10/– note (50p) and the £1 note – have now, however, been replaced by coins. Money also needs to be portable, easy to carry, convenient to handle, passing easily from one person to another.

One of the great disadvantages of cattle was that they were not easily divisible! In our own monetary system the smallest unit of legal tender is the penny so that even the smallest transactions can be made. Divisibility is thus an important characteristic of good money.

During Elizabethan times the coinage was frequently clipped or debased by the admixture of inferior metals. This gave rise to what is generally known as Gresham's law, after Sir Thomas Gresham, which states that bad money drives out good. Money, therefore, should be uniform – of a standard shape or pattern so that one coin or note is of equal value with the next. It must also be difficult to counterfeit since widespread forgery could play havoc with the management of the economy.

Finally, money should be stable in value. In Germany in 1923 the monetary system collapsed and hyper-inflation was rife. Then money no longer had any real meaning. Wage agreements had to be negotiated daily and a sackful of banknotes was insufficient to buy a loaf of bread. Nothing on this scale exists anywhere today although inflation rates of several hundred per cent are to be found, inter alia, in Israel and Brazil. However, even in Britain and the western democracies levels of inflation running into two figures have been worrying enough and have created distortions in the economic system. In recent years for example, there has been a tendency for people to put money into property because this seemed to provide a better investment than almost anything else.

TYPES OF MONEY

There are three kinds of money in the modern economy:

(a) Coins.
(b) Paper money.
(c) Bank deposits.

Coins are legal tender up to specified quantities, i.e. they do not have to be accepted in settlement of a debt beyond stipulated amounts. However, there is no such legal bar to the acceptability of notes. Modern banknotes are derived from the receipts which the 18th century goldsmiths issued in exchange for gold deposited with them in their vaults. In due course these receipts passed from hand to hand becoming as acceptable as the gold they represented. Until 1931 it was possible to exchange banknotes for gold at the Bank of England.

Today, however, both coins and paper money can only be regarded as the small change of the monetary system. By far the largest part of the money supply now consists of bank deposits. Because bank deposits can be readily converted into notes and coins or transferred almost instantly from one person to another, they too are regarded as money. Cheques, however, are not money but only instruments for the payment of money. Bank deposits can be increased by an expansion of bank lending or decreased by the calling in of loans during a "credit squeeze". They are, therefore, not merely the largest element of the money supply but also the most volatile.

Not all bank deposits, however, are equally liquid and as we shall point out in Chapter 22 there are various official definitions of what constitutes the money supply. There is no single definition which is altogether satisfactory, and its measurement in any meaningful sense is certainly an immense problem.

THE FUNCTIONS OF MONEY

We have discussed what money is and what characteristics it should display as well as the various types of money. We must now return to the aphorism with which this chapter opened – "money is as money does". What then are the functions of money? What precisely does money do, or what ought it to do? There are, in fact, five generally accepted functions of money:

1. Medium of exchange.
2. Measure of value.
3. Unit of Account.
4. Store of value.
5. Standard of deferred payments.

It is as a medium of exchange that money makes a barter system irrelevant. In particular it obviates the problem of the double coincidence of wants because it is always possible to make up for any difference in value by the giving or receiving of "change". It is the essential and most important function of them all.

A major problem of barter was the determination of value. Another vital function of money, therefore, is as a measure of value whereby each item produced has its own determinable value. The price system is made possible by this function of money. This function can perhaps, therefore, be regarded as the most basic of all the functions of money. We must, after all, put a value on something before we tender money as a medium of exchange.

A third problem with barter was divisibility. An important quality of money is that it should be divisible into small units. This characteristic of money enables it to perform another vital function – as a unit of account. It is thus possible to keep a set of accounts, to calculate profits, draft balance sheets and measure the national income. The unit of account function of money is very closely associated with the measure of value function: indeed, some writers treat them together as a single indivisible function.

Money should also provide a good store of value (i.e. wealth). Thus, money does not have to be used up in a short or indeterminate period of time like apples or clothing. Money may be invested at interest with little, if any, loss of liquidity or uncertainty about repayment. To adequately fulfil this function the quality of stability of value is highly important. Hence when inflation is endemic, as we have seen, real assets such as gold and property are often preferred to money and financial assets generally.

Finally, money represents a standard of deferred payments. In modern society by no means all transactions are settled in full and at once. Nearly all housebuyers need to raise mortgages and take out insurance policies; and many people borrow for shorter periods by means of overdrafts, or on hire purchase or against credit cards. None of these would be possible unless money also acted as a standard of deferred payments.

THE VALUE OF MONEY

One of the important characteristics of money, as we have seen, is that it should be reasonably stable in value. Given this stability money can then function reasonably as a store of value.

The value of money will rise or fall in line with its purchasing power. If, as in our recent history, inflation predominates then money will, in general, buy less goods and services today than was the case a year ago. This may not be true of everything, however. The prices of some goods, e.g. computers, have fallen dramatically in the recent past, and many domestic appliances – washing machines, freezers, etc., are much cheaper in real terms (i.e. after allowance for inflation) than they were twenty or thirty years ago.

Measuring the value of money, therefore, is no easy task. The best known yardstick, the Index of Retail Prices, is based on a large selection of commodities weighted in importance in relation to the average consumer. So the index includes expenditure on smoking and on mortgage payments although these items will not necessarily form any part of some people's expenditure. The Index, therefore, is an average – no more than that – of aggregate (i.e. total) consumer spending.

In the example below we consider an economy with just two commodities – A and B – each of which accounts for half of total spending. Hence the index which includes them will give each of them equal weight. Let us assume that over a year the price of A increases by 20 per cent while that of B rises by only 5 per cent. Because the two commodities are equally weighted the average price increase is $12\frac{1}{2}$ per cent.

Table 21.1: A simple price index.

Commodity	Actual Prices (p)		Price Relatives*		Weight	Weighted Price Relatives*	
	Year 1	Year 2	Year 1	Year 2		Year 1	Year 2
A	50	60	100	120	50	5,000	6,000
B	200	210	100	105	50	5,000	5,250
						10,000	11,250
			Price indices			100	112·5

* A price relative simply converts actual prices into percentage terms; while a weighted price relative is found by multiplying the price relative by the appropriate weight.

Suppose, however, that A was three times more important in total spending than B. In this case A would be weighted 75 against a weighting of only 25 for B.

Commodity	Actual Prices (p)		Price Relatives		Weight	Weighted Price Relatives*	
	Year 1	Year 2	Year 1	Year 2		Year 1	Year 2
A	50	60	100	120	75	7,500	9,000
B	200	210	100	105	25	2,500	2,625
						10,000	11,625
			Price indices			100	116·25

In this situation the greater weight allocated to A means that the greater increase in its price has a more marked effect on the price index. Figure 21.1 below shows the weighting of the main groups of the RPI in 1989 compared with those 15 years earlier. It will be noted that food and clothing – two of the basic requirements of life – had become less important constituents of the average person's spending in 1989, though housing had become a bigger item.

The increased weighting on alcoholic liquor is probably more due to higher living standards than to the relatively small reduction in the real (i.e. after allowance for inflation) price of drink. Larger weightings for transport, private motoring being much more widespread than in 1974, can also be associated with rising living standards.

Figure 21.2 shows changes in relative prices over the thirteen years to 1987. It shows the price increase for each group as a percentage of the all-items index. For instance, over the period the all-items index rose from 100 to 394·5 while tobacco moved from 100 to 602·9. This figure is 152·8 per cent of 394·5: hence the relative increase in the price of tobacco to the index generally was 52·8 per cent.

QUASI-MONEY AND NEAR MONEY

Earlier in this chapter we stated that money consisted of notes and coin and bank deposits. Of these elements bank deposits are by far the most important. In fact this simple division is really quite inadequate for any sensible discussion because of the different nature of bank deposits. Some, for example, are available on demand while others may be of much longer duration. Some will be held by overseas investors. Then there is the question of Treasury bills and national savings: how do these fit into the monetary picture?

The main elements of what is called *near money* are National Savings Bank deposits, loans at short notice to the discount houses and government securities close to maturity. Near money must have a precise monetary value, must be highly liquid and completely safe against loss. *Quasi money*, on the other hand, consists of short-term instruments such

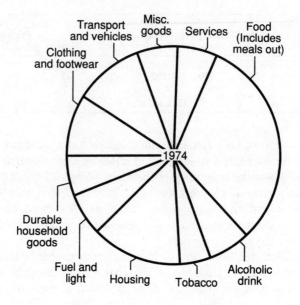

Source: Central Statistical Office.

Figure 21.1: Changes in Spending 1974–1989.

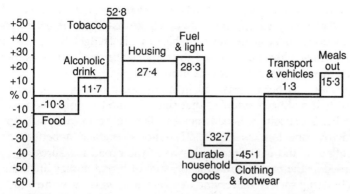

Note: Width of bars indicates 1987 weights in RPI. Source: Department of Employment.

Figure 21.2: Changes in Relative Prices: 1974–1987.

as eligible bills and government securities generally. Such instruments may fluctuate a great deal prior to maturity.

THE LEVEL OF BANK DEPOSITS

As we have already seen the money supply consists mainly, in our modern cheque book and credit card economy, of bank deposits. The level of bank deposits is not fixed and can expand or contract in given circumstances. The chief factors influencing the level of bank deposits are:

1. The level of national income.
2. The banks' opportunities for lending.
3. Government fiscal policy i.e. borrowing to meet a shortfall in tax revenue or the achievement of a surplus.
4. Government monetary policy – by which it attempts to influence directly the level of bank deposits.

THE MONEY STOCK AND LIQUIDITY

Successive governments have attached varying degrees of importance to the control of the money supply however it is defined. A number of different measures have been used to measure the money stock and liquidity generally. Some used in the past have been eclipsed by methods considered more appropriate today.

The narrowest measure of all consists of three elements:

(i) Notes and coin in circulation.
(ii) Cash in banks' tills.
(iii) Banks' operational deposits held at the Bank of England.

Some economists would like to see MO, the *narrow money* measure, used to control the money supply but others argue that it is subject to too many distortions to be generally reliable. In his Budget Statement in March 1990, the Chancellor stressed the importance that this measure is being given in attempts to control the money supply.

Broad money has been measured in many ways over a long period. Until recently it had been assumed that since the money supply consisted mainly of bank deposits a broad measure had to be more satisfactory than a narrow one but, as Figure 21.3 shows, there is a better "fit" between inflation and MO than with two of the broad measures. M4 is now regarded as the most significant measure of broad money, including as it does building society shares and deposits. M4, which was introduced as a new definition of the money stock in 1987, consists of:

	As at 30 September 1989*
	(£m)
(a) Notes and coin in circulation with the public	14,811
Add (b) Sterling bank sight deposits of the U.K. private sector	123,112
	137,923
Add (c) Sterling bank time deposits, including bank sterling CDs	146,887
Equivalent of former "M3":	284,810
Add Private sector holdings of building society shares and deposits and sterling CDs	140,703
	425,513
Deduct Building society holdings of items (a), (b) and (c)†	18,386
M4 measure of money supply:	407,127

* Source: Bank of England Quarterly Bulletin.
† Deducted in order to avoid "double counting".

M4 recognises that the distinctions between banks and building societies are becoming increasingly blurred.

The need for a monetary aggregate which includes foreign currency deposits of U.K. residents with U.K. financial institutions, is met by the new M4c, consisting of:

M4, *plus*

Foreign currency deposits placed with banks and building societies by the rest of the U.K. private sector.

Figure 21.3 shows the relationship between the official U.K. monetary aggregates and the Retail Price Index between 1979 and 1989.

Money and inflation Year on year increase

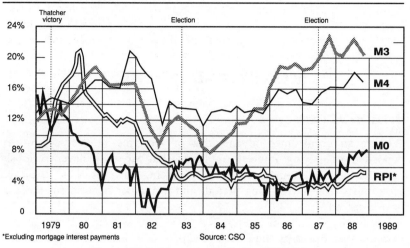

Figure 21.3: Money and Inflation 1979-89

QUESTIONS

1. What are the deficiencies of barter?

2. Discuss the various functions of money. To what extent are they fulfilled today in (a) the United States and (b) in Argentina?

3. What are the problems in defining money? To what extent are (a) Treasury bills and (b) building society deposits money?

4. Distinguish between narrow money and broad money.

CHAPTER 22

MONEY AND INTEREST

INTRODUCTION

We are so accustomed to the idea of receiving interest on money deposited or paying interest on loans that we may never seriously consider why it is imposed. This problem, however, has perplexed economists over a very long period, and a number of different theories have emerged.

Essentially the rate of interest is a price, and as such it is determined like all other prices by the forces of supply and demand. Earlier economists held the view that interest was the price paid for forgoing spending, while for Keynes and his successors interest was the price of money itself. For the classical economists interest was a real phenomenon explained in terms of savings and investment whilst Keynes' view was that it is determined purely by monetary forces.

CLASSICAL THEORY

To the 18th century economists, Adam Smith and David Ricardo, interest was to capital rather as rent is to land, a reward to a factor of production such as we have discussed earlier in this book. Later economists discovered that interest was more complex and that the rate of interest was determined by the forces of supply and demand – the supply of savings on the one hand and the demand for loanable funds on the other. The demand for money was a derived demand: it was not wanted for itself.

Savers, it was asserted, will be influenced by their time preference since saving means abstaining from spending – forgoing present consumption. £100 today is considered more desirable than £100 in the future. Thus, given an interest rate of 10 per cent, we can say that its future value in one year will be £110 (£100 × 1·10) whilst the present value of £100 receivable in 12 months' time is £90·91 (£100 ÷ 1·10).

To the extent that investment is profitable a firm will be be willing to pay interest. The lower the rate of interest the more projects it will be able to undertake, and the greater its demand for investment funds. For savers, on the other hand, the higher the rate of interest the greater their

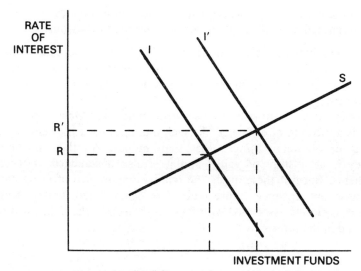

Figure 22.1: The Classical Theory of Interest.

willingness to forgo current spending. Interest, therefore, could be explained by the willingness of savers to defer consumption on the one hand and the readiness of entrepreneurs to make investments now.

Figure 22.1 illustrates the situation where the rate of interest (R) is found at the intersection of the S (supply of savings) curve with the I (demand for investment) curve. An increase in the demand for loanable funds is represented by a rightward shift of the I curve to I'. Savers will respond to this increase in demand by providing further funds – a movement along the S curve – so that savings again equal investment, and the equilibrium interest rate will move up from R to R'.

OBJECTIONS TO THE CLASSICAL APPROACH

Plausible though the classical theory may appear to be there are, in fact, many objections to it. The great twentieth century economist, John Maynard Keynes (1883–1946) attacked it, as well as later ideas developed out of the basic theory, on the grounds that:

1. The demand for investment funds was not interest-elastic as the classical economists maintained.

2. It ignored the influence of government policy towards investment.

3. It assumed the rate of interest was the only determinant of savings and investment.

4. It did not explain short-term variations in interest rates.

5. It ignored psychological factors in investment behaviour.

As Keynes himself bore witness the self-adjusting mechanism of the market – so fundamental to the classical economists – was clearly not working in the 1930s. Even very low rates of interest were unattractive to borrowers.

Money, as we have seen, fulfils several functions. Most important of all it is a medium of exchange. As such money is needed essentially as a means of obtaining things other than money. Another function of money is as a store of value; and it is also a standard of deferred payments. Both of these imply the relative importance of using money not now but at some future date. The demand for money, Keynes argued, is closely associated with these twin needs – the need for money now and in the future.

KEYNES AND LIQUIDITY PREFERENCE

Lord Keynes identified three motives for holding money and we now examine each of these in turn:

1. The transactions motive.

2. The precautionary motive.

3. The speculative motive.

The transactions motive: Consumers and firms require money to facilitate current transactions. The extent to which money is needed for this purpose will depend on the needs of the individual or the firm in relation to the frequency with which income is received. A wage-earner receiving £200 a week, all of it spent before the next pay-day has only this one motive – to hold it for transactions purposes; and his average requirement to meet his transactions needs will be £100. A salary earner on £1,200 a month may decide to set aside £100 each month in savings: he will therefore maintain an average balance of £550 (£1,100 ÷ 2) a month for transactions purposes. Similarly firms will require transactions balances to meet day to day expenditure – to pay wages, to buy raw materials and meet other regular commitments; and so do government departments.

For most individuals the balances held for this purpose are relatively stable since the commitments for which the money is held are known in advance and are reasonably predictable. For the community as a whole this is also true. Thus transactions balances, related at the micro-level to individual incomes, are related at the macro-level to the size of the national income.

The precautionary motive: Money is also required for events which cannot be precisely predicted – to meet, for example expenditure arising out of accidents, illness, loss of earnings or repairs to the family car. Businessmen will also need additional liquidity to meet unforeseen expenditure such as a sudden rise in the price of materials.

The proportion of funds set aside for this purpose will vary from individual to individual, and from firm to firm; but for the economy as a whole Keynes believed that precautionary balances could also be closely related to the national income. In a sense, therefore, the precautionary motive is little more than a part – a specialised extension – of the transactions motive.

The speculative motive: Most important of all, Keynes asserted, is a third motive – the speculative motive. This he established, despite the fact that for many people (and indeed firms too), only two motives have much relevance. Keynes argued that since the amount of money in existence – chiefly bank deposits it will be remembered – greatly exceeds the demand for "active" balances as he called the transactions and precautionary balances, there must be a third motive for holding money. Why though should some people wish to hold "idle" balances?

Keynes looked at this phenomenon by reference to the price of bonds i.e. gilt-edged stocks. The return or yield on such stocks varies inversely with their prices. Thus, for example, at a price of £30 $2\frac{1}{2}$ per cent Consols will yield 8·33 per cent.

$$\frac{2\frac{1}{2}}{30} \times 100 = 8\cdot33 \text{ per cent}$$

If investors believe that interest rates are likely to rise then they will not invest at the current price but remain liquid expecting the price of the

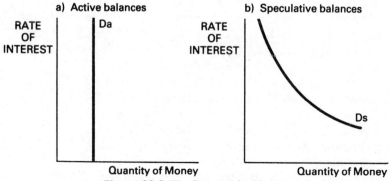

Figure 22.2: The Demand for Money.

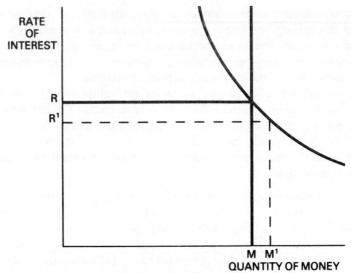

Figure 22.3: Liquidity Preference.

stock to fall and the yield to rise. At £20, for example, the same stock will yield $12\frac{1}{2}$ per cent.

Keynes regarded the demand for active balances as fixed relative to the quantity of money in the economy. It was completely interest-inelastic [Figure 22.2(a)]. An increase in incomes, however, would be reflected by an increase in the demand for such balances – a rightward shift of the curve Da. The demand for speculative balances, on the other hand, was interest-elastic [Figure 22.2(b)]: the interest rate did have considerable impact on the demand for this kind of money.

Thus interest rates and investors' expectations about their future course are the important determinant of the demand for money. When the Da and Ds curves are combined we get the total demand for money curve – what Keynes called "liquidity preference". Figure 22.3 shows this liquidity preference curve. It will be observed that like all demand curves it slopes downwards from left to right.

With the supply of money at M the rate of interest is R. An increase in the money supply to M' will cause interest rates to fall to R'. Eventually the curve flattens out since below a certain level the attraction of remaining liquid against that of holding bonds he considered to be overwhelming. At such a level speculators must conclude that interest rates can move only one way – upwards.

The volume of speculative balances then is determined by quite different considerations to those influencing the demand for "active" balances. Clearly the size of the national income is not so important. Investors' expectations about future interest rates – which are highly volatile – are the determining factor. Keynes' theory explained for the first time the paradox of the demand for "idle" balances in preference to interest-earning or tangible assets.

KEYNES AND THE MONEY SUPPLY

As we have already seen the demand for money is highly complex. Of the three motives for holding money, two of them – the transactions and precautionary motives – are chiefly influenced by the level of national income while the speculative motive is influenced by investors' expectations about the level of future interest rates.

In the short term Keynes regarded the money supply as fixed and was more interested in changes in the level of income. A change in income, Keynes maintained, altered the demand for active balances relative to that for speculative balances. Thus an increase in the level of income would force up interest rates given that the money supply was held constant (Figure 22.4).

In Figure 22.4 the curves Y and Y' represent different levels of money income. With the money supply at M the rate of interest will be R but rises to R' at the higher income level Y' where the demand for active balances will be greater.

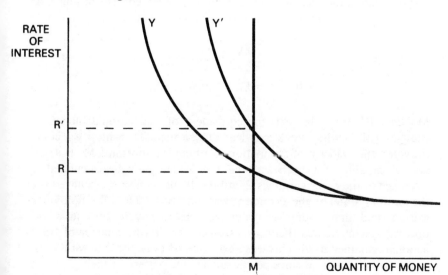

Figure 22.4: Income and the Interest Rate.

THE QUANTITY THEORY OF MONEY

Until Keynes' time economists generally believed that while the money supply did not influence specific commodity prices it did, nonetheless, affect the overall price level. Keynes' views still command a very large measure of support although they have naturally been modified and refined by later writers. In more recent times, the Chicago School led by Milton Friedman (1912–), has made a forceful challenge to the Keynesians emphasising the greater importance they attach to the supply of money.

The germ of their ideas is the quantity theory of money initially developed by Irving Fisher (1867–1947). The quantity theory is based on the fundamentally simple equation:

$$MV = PT$$

where M = the quantity of money in the economy,
V = the velocity of its circulation,
P = the general level of prices and
T = the total number of transactions in a given period

The meaning of this essentially simple equation can be understood if we look at a simple economic model. Let us suppose that in the economy there are 1,000 transactions a year at an average price of £2 so that total turnover amounts to £2,000. Since the money stock consists of only £500 we can see that this money is used four times in the period in question.

$$MV = PT$$

$$£500 \times 4 = £2 \times 1,000 = £2,000$$

MV and PT then are each the equivalent of the national income. A change in the money stock (M) leads to an increase in money incomes provided the velocity of circulation (V) remains constant. M, P and T are all capable of being measured but V can only be calculated by reference to the other variables. Until the 1930s economists believed that the normal state of the economy was one in which full employment existed; and that booms and slumps were merely hiccups in a well ordered system. It was therefore assumed that T (the number of transactions) remained fixed. This was also assumed to be the case with V (the velocity of circulation) since people change the pattern of their payments only slowly. So, if V and T can be considered fixed it follows that an increase in the money stock (M) must lead to an increase in P, the overall level of prices.

FRIEDMAN AND MONETARISM

Milton Friedman challenged the Keynesian views on money with his radical redefinition of the quantity theory. In Friedman's view, while money has certain special qualities it is nevertheless possible to substitute a number of other assets – real as well as financial – for money. Thus in recent years house property and antiques have proved to be better investments than gilt-edged stocks; and since the late 1950s investors generally have purchased ordinary shares in preference to gilts thus reversing the once traditional structure of yields. Today ordinary shares in general provide relatively low immediate returns because investors believe that over time company profits and dividends will increase.

The precise form in which individuals choose to hold assets will obviously vary considerably, depending on taste, temperament and convenience as well as on the money return. Owner-occupied homes, for example, are presumed to provide an implicit return equivalent to the rent which would otherwise be payable.

Friedman argues that an increase in the money supply will lead people to consider holding assets other than money, and that increased demand for these assets will lead inexorably to an increase in the price level. This will lead to an increase in money incomes (but not real incomes) as wage demands reflect past price increases and anticipate future ones.

Keynesians believe that there is a close relationship between the demand for money and the rate of interest, while the Friedmanites recognise no particular relationship between them. In their extreme forms neither theory seems completely tenable today. Both schools of thought contain an element of the truth. However, because of the problems of defining the money supply and measuring the relative importance of different kinds of assets it may never be possible to ascertain precisely the relationships between the money supply, the rate of interest and the general level of prices.

THE STRUCTURE OF INTEREST RATES

In our analysis we have dealt with interest as though there were only a single rate at any one time. This we know is patently not the case. There are, in fact, very many interest rates. Interest rate differentials are determined by three main considerations – time, risk and the rate of inflation.

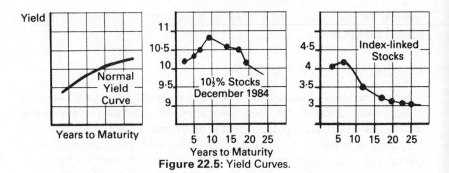

Figure 22.5: Yield Curves.

Time: In general short term loans and government securities carry lower interest rates than long term debts. Savers are willing to provide funds at relatively low rates of interest knowing that they can obtain their funds immediately or at very short notice; or, in the case of government stocks that the capital value of their investment will move closer to par (£100) as the maturity date approaches. In short they are prepared to sacrifice profit for liquidity.

Savers will generally require a higher return the longer the term, other things being equal. Economists speak of the "term structure of interest rates", and yield curves can be drawn to reflect the pattern of interest rates for a variety of stocks with different redemption dates (Figure 22.5).

Risk: The degree of risk is a second important factor in interest rate determination. British government securities are risk free. Banks and building societies may be considered only slightly risky, but among industrial companies the risk factor will be extremely variable – low for "blue chip" companies such as ICI and GEC but much higher for smaller, newer companies, especially those in the field of high technology. Furthermore any company which has a large proportion of debt to equity capital – one which is highly geared – must be considered a relatively poor risk.

Inflation: When inflation is running at a high level nominal interest rates will also be high. The real (adjusted for inflation) rate of interest will be lower than the nominal rate. Thus if the nominal rate is 9 per cent and inflation is running at 5 per cent the real or "true" rate of interest is approximately 4 per cent.* Real rates of interest can also be negative especially if taxation is taken into account. Thus a building society

* Actually 3.8 per cent [(1·09 ÷ 1·05) − 1] × 100.

mortgage rate of 10 per cent would be a net 7·5 per cent for a person paying tax at 25 per cent. If inflation was running at 9 per cent the real "cost" of the borrowing would be around − 1·5 per cent.

Some British government securities are index-linked as to both capital and interest. Thus an initial return of 2½ per cent will increase with the rate of inflation to provide a continuing real return of 2½ per cent on the initial investment. Its capital value will also rise in line with the rate of inflation.

YIELD CURVES

As mentioned earlier yield curves can be drawn at specific dates to show the relative time preferences of investors. The normal pattern is the upward sloping yield curve which flattens out as the maturity dates lengthen [Figure 22.5(a)].

Sometimes, however, the curve may slope downwards reflecting investors' belief that in the longer term interest rates in general are likely to fall. An interesting pattern was to be found in December 1984 in the case of both 10½ per cent and 2½ per cent index-linked stocks [Figure 22.5(b) and (c)]. In each case the curve rises at first (normal trend) but then it falls back reflecting investors' expectations that interest rates in the long term are likely to fall.

THE LEVEL OF INTEREST RATES

We have seen that in general, and at most times, interest rates will increase the longer the term, the greater the risk and the higher the level of inflation; but what determines the actual level of interest rates?

All interest rates are related to each other and most important of all are short term rates which are the most responsive to change. In the U.K. the pivotal factor is the action of the Bank of England through its day-to-day operations in the money market. As we shall see more clearly later the central bank, as lender of last resort, makes funds available to the discount houses and the rate it charges them influences the rates at which they are willing to discount commercial bills, treasury bills and certificates of deposit.

In turn the banks who traditionally supply the discount houses with funds will raise their rates, and this will have repercussions in the money markets in general. The banks will increase their base and deposit rates forcing other institutions such as the building societies and finance companies to adjust their rates too.

Fundamental economic considerations will, of course, influence the

Bank of England. Long term interest rates, however, will be even more affected by factors such as the exchange rate, the balance of payments and the rate of inflation.

QUESTIONS

1. How did the classical economists explain the demand for money?

2. Keynes wrote of three motives for holding money. How did he explain them?

3. Is the monetarism of Milton Friedman merely a restatement of the old quantity theory?

4. What are yield curves?

CHAPTER 23

BANKING AND THE CREATION OF MONEY

INTRODUCTION

The Banking Act 1987 requires that a bank carries out the following services:

1. The acceptance of deposits.
2. The making of loans.
3. The provision of foreign exchange.
4. Bill finance and the handling of documents for foreign trade.
5. Corporate finance and investment management.

The Act does not specifically mention the transmission of money or the provision of cheque facilities both of which might also be regarded as characteristic of the modern bank! The requirements, however, are intended to be wide enough to cover a wide range of institutions such as the merchant banks and the foreign banks as well as specialised banks such as the discount houses.

TYPES OF BANK

Banks may be divided broadly into two kinds – the deposit banks, those banks which carry out the functions we most associate with banking, and the secondary banks, a diverse collection of banks including the merchant banks, British overseas banks and foreign banks.

Another term used to describe the deposit banks today is "retail banks". This clearly distinguishes them from those institutions who do not provide cheque book and money transmission services. Other banks, in contrast, are referred to as "wholesale banks". However, the terms "retail" and "wholesale" may also be related to the *activities* of the banks. The major retail banks certainly do a large amount of wholesale business – the placing and receiving of large deposits with other financial intermediaries.

Under the 1987 legislation, any institution which accepts deposits from the public must be authorised to do so by the Bank of England, unless it is deemed to be an *exempted institution*. What were "recognised banks" and "licensed deposit takers" (LDTs) under the 1979 Act are now known as *Authorised Institutions*. Exempted institutions include building societies, insurance companies, the National Savings Bank, as well as the E.C. Central Banks.

FINANCIAL INTERMEDIATION

Financial intermediation is the process by which banks and other financial institutions operate to assist their customers in the placing or obtaining of funds. Within the economy as a whole some individuals, firms and institutions will be in surplus while others will be in deficit. It is the job of the intermediary to try to match the needs of both of them. It is more convenient; it is safer; and in the long run it is cheaper to have these functions carried out by a specialist firm than for the parties to attempt to match their needs directly.

Financial intermediaries carry out three main functions: – aggregation, maturity transformation and risk transformation.

Aggregation: Typically individuals save in relatively small amounts. It is the task of the intermediary to collect such small amounts together – the surplus – and to lend larger sums to those in deficit.

Maturity transformation: In the case of the banks a large percentage of depositors' funds are on current account – technically repayable on demand – and most other deposits are relatively short term. Bank lending is often of longer duration.

Risk transformation: "Neither a borrower, nor a lender be", Shakespeare's famous dictum (*Hamlet*) is very applicable to individuals. A loan to the best of friends or the most reliable of people can go wrong. Financial intermediaries, however, are experts at making loans and by spreading their activities they reduce the level of risk considerably.

THE DEPOSIT BANKS

The deposit or retail banks comprise the London and Scottish clearing banks, the Northern Ireland banks, Girobank and a few smaller banks such as The Yorkshire Bank and the Cooperative Bank.

Sterling deposits feature prominently in the balance sheets of the retail banks but overall the dominance of foreign currency business is an important feature of the U.K. banking scene.

We will obtain a fairly good picture of what a commercial bank does by looking first at its balance sheet. Table 23.1 shows in abbreviated form a

Table 23.1: Balance Sheet of Barclays Bank at 31 December 1989.

Liabilities	£m	%	Assets	£m	%
Deposits and			Cash and		
current accounts (A)	103,806	81·3	short-term funds (B)	20,192	15·8
Other accounts	14,270	11·2	Items in course		
			of collection	708	0·6
Loan capital	1,547	1·2	Investments	1,938	1·5
Shareholders' funds	7,993	6·3	Trading assets of		
			securities business	7,837	6·1
			Advances (C)	94,244	73·8
			Investments in		
			associated companies	435	0·3
			Property and		
			Equipment	2,262	1·8
	127,616			127,616	

recent balance sheet of Barclays Bank plc, one of Britain's largest banks.

It will be noted that the items are listed in order of liquidity, the very reverse of the usual method of presentation of a balance sheet. This is because for a bank, even more than for other concerns, liquidity is of paramount importance. Shareholders' funds and loan capital are also much smaller in relation to total assets than in balance sheets of other firms. In an industrial firm this might be a sign of weakness but banks are very different kinds of institutions. Capital structure is, of course, important and the Bank of England, under the Banking Act, has powers to regulate the capital ratios of the banks.

In the balance sheet of a deposit bank the items of really central importance are those marked on the balance sheet:

A. Deposits and current accounts.
B. Cash and short-term funds.
C. Advances.

A: Deposits and current accounts. A very large proportion of these will be current account deposits withdrawable on demand. It is a huge item (over 80 per cent of total funds) and, in theory, if there were a substantial demand by depositors for the return of their money this could cause an enormous strain on a bank's liquidity and force it to sell investments prematurely and call in its loans. It is highly unlikely, however, that this would ever happen. This is because most withdrawals take place not for cash but by means of cheques drawn on bank deposits, the only significant part of the money supply today. Barclays is one of the biggest banks in the U.K., and a large part of the withdrawals of some of its customers would be returned as deposits by others.

B: Cash and short-term funds. Further details of this item are provided in a note to the balance sheet:

	£m
Cash in hand and with central banks	1,802
Money at call and short notice	10,986
British and other government treasury bills	2,963
Other bills	1,953
Certificates of deposit	2,488
	20,192

Less than one-sixth of its liquid funds – a very small proportion indeed of total funds – are earning no interest. Money at call or short notice represents funds advanced on a "call" basis (i.e. repayable on demand) traditionally to the discount houses but also to stock exchange firms, local authorities and other financial institutions. It will also include certificates of deposit, which although of fixed term, are readily negotiable in the money markets, and hence extremely liquid. The "longest money" in this category is, in fact, normally repayable in 30 days.

By convention the clearing banks do not normally purchase British Government Treasury bills direct from the Bank of England. They prefer to acquire them when they are closer to maturity thus keeping their balance sheets extremely liquid.

Other bills will include short-term borrowings by local authorities and first class companies both in the U.K. and abroad. Certificates of deposit represent claims on other banks which can be readily negotiated in the money markets.

C: Advances

	£m
Lendings to customers	74,685
Equipment leased to customers	4,383
	79,068
less provisions for bad and doubtful debts	2,499
	76,569
Placings with banks (over 30 days)	12,120
Other accounts	5,555
	94,244

Advances are the least liquid of a bank's assets but the most profitable. Over recent years bank lending has become an even more important item in the balance sheet. In the depressed 1930s lending might have comprised no more than 30 per cent of total assets. Even in 1959 the Radcliffe Committee noted that advances represented only about 40 per cent of deposits. However, by the mid-1970s 70 per cent was more usual. In the case examined above, Barclays total lendings account for nearly 91 per cent of deposits and nearly 74 per cent of total assets.

This apparently inexorable rise in bank lending is, however, constrained by several factors:

1. The level of deposits in the economy.
2. The banks' ability to compete effectively for them.
3. The requirements laid down by the Authorities as to:
   (a) the adequacy of a bank's capital base
   (b) liquidity requirements including deposits with the Bank of England.
4. The demand for advances.
5. The banks' attitude to risk in meeting this demand.

HOW THE BANKS CREATE MONEY

The deposit banks, unlike the other banks, are actually able to create money. Bank deposits, it will be remembered, are the largest element of modern money with coins and notes the "small change" of the financial system. It will, therefore, be appreciated that if a bank lends say £1,000 to one of its customers it can actually increase the amount of money in the economy. It will be easier to think about this if we consider a very small bank whose assets and liabilities are as follows:

	£		£
Deposits	49,000	Liquid assets	10,000
		Advances	39,000
	49,000		49,000

If this bank now lends £1,000 to a customer, crediting £1,000 to his current account, the bank's balance sheet will look like this:

	£		£
Deposits	50,000	Liquid assets	10,000
		Advances	40,000
	50,000		50,000

Thus the act of lending has increased the level of deposits and hence the money supply.

The customer will now proceed to use the borrowed money and the £1,000 will be deposited in the account of another person. It could, however, be used to reduce someone else's borrowing with another bank so neutralising the money creating action of the first bank. Thus it is that while lending creates deposits the repayment of bank credit effectively destroys money.

The limit to a bank's ability to create money is determined primarily by the recognition of the fact that banks must adhere to some minimum level of liquidity. This prudential level may be reinforced by a legal or quasi-legal requirement to maintain a certain minimum of its assets in some prescribed form. At one time there was a liquidity requirement of 28 per cent. More recently, and using different definitions of liquidity this was reduced to only $12\frac{1}{2}$ per cent. Today, however, the system is rather more complex (we examine this in Chapter 28) but taking Barclays as an example we see that its own liquidity in the balance sheet in question amounted to some 16 per cent or about one-sixth of total liabilities.

Returning to our example, if it is the bank's objective to retain, say, a 20 per cent liquid ratio then the situation described above – with liquid assets of £10,000 and total deposits of £50,000 – represents an equilibrium position and no further lending is possible. If, however, another customer now deposits cash of £500 the balance sheet will look like this:

	£		£
Deposits	50,500	Liquid assets	10,500
		Advances	40,000
	50,500		50,500

Liquid assets now represent more than 20 per cent of total deposits so the bank can grant further loans of £2,000 to reach a new equilibrium position. Thus the deposit of £500 has led to an overall increase in deposits of £2,500 – a multiple of 5.

	£		£
Deposits	52,500	Liquid assets	10,500
		Advances	42,000
	52,500		52,500

The money-creation multiplier, as this is called, is broadly the reciprocal of the liquidity requirement. Thus when the required ratio was $12\frac{1}{2}$ per cent the multiplier was 8 $(100/12\frac{1}{2})$.

In practice, of course, we cannot look at one bank in isolation. Most "new" deposits are simply somebody else's old ones. So real growth, once the banks have reached equilibrium, can only come from "external events" such as the sale of goods overseas or government borrowing, another means of money creation. The most important growth, however, is that which comes about through the expansion of the economy resulting in an increase in national income.

LIQUIDITY VERSUS PROFITABILITY

Bankers make a living by lending money and, as we have seen, this can take a variety of forms. They must also retain a measure of liquidity whether or not this is imposed upon them. By its very nature short-term lending – with the ability to call in the loan immediately – is not very profitable. However, since the banker must maintain a prudent degree of liquidity he will endeavour to achieve this as profitably as he can. Hence the item "money at call and short notice" and others similar to it in bank balance sheets. Absolute liquidity in the form of coins and notes generally accounts for less than two per cent of total deposits. The remainder of a bank's assets, with the exception of property and fixed assets are all financial assets and hence, to a greater or lesser degree, profitable.

THE CONTROL OF CREDIT

As we have seen a number of factors inhibit the growth of credit and hence the money supply. Not the least of these is the bank's own policy in regard to lending and its perceived need for liquidity. However, there are some external controls too. It was mentioned earlier that the liquidity ratio was once 28 per cent. This was the situation until 1971. For the next ten years the concept of liquidity was somewhat modified and the banks had to maintain a ratio of eligible reserve assets to eligible liabilities (mainly short-term deposits) of $12\frac{1}{2}$ per cent. Reserve assets were strictly defined and did not include all liquid assets; so the apparent relaxation in the requirements of the Authorities was nothing like as great as it might seem. From 1981 onwards a new system has been in operation and we shall examine this in Chapter 27.

QUESTIONS

  1. What is financial intermediation and what purposes does it serve?
  2. What are the major assets and liabilities of a major clearing bank?
  3. "Banks create money. But there are limits to this growth." How would you explain this statement?

CHAPTER 24

THE BANK OF ENGLAND

INTRODUCTION

The Bank of England, the central bank of the United Kingdom, is a unique institution in this country. Founded in 1694, it was originally a joint stock, profit-oriented bank although from the outset it enjoyed a special relationship with the government of the day. Gradually, the importance of this connection increased so that when the Bank was nationalised in 1946 this was little more than confirmation of an already established state of affairs. The Bank of England differs from a commercial bank in a number of ways:

1. Its capital is owned by the state.
2. It is not motivated by profit in the usual sense.
3. It does not accept ordinary commercial business – private or corporate.
4. Its functions are altogether different from those of the commercial banks.

The Bank of England is a bridge between the public sector (to which it belongs) and the private sector, and is an indispensable part of the financial system. Its principal officers are the Governor and Deputy Governor and sixteen directors appointed by the state. Most of its directors – distinguished men and women from various walks of life – work only on a part-time basis.

The Governor of the Bank of England is a person of considerable influence. His public utterances are listened to with respect and carry a great deal of weight. At times, however, there is a conflict of view between the Treasury and the Bank of England. In such cases the Bank is, in the last resort, subservient to the government through the Treasury – a power enshrined in the Bank of England Act, 1946.

The Bank's functions may be summarised briefly under the following headings:

1. Supervision of the banking system.
2. The bankers' bank.

3. External functions.

4. Management of the monetary system.

PRUDENTIAL REGULATION OF BANKS

At the time of the secondary banking crisis of 1973/74 there was no formal system of bank regulation in the U.K. Several financial institutions during that period had collapsed; and over twenty others which had got into severe difficulties were assisted towards recovery by the English and Scottish clearing banks – the so-called "lifeboat operation".

The existing system of supervision came about primarily because of a European Community requirement that the U.K. should harmonise its banking laws with those of its partners in Europe. The Banking Act 1987, which replaced the Banking Act 1979, deals, *inter alia*, with:

1. Control over bank names.

2. Authorised Institutions. Any institution which accepts deposits from the public must be authorised to do so by the Bank of England, unless it is deemed to be an *exempted* institution.

3. A deposit protection scheme.

To be classified as an Authorised Institution the institution must satisfy criteria as to capital adequacy, liquidity, "large exposures" (over 10 per cent of capital) and foreign currency exposure.*

THE BANK OF ENGLAND AS BANKER

1. Banker to the Government

As a banker to the government of the day the Bank of England carries out not only the functions we would expect of any bank but also some highly specialised operations peculiar to it as the central bank. These functions may be summarised as follows:

1. Maintenance of central government accounts and those of government departments. The accounts may be broadly divided into:
    (i) Consolidated Fund (Exchequer accounts)
        Receipts from gilt-edged issues
        All central government expenditure
    (ii) National Loans Fund accounts
        Nationalised industries

---

* In 1985 seventeen U.K. commercial banks announced the appointment of an Ombudsman to arbitrate on the complaints of personal customers.

Table 24.1: Distribution of the National Debt at 31 March 1989.

		End-March 1989	
Market holdings		£m*	%
Sterling marketable debt:			
Government and government-			
guaranteed stocks: index-linked		16,739	10·0
other		105,470	63·1
Treasury bills		3,286	2·0
Sterling non-marketable debt:			
National savings: index-linked		2,844	1·7
other		27,070	16·2
Interest-free notes due to the IMF		3,660	2·2
Certificates of tax deposit		2,274	1·4
Other		595	0·4
	Total	161,938	96·8
Foreign Currency debt:			
North American government loans		1,316	
Foreign currency bonds		20	
Floating-rate notes		2,373	
ECU Treasury bills		1,562	
	Total	5,271	3·2
Total market holdings		167,209	100·0
Official holdings		30,147	
	Total	197,356	

* Nominal values
Source: Bank of England Quarterly Bulletin

Local authorities
Public boards, etc.
2. Provision of temporary "ways and means" advances.
3. Advice on a range of banking and related matters.
4. Management of government borrowing (i.e. the National Debt) by means of the issue of Treasury bills and gilt-edged stocks (see Table 24.1).

(a) new issues and redemptions
(b) payment of interest
(c) maintenance of registers.

Most of the debt consists of marketable securities listed on the Stock

Exchange. The non-marketable portion consists mainly of National Savings investments. Although the debt may appear to be huge it represents less than half of the gross domestic product for one year, and its proportion to GDP has steadily declined ever since World War II.

2. Banker to the U.K. banks
The Bank's functions under this heading comprise:

1. Provision of notes and coin as required.

2. All authorised institutions are required to keep 0·45% of their eligible liabilities with the Bank of England as non-interest bearing deposits.

3. Settlement of clearing house indebtedness. London clearing banks must keep rather larger balances than other banks for this purpose.

4. Consultation and advice.

3. Banker to overseas central banks and international organisations.
The Bank's functions in this category approximate in some degree to those which it provides to the U.K. government and the other banks in this country.

1. Maintenance of working balances for the settlement of inter-government and trade indebtedness.

2. Management of their gilt-edged and other sterling funds.

3. Settlement of their foreign exchange operations.

4. Promotion of stability in international affairs.

The Bank of England works closely with a number of international bodies, among them the Bank for International Settlements, the International Monetary Fund (and its agencies) and with the International Bank for Reconstruction and Development (the World Bank).

4. Lender of Last Resort
When there is a shortage of funds in the money market as a whole the Bank of England will give assistance to the discount houses who normally obtain their short-term funds from the clearing banks. The basis of the clearing banks' advances to the discount houses is that the money lent is repayable at call. Thus the Bank of England indirectly assists the clearing banks, the cornerstone of the banking system, to adjust their liquidity requirements. The important role of the discount houses is discussed in Chapter 25.

5. Responsibility for the Note Issue
The Bank obtains coins from the Royal Mint but prints and issues

Table 24.2: Balance Sheet of the Bank of England as at 28 February 1989.

Liabilities		Assets	
	Issue Department		
	£m		£m
Notes in circulation	14,112	Government debt	11
Notes in banking department	8	Government securities	9,695
		Other securities	4,414
	14,120		14,120
	Banking Department		
	£m		£m
Capital	15	Notes and coin	9
Reserves	675	Cheques in course of collection	496
Public deposits	550	Treasury and other bills	1,742
Bankers' deposits	1,413	Investments	681
Other accounts	1,458	Advances	865
Treasury	56	Premises, equipment etc.	374
	4,167		4,167

banknotes itself. Although at one time the note issue was backed by gold, today virtually the whole of the issue is fiduciary (i.e. not backed by gold).

Before going on to consider the remaining functions of the Bank let us look at its balance sheet. This reflects its various activities and also the contrast between its special position in the monetary system with that of the commercial banks.

An interesting aspect of the balance sheet is its division into two parts – the Issue Department and the Banking Department. In fact, these are not really separate departments at all; the division is no more than an accounting convention. The Issue Department shows as liabilities the total value of the notes and coin in circulation, and separately that held by the Bank of England itself. On the assets side of the balance sheet we see how the issue has been financed. The small item, government debt, is of historic significance only. The vast majority of the backing for the note issue – there is no longer any gold – consists of government stocks and the same kind of short-term securities that might be held by any bank.

In the Banking Department perhaps the most confusingly named item is Public Deposits. These are, in fact, the balances on government accounts including those of the Exchequer and the National Debt Commissioners. Another big item is Bankers' Deposits, and of this amount some £1,135m represents the 0·45% deposits made by the banks in terms of the cash ratio requirement.

On the assets side the first three items are similar to those to be found in a commercial bank's balance sheet. The first item – notes and coin – is almost a reflection of the liability item in the Issue Department; but it also contains some coin. The investments are almost exclusively British Government stocks.

EXTERNAL FUNCTIONS OF THE BANK

The Bank of England's external functions are hardly less important than the domestic ones we have already examined. Indeed it is possible to envisage the former being handled by some other institution. Many of the external functions are, however, inextricably linked with government. We will briefly examine each of these in turn.

1. Management of the Exchange Equalisation Account
This account holds the nation's gold and foreign currency reserves, the ultimate means of settling our international indebtedness.

2. Management of the sterling exchange rate
At one time sterling's relationship with the U.S. dollar was very closely controlled between a few percentage points. In more recent times market forces have largely been allowed to determine not only this key exchange rate but those with other currencies too. The deutschemark rate has become an increasingly important indicator.

3. Exchange Control
Exchange controls may be imposed to limit the flow of funds both into and out of a country, and so influence exchange rates. They may be applied to both current and capital movements. They have been used extensively in the U.K. in the past.

(a) Exchange controls were suspended in the U.K. in 1979, and have now been formally abolished.
(b) The Bank, however, acts as an agent of central banks in other countries and so helps to enforce their exchange control regulations.

4. International connections
As mentioned previously it also co-operates with a number of international agencies such as the IMF and the World Bank.

MANAGEMENT OF THE U.K. MONETARY SYSTEM

Perhaps the most important of all the Bank's functions is to assist in the formulation of and to carry out the execution of the government's monetary policy. Monetary policy must be distinguished from fiscal policy which is concerned with taxation, subsidies and tax incentives.

Monetary policy is concerned with the control of credit, interest rates and the supply of money. Clearly, therefore, there will be some degree of overlap with fiscal policy. If, for example, the government were to embark on a large programme of deficit financing by means of tax cuts this will encourage spending. It could also lead to an increase in the volume of credit and thus an increase in the money supply. It is, therefore, extremely important that government harmonises policy in these two areas.

The Bank of England has various means at its disposal to implement monetary policy. Among the methods which it has used in the past, some of which are still in current use, are:

1. The imposition of cash or liquid assets ratios on the lending institutions.

2. The issue of government stocks to fund the Central Government Borrowing Requirement.

3. Open market operations by means of which government controls the money supply through the purchase and resale of its own gilt-edged securities.

4. Special deposits – compulsory extra deposits placed with the Bank of England thus reducing abruptly the capacity of the commercial banks' scope for lending.

5. Supplementary deposits – non-interest bearing deposits with the Bank of England imposed upon the banks when their total deposits (caused mainly by extra lending) exceeded specified targets – a penal imposition on the banks.

6. The use of an official bank rate or minimum lending rate to influence all other rates.

7. Moral suasion. Sometimes when restrictions cannot easily be imposed or when these might seem undesirable the Bank may use its moral authority to influence the banks' pattern of lending. Examples of moral suasion include:

   (a) Quantitative restrictions which place a "ceiling" on bank lending. These are intended to limit the growth of advances in the aggregate.
   (b) Qualitative restrictions which restrict lending to certain

categories of business or limit the growth of consumer credit. Sometimes, however, these may be coupled with a positive exhortation to assist specific sectors of the economy.

It must be stressed again that these are methods which have been used in the past. Not all of them are in use today. In Chapter 27 we shall consider in detail the present methods used to implement monetary policy.

QUESTIONS

1. How does the Bank of England differ from other banks?

2. Discuss the role of the Central Bank as banker. What functions, if any, does it carry out like any other bank? Which of its functions are unique?

3. What additional "non-banking" functions does the Bank of England fulfil?

4. Discuss the various methods the Bank may adopt to control the money supply. Does it merely carry out government policy?

CHAPTER 25

THE MONEY MARKETS

INTRODUCTION

In previous chapters we considered first the deposit banks and secondly the Bank of England. These may be regarded as the basic institutions of the U.K. financial system but they are very far from being the only ones. Broadly speaking we can divide the financial institutions into two kinds:

1. Those which deal mainly with the provision of *short-term* finance. These operate in the money market which may for convenience be divided into four sectors:

    (a) The discount market.
    (b) The parallel money markets.
    (c) The foreign exchange market.
    (d) The financial futures market.

2. Those which are concerned in large measure to provide *longer-term* finance. The fulcrum of this market is the Stock Exchange which acts as a magnet in attracting new funds. It does not, however, raise new capital itself. The principal institutions involved in this market are:

    (a) The insurance companies.
    (b) The pension funds.
    (c) Unit trusts.
    (d) Investment trusts.
    (e) Merchant banks.
    (f) Finance corporations.

Also included in this sector are those institutions who, while obtaining most of their funds *short term*, lend or invest a large part of these funds on a *longer term* basis. Amongst the most important of these we must mention:

    (g) Finance (hire purchase) companies.
    (h) Building societies.
    (i) The National Savings Bank.

In practice, however, it is not really possible to draw a dividing line between the two markets because nearly all the institutions have dealings in both the short- and long-term markets. We will consider the capital market in some detail in the next chapter. We first turn our attention to the money markets and the institutions that comprise them.

THE LONDON MONEY MARKET

This is a general term to describe the complex network of firms dealing in short-term money. Typically such funds will be placed for three months or less, but there is a substantial volume of business in money for up to one year and a smaller amount will be placed longer term – perhaps for up to as much as five years.

Until the mid 1950s there was really only one money market apart from the foreign exchange market. This was the discount market. Since that time the relative importance of the discount market has declined and there has been substantial growth in what have come to be known as the parallel money markets – so-called because they operate alongside the traditional discount market.

THE DISCOUNT MARKET

The chief operators in this market are:

1. The deposit banks.
2. The Bank of England.
3. The discount houses.
4. The merchant banks.

In previous chapters we have examined the roles of the commercial banks and the central bank; and we have seen how important it is for the banks to include short-term financial instruments among their assets. We have also recognised in some measure the way the Bank of England uses short-term assets, and the importance it may attach to them in relation to monetary control.

The traditional business of the discount houses has always been the purchase of Treasury bills from the Bank of England while that of the banks included the acceptance and discounting of bills of exchange. The merchant banks were – and still are – closely involved in the financing of overseas trade.

Until recently the core of the discount market comprised the eight members of the London Discount Market Association (LDMA) together with a number of small bill-broking firms. To ensure adequate competition in the money market, the Bank of England has now allowed firms which meet certain requirements to be accorded a dealing relationship with the Bank. In effect such firms are included in the Bank's dealing arrangements in "eligible bills" and are expected to operate actively in the Bank's money market operations.

1. THE DISCOUNT HOUSES

A very large part of the business of discount houses is concerned with the acquisition and sale of very short-term monetary instruments. The purchase of the government's 91-day Treasury bills has steadily declined in importance. This is due, at least in part, to the greater reliance by government on longer term finance and also because of the growth in, and attraction of, other forms of short term business.

Members of the LDMA still borrow substantial funds from the clearing banks on a call basis at very fine rates of interest, thus providing the banks with the opportunity to achieve some profit while remaining extremely liquid. By convention the Bank of England assists the discount houses as lender of last resort if and when they are required to repay these call loans to the banks.

2. THE MERCHANT BANKS

The former 16 members of the Accepting Houses Committee absorbed into the British Merchant Banking and Securities Houses Association, include some of the most famous names in British banking – Hambros, Rothschilds and Morgan Grenfell to mention just three of them. Like the discount houses they rose to prominence in the 19th century with the increase in international trade. Their traditional business came to be the acceptance of bills of exchange whereby they guaranteed the payment of a bill in the event of the default of the principal debtor. Such is their reputation that their acceptance of a bill renders it a "fine bill", one which will be readily negotiated by another financial institution, typically a discount house.

Like the discount houses they have expanded their interests in many other directions in recent years, and would be almost unrecognisable to their forebears. The discounting of bills is no longer a significant part of their business.

The difference between the business of the retail banks, discount houses and the merchant banks is perhaps made clearer when we compare the structure of their balance sheets (see Table 25.1).

SHORT-TERM FINANCIAL INSTRUMENTS

It is now appropriate to consider the more important of the various securities handled in the discount market:

Table 25.1: Composite balance sheets of some financial institutions as at 27 December 1989.

	(£m)		
	Retail Banks	Merchant Banks	Discount Houses
Sterling Deposits	266,422	28,916	14,523
Other currency deposits	63,482	15,623	403
Other Funds and Capital	61,797	6,996	350
	391,701	51,535	15,276
Notes and Coin	3,861	3	—
Balances with Bank of England (including cash ratio deposits)	1,064	62	14
Market (ie. short term) Loans	54,440	16,409	7,650
Bills	10,990	453	6,946
Advances	213,441	12,699	—
Investments	12,525	2,074	216
Other currency assets	95,380	19,835	450
	391,701	51,535	15,276

Source: Bank of England Quarterly Bulletin

1. Bills of Exchange

A bill of exchange is defined in the Bills of Exchange Act 1882 in the following famous words:

'A bill of exchange is an unconditional order in writing addressed by one person (A) to another (B) signed by the person giving it requiring the person to whom it is addressed to pay on demand, or at a fixed or determinable future time (C) a sum certain in money (D), to or to the order of a specified person or to bearer (E)'

A bill of exchange may take several forms. One example is that given in Figure 25.1 below.

The person to whom money is owed (A in the above definition) is known as the drawer of the bill whilst the person to whom it is addressed (his creditor – B in the above definition) is called the drawee. Most bills will be drawn (i.e. issued) as a result of a trading transaction and the bill of exchange has come to be the single most important, certainly the most basic, document used in international trade. Except in cases where payment is due on arrival of the goods it is necessary for the importer (the drawee) to accept the bill. In doing this he agrees to pay the amount due (the 'sum certain in money') not later than the due date.

```
                                                        131 High St
                                                            Bloxted
  £3,044                                       17th January, 199—.


                Three months after date (C), pay to me or my order (E)
                Three thousand and forty-four Pounds (D).


  To J. Higgs (B),
     121 New St,
        Brummagem                                    Henry Bloggs (A)
```

Figure 25.1: A bill of exchange

The drawer, however, may know little about the financial probity of the drawee, and in such circumstances it would be foolhardy to agree to the release of the goods against his acceptance of the bill. What the drawer requires is a good acceptance and this is what the accepting houses are in business to provide.

With the accepted bill in his possession the drawer can now do one of four things with it:

1. He can hold it until maturity in full confidence it will be paid.

2. He can transfer it to someone else in payment of a debt. In such a case he is said to negotiate it.

3. He could borrow against the security of the 'acceptance' (i.e. the accepted bill).

4. He could discount the bill with his bank – this is tantamount to selling the bill (for less than its face value of course) except that the bank has recourse to the drawer in the event that the bill is unpaid at maturity.

The banks who discount such bills do not necessarily hold the bills until maturity. They may rediscount them with discount houses or other financial institutions depending on their liquidity requirements.

As mentioned previously most bills of exchange are issued as a result of a trading transaction. Sometimes, however, bills may be issued purely as evidence of indebtedness. Such bills, known as accommodation bills, are much less common. The most highly rated of these bills are known as "bank bills".

2. Treasury Bills

Treasury bills are bills drawn by the Treasury on the Bank of England and are redeemable 91 days after issue. They are sold by tender (i.e. to the highest bidders) every Friday. Until 1971 the discount houses submitted a joint tender but they now bid individually, competing among themselves and with other financial institutions (although not with the clearing banks who by convention never bid). The number of bills – in units of £5,000 – issued each week depends on the government's need for short term finance. The bills are issued at a discount. Thus a bill might be issued for £4,875 and be redeemable 91 days later for £5,000 to yield a profit of £125 – $2\frac{1}{2}$ per cent of the face value representing an interest rate of about 10·4 per cent per annum.

The discount houses' purchases of Treasury bills are mainly financed by funds they acquire at call (i.e. repayable on demand) from the London clearing banks. The banks are happy to provide funds at a low rate of interest for this purpose because, as previously mentioned, the Bank of England in its role as lender of last resort, is prepared to assist the discount houses at any time they should need funds. Although the banks do not tender for them, Treasury bills do, as we have seen, appear as assets in their balance sheets. Typically the banks acquire their Treasury bills a few weeks after issue to form part of their liquid portfolio. They may rediscount them later or hold them until maturity.

3. Certificates of Deposit

These financial instruments are issued by banks for periods of three months to five years in return for deposits. Usually the interest rate is fixed but sometimes the rate is variable with prevailing interest rates. Where the rate is fixed a sharp increase in interest rates will adversely affect the values of a CD whereas a fall in rates will enhance its value. CDs are negotiable instruments and the longer-dated ones assist the banks to facilitate medium term lending.

Certificates of deposit were first used in the eurodollar market in the 1950s. It was not, however, until the late 1960s that the first sterling CDs appeared. Since that time these have become increasingly important means of short term and medium term finance. They have developed, however, much more as a medium of inter-bank borrowing than as a means of attracting funds into the banking system.

4. Government Stocks

In addition to Treasury bills the British government issues marketable securities of many kinds. These may be classified as follows:

(a) Short-dated stocks (redeemable within 5 years)
(b) Medium-dated stocks (5–15 years)
(c) Long-dated stocks (over 15 years)
(d) One-way option stocks (with no date set for redemption)
(e) Index-linked stocks

It is, of course, the short-dated stocks which are of most interest in the money markets but we shall consider all of them briefly in this section.

With the exception of the one-way option stocks all the funds are dated and some of them carry two dates e.g. 1999–2001 indicating respectively the earliest and latest dates at which they may be redeemed. Most stocks carry fixed rates of interest but an increasing number of them are now index-linked, both interest and capital being linked to the rate of inflation. An experiment with variable interest or floating rate stocks was tried in the mid-1970s but all the issues made during that period have now been redeemed. They were not popular with the institutions who are today the main buyers of gilt-edged stocks.

The one-way option stocks are "low coupon" issues providing nominal interest rates as low as $2\frac{1}{2}$ per cent. Typical of these is $2\frac{1}{2}$ per cent Consols (Consolidated Stock) which was first issued at a time when interest rates were much lower. Because these stocks carry no definite redemption date (for Consols it is actually "1923 or after") they are redeemable only at the option of the government, and today this possibility must be considered remote. Therefore the prices of such stocks are determined only on the basis of immediate and permanent return. For all other stocks the relative proximity of the redemption date is always a relevant consideration.

Today's index-linked stocks invariably carry low coupons but these are a very different situation. A $2\frac{1}{2}$ per cent coupon on one of these represents a real return because both the interest payments and the capital (redemption value) are linked to the Retail Prices Index.

The institutions of the discount market all purchase gilt-edged stocks – mainly in the short-dated category – with a range of maturity dates to meet liquidity and profitability targets. All such stocks, being marketable, can be sold for "cash" settlement (i.e. on the day following sale) but this may involve losses when interest rates move higher.

THE PARALLEL MARKETS

Until the 1950s the traditional discount market was the only money market in London. It is not, and never was, a market having a fixed location, most of its business being handled over the telephone, deals involving millions of pounds being negotiated by word of mouth. Dictum meum pactum – "My word is my bond" – the motto of the Stock Exchange can also be regarded as the guiding maxim of all city markets.

During the 1950s and 1960s the government's monetary policy was often severely restrictive and this gave the clearing banks particular problems because they were then obliged to keep some 28 per cent of their deposits in liquid form. This restriction did not apply to any of the other financial institutions who were thus placed in an advantageous competitive position vis-a-vis the banks.

This situation also gave rise to a rapid increase in the number of banks – the so-called "secondary banks" – and a large number of foreign banks moved into London. All the major banks acquired or formed subsidiary companies so that they could participate more effectively in the market for short term funds. One important development contributing to the development of this "parallel" market was that the local authorities, who traditionally obtained the bulk of their short term needs from a government department were obliged, from 1955 onwards, to obtain their funds at market rates of interest.

THE ROLE OF THE BROKER

In the traditional market only a limited number of institutions are involved. These used to deal primarily in Treasury bills and bill business generally. The parallel markets encompass the clearing banks and merchant banks too, but also include many other institutions including the local authorities, finance houses, large U.K. companies and British and foreign overseas banks.

Such a complex network gave rise to the need for money brokers who could bring together those having a shortage of funds with others experiencing a temporary surplus of liquidity. The discount houses themselves operate as principals in the parallel markets but have also adopted the role of bill brokers. We will now examine the major markets which comprise the parallel markets.

1. The Local Authority Market

As mentioned previously this market arose from the need of local authorities for short term funds following a change in government financing. This led banks and other institutions to actively seek funds which they could then on-lend to the local authorities. The period of such loans ranges from two days to just under a year. Local authorities also issue accommodation bills and negotiable bonds (popularly called "yearling bonds" because they typically have a term of just one year).

2. The Inter-Bank Market

Until 1971 the non-clearing banks were not subject to a liquidity ratio and there was therefore considerable scope for brokers to operate to relieve liquidity shortages in the market. Those banks with surpluses were thus enabled to find profitable short term outlets with others whose liquidity was low. Today this very important market is also used by the clearing banks, and a very frequently quoted interest rate is the three month inter-bank offered rate (LIBOR). Inter-bank transactions are not limited to sterling, there being very considerable business in other currencies too.

3. The Euro-Currencies Market

Despite its name this market is not restricted to European currencies. Indeed the market originated in U.S. dollars in the 1950s when interest rates in the United States were restricted by federal regulations. There were even fears that exchange controls might prevent the free movement of U.S. dollars following the convertibility of sterling in 1958. The growing U.S. trade deficit contributed to the supply of U.S. dollars in Europe and these funds – called eurodollars – became in effect a sub-currency of the U.S. dollar. The term eurocurrency today includes Swiss francs held in London, German marks in Tokyo and even Japanese yen maintained in New York!

4. Certificates of Deposit Market

We have already seen that CDs are among the most important of the assets of the discount houses and the merchant banks. They are issued by banks and building societies for a minimum period of three months and up to a maximum of five years, the minimum amount being £50,000. Rates of interest are fixed (or determinable, often by reference to LIBOR) at the outset so that changes in interest rates can involve a profit or a loss when a CD is sold on the secondary market. Nowadays a great deal of CD business is inter-bank so this market can be regarded as providing some of the medium term funding necessary to the banks.

5. Sterling Commercial Paper Market

The borrowers in this market are companies with net assets of at least £50m. Subject to investor protection requirements introduced in the Financial Services Act 1986 such companies are permitted to issue short-term debt securities without publication of a prospectus. The term of such securities can range from seven days to a year in minimum denominations of £500,000. The attraction for the issuers is that borrowing in this way is cheaper than by conventional means.

THE FOREIGN EXCHANGE MARKETS

Like the other markets this market has no set place of business, and even more than other markets requires complex telephone, telex and computer links for its efficient operation.

The principal business of the market is the settlement of commercial transactions between a buyer in one country and a seller in another. The participants in the market, however, are the banks. Two kinds of transaction predominate – "spot" transactions are for immediate settlement while "forward" deals are designed to hedge the risks involved in acquiring or selling a currency in the near future. At one time most major currencies were traded within narrow limits with the central banks intervening if these limits were pressed too closely. Today, however, supply and demand factors are even more important determinants of exchange rates. A fuller discussion of this important topic is reserved for Chapter 37.

THE LONDON INTERNATIONAL FINANCIAL FUTURES EXCHANGE (LIFFE)

Many commodities (e.g. wool, copper etc.) can be bought or sold "spot" or "forward" and this market makes it possible for dealers to execute forward contracts in money. In this market, in other words, money is treated just like a commodity. This is the one financial market which does have a specific location – the Royal Exchange building in the City of London. First opened in 1982 this market enables operators to deal in financial futures. A number of different contracts are available, the principal one being the eurodollar three-month time deposit. Thus it would be possible now to fix a rate for a time deposit commencing at a specific future date, a very useful facility for financial institutions in general, and for corporate treasurers.

QUESTIONS

1. "The London Money Market is not confined to a single place, nor is it a singular institution." Discuss.

2. Why is the bill of exchange such a versatile monetary instrument?

3. Government stocks earn interest but Treasury bills are issued at a discount. Explain the differences between them.

4. What are the parallel markets?

CHAPTER 26

THE CAPITAL MARKETS

We now turn to those institutions that deal primarily not in short-term funds but provide permanent or long-term funds for government, local authorities and businesses of every kind. Generally speaking the provision of such funds is not the role of the commercial banks, still less that of institutions such as the discount houses. In some countries (e.g. West Germany) the banks do provide long-term finance including equity capital. In the U.K., however, the banks have always seen their main role as the privision of working capital finance – broadly the financing of stocks and debtors – because of the self-liquidating nature of such finance. In recent years, however, they have departed from this position and now provide some medium- and even some long-term finance for industry. They have also entered the mortgage market in competition with the building societies.

We will consider each of the main providers of long-term finance in turn.

MERCHANT BANKS

The British Merchant Banking and Securities Houses Association was formed on 1 January 1988. It includes all 16 members of the previous Accepting Houses Committee together with most members of the previous Issuing Houses Association. It is to their role in the financing of new issues that we now turn.

When a company wishes to "go public" or an existing quoted company makes a further issue of shares to existing shareholders (a rights issue) it will usually turn to an issuing house for advice. The issuing house will examine the company's past record and future prospects very thoroughly and recommend the best way of raising the finance required. It will advise on the timing of the issue and on its pricing. It will also arrange for issues to be underwritten by means of which the success of the issue will be guaranteed. If, for any reason, the public fail to provide the funds, the issue will nevertheless be taken up in full by the underwriters. Usually the issuing house itself will be the principal underwriter; but it will use a number of sub-underwriters, paying them a part of the commission, to cover the full issue.

Issuing houses can arrange for a company to "go public" in a number of different ways. The method most favoured is the public offer for sale whereby the issue is advertised in at least one national newspaper. The price will usually be established by the issuing house but sometimes the issue is made by tender, those investors making the highest bids being successful. An alternative method, the placing, may be used for smaller issues but this is not a public issue and the shares are normally allocated to the clients of the institutions involved in the sale.

Ordinary share issues are much more important than loan capital issues whilst preference share issues are negligible. One reason for this is that company borrowing from the banks is now much more widespread than it used to be.

Issuing houses may also be involved in the sale of fixed interest securities, but government issues of dated stocks as well as Treasury bills are made through the Bank of England.

THE STOCK EXCHANGE

As we have seen the Bank of England and the issuing houses play an important part in the raising of new capital. A popular misconception is that new capital is raised on the Stock Exchange but this is not really the case. The very existence of a stock market, however, makes it possible for large sums of money to be raised by industry and government. The Stock Exchange therefore is extremely important in economic terms. Its functions may be summarised under four headings:

1. As a Secondary Market in Stocks and Shares
Investors in shares which are quoted on the Stock Exchange know that they can dispose of them at any time – or increase their holdings – because there is a market organised for this very purpose. Because of this:

(a) Securities will be more readily marketable.
(b) The differences between bid (selling) and offer (buying) prices will be narrower than they would otherwise be. It follows that.
(c) Issuers of securities will obtain their capital requirements more cheaply than would otherwise be the case.

Thus the existence of a sophisticated stock market reduces the cost of capital to borrowers.

2. As a Channel for New Funds
The existence of an excellent and well regulated secondary market in

stocks and shares is beneficial to investors and seekers of capital alike. The Stock Exchange, therefore, acts as a kind of magnet for the investment of huge sums of money. This money is used by government and business to build schools and hospitals, and factories and offices all of which make a real contribution to the national income.

Without new investment there would be no economic growth. The importance of investment in the strict economic sense (i.e. in contrast to consumption) cannot therefore be overstated. This function is therefore by far the most important. However, it really is quite impossible to separate one of them from the others: they are inextricably connected.

3. As a Guarantor of Standards
Although the Stock Exchange does not actually raise new capital it will only grant quotations to those companies who meet certain standards and who agree, by executing a listing agreement, to abide by certain standards of behaviour. Companies must, for example, announce all "price sensitive" information – dividends, share issues, take-over announcements, etc. – to the Stock Exchange before the news reaches any other person or body.

4. As an Economic Barometer
Since 1935 the Financial Times Ordinary Share Index has been the most widely quoted, if not the best, of the Stock Exchange indices. Today, two other indexes – the All-Share Index and the FTSE 100 Index – are regarded as more useful indicators. As economic barometers these indexes tend not so much to reflect the current economic situation as what investors expect it to be like in 12 to 18 months' time. Stock prices sometimes get out of line. They may advance too rapidly and then fall back, not so much because of bad news but because investors were perhaps too enthusiastic in the first place; likewise investors sometimes tend to overreact to bad news.

Whereas the issuing houses act as midwives to new issues it is the Stock Exchange which, by means of the grant of a quotation, gives them birth. A very large part of total stock exchange investment is undertaken by individuals but over the past 40 years or so this proportion has been steadily declining.

THE PENSION FUNDS

The greatest growth of all in recent years has come from the pension funds who now represent the largest of the institutional groups in terms of Stock Exchange investment. Their growth has been particularly due to the greater emphasis on pensionable employment in the 1970s influenced to a large extent by government legislation.

Another important and related factor is the tax treatment of the pension funds themselves and their contributors. Pension funds are generally free of all taxes: thus funds invested in them grow very much faster than if the income and capital gains were to be taxed as they arose. Contributors, whether as employees or as self-employed persons, therefore enjoy very considerable benefits. In most cases the whole of both the employers' and the employees' contributions can be offset against tax, and this reduces the net cost considerably. In the case of self-employment a maximum of $17\frac{1}{2}$–40 (according to age) per cent of net relevant earnings can be invested in a pension fund giving the contributor a large tax saving. The tax advantage of saving to provide a pension is brought out clearly in Table 26.1:

Table 26.1: Tax Saving in Pensionable Employment.

	No pension arrangement	Pension arrangement
Income (after personal allowance)	15,000	15,000
less Pension contributions	—	2,000
	15,000	13,000
less Taxation (say 25 per cent)	3,750	3,250
Net income	11,250	9,750

The net cost of the employee's pension contribution is thus only £1,500 (75 per cent of the gross amount) owing to the tax saving of £500. For higher rate taxpayers this advantage is even more substantial, while for companies there is a similar saving in corporation tax

INSURANCE COMPANIES

The other great investing group consists of the insurance companies. Most forms of insurance – fire, accident, motor and so on – do not give rise to the substantial investment of funds. This is because in each case the premiums are only about sufficient to cover the costs of administration and the expected claims arising from year to year. With the life assurance companies it is a different matter. Their substantial funds are invested long term. Over the years because of rising living standards and generous tax advantages the funds invested by the life insurance companies have steadily increased.

Tax relief on life assurance premiums was abolished following the 1984 budget, but life assurance still remains an excellent means of producing a tax free lump sum quite apart from their more obvious advantages – to provide family protection and as a useful means of building up a retirement "nest egg".

Like the pension funds life assurance companies invest heavily in British government securities which give them a large stable base; but in recent years they have become increasingly interested in equities and in property in the pursuit of growth in both income and capital.

UNIT TRUSTS AND INVESTMENT COMPANIES

Despite the very tangible tax advantages in particular of the pension funds some individual investors choose to invest directly in the stock market. Many investors, however, do not have sufficient capital to invest in a broad range of securities and thus avoid the risks involved in acquiring just one or two stocks. Unit trusts and investment companies are both media for investing small sums in a broad range of securities – diversification – without the risks associated with investment in just one or two securities. They are very appropriate investments for small investors.

Investment companies, first established in the 1860s, are limited companies whose chief, if not their sole, aim is to invest their equity and loan capital in other companies. They may, however, also purchase property and commodities if they consider these to be worthwhile investments. In general they aim to achieve capital growth rather than high income.

Unit trusts were first set up in the 1930s, but it was not until the 1950s that the movement really took off and there has been substantial growth again in recent years. Unlike investment trusts they can be widely advertised, and because unit trust prices are closely allied to the underlying value of the trust's securities they have been much more popular than investment trusts. The typical unit trust management company will offer at least six different funds – income, capital growth, overseas, etc. – to meet the requirments of a wide variety of investors. The major unit trusts which are authorised by the Securities and Investments Board under the Financial Services Act 1986, are only allowed to invest in prescribed investments (principally securities); and there are a number of other rules imposed on them to protect investors. Investment companies, subject only to their memorandum, can invest more widely – in property and in gold or other commodities.

FINANCE CORPORATIONS

Pension funds, insurance companies and unit trusts channel a great deal of the nation's savings into productive investment but their principal objective is to find safe and profitable havens for the funds entrusted to them. Their investors are mainly individuals of modest means who cannot afford to take undue risks. The major institutions have been criticised on the grounds that new firms and new industries are starved of funds because of the conservative approach to investment of the banks and the big institutions. This tendency was recognised in the MacMillan Report as long ago as 1931, and the expression "MacMillan Gap" has been used to describe the problem of financing this important part of the economy. The same problem was highlighted by the Wilson Committee in 1978.

Finance corporations are companies formed to meet this need – to provide not only loan capital but equity finance as well. The most important of them, Investors in Industry (3i) had its origins in the years after World War II when the financing needs of British industry were acute. The best known of its investment divisions is ICFC (formerly Industrial and Commercial Finance Corporation), the leading organisation in the U.K. geared to provide small businesses with long term capital. Its Venture Division supports high growth enterprises with risk capital while its Head Office Division is committed to financing larger enterprises, providing loan and equity capital of up to £35m and £5m respectively.

In recent years many of the merchant banks have been more active in this field, and the clearing banks too – encouraged by the government's Loan Guarantee Scheme – have been more willing to provide longer term loans for the purchase of fixed assets. Another important development has been the setting up of the government's Business Expansion Scheme whereby higher rate taxpayers can obtain considerable tax savings when they invest in new or expanding ventures. Most important of all has been the creation by the Stock Exchange of the Unlisted Securities Market. Many companies which could not previously have done so are now able to raise equity capital on this market.

FINANCE HOUSES

The finance houses, better known perhaps as hire purchase companies, provide not only consumer finance but industrial hire purchase and leasing arrangements for business. Such finance as they provide is invariably linked to specific purchases of medium- to long-term assets.

They thus affect the level of investment in the economy both indirectly (through consumer finance) as well as directly. Some of the finance houses are subsidiary companies of the major banks. They acquire their funds from the general public and in the parallel markets.

BUILDING SOCIETIES

Capital formation does not only occur in the business and government sectors of the economy. One of the critical measures of economic activity is the level of new "house starts". The building societies, by making funds available for house purchase, therefore perform a vitally important role in the economy.

Unlike the finance houses they are not linked with the big banks. Under powers granted by the Building Societies Act, 1986, they are now competing strongly with the banks through making unsecured advances and by providing a range of financial services. They are now funding themselves increasingly through the wholesale money markets: by law this is limited to 40 per cent of liabilities.

They remain largely dependent on the funds deposited by their members, but building societies are, of course, long-term lenders. They are, however, easily able to meet their commitments by their readiness to vary the rates paid to investors in line with market conditions.

QUESTIONS

1. What functions does the Stock Exchange fulfil?
2. Who are the chief investors on the Stock Exchange today?
3. "Building societies are long-term investors but short-term borrowers." How true is this statement?
4. "The MacMillan Gap highlighted in 1931 no longer exists." How true is this statement today?

CHAPTER 27

MONETARY POLICY

ECONOMIC POLICY

The Radcliffe Committee reporting in 1959 identified four principal objectives of economic policy:

1. Maintenance of employment at a high level.
2. Stable prices.
3. Economic growth.
4. Balance of payments equilibrium.

Laudable though these objectives may be, it seems, extremely difficult to achieve them in the U.K. A high level of employment, for example, tended to push wages and hence prices up. It also created an imbalance between exports and imports. Furthermore the competition among firms for labour tended to reduce labour productivity since workers were not always fully employed.

Governments will differ in the emphasis they place on each of the above objectives. For many years the main emphasis was on employment and the balance of payments, but this adversely affected the pursuit of stable prices and economic growth. In the early 1980s great stress was placed on bringing down inflation, but this had severe effects on jobs and on economic growth. The pursuit of an expansionary policy from 1987 resulted in an increase in GDP and a fall in the level of unemployment; but was accompanied by a marked rise in the rate of inflation and a serious balance of payments deficit. Some indication of the success or otherwise of recent governments in each of these key areas is shown in Table 27.1.

In carrying out its economic policy the government uses two principal means – fiscal policy and monetary policy. Fiscal policy is concerned with taxation, subsidies and government spending and is dealt with in Chapter 34. Monetary policy, in contrast, is concerned with interest rates, the money supply and bank lending.

Monetary policy is broadly neutral in its effects whilst fiscal and other measures can be used more discriminately – the redistribution of

Table 27.1: Employment, prices, growth and the balance of payments 1978–88.

Year	Unemployment* as a percentage of working population	Annual change in RPI (%)	Annual change in GDP (%)	Balance of payments (current account) (£m)
1978	4.3	8.3	3.2	936
1979	4.0	13.4	1.8	−550
1980	5.1	18.0	−2.4	2820
1981	8.1	11.9	−1.5	6628
1982	9.5	8.6	1.9	4587
1983	10.5	4.6	2.3	3758
1984	10.7	5.0	1.7	1885
1985	10.9	6.1	3.9	3203
1986	11.1	3.4	3.2	66
1987	10.0	4.2	4.5	−3671
1988	8.0	4.9	4.4	−14617

* Seasonally adjusted and excluding claimants under 18 years
Source: Annual Abstract of Statistics & Economic Trends

incomes and lower rates of corporation tax for small businesses are two examples. However, fiscal policy is not always sufficiently specific for government, and so other means are used to supplement both fiscal and monetary measures. Government regional aid schemes and home improvement grants come into the category of direct measures; and so do statutory and voluntary incomes policies.

THE IMPORTANCE OF MONEY

As we saw in Chapter 21 money must be capable of fulfilling five different functions. The extent to which these are important will vary from place to place and from time to time. In our society, for example, money is more important as a medium of exchange than as a store of value because there are many "near money" instruments which can be substituted for money; and there is also a good and active market in securities.

While the functions of money are indeed important economists believe that money does more than merely fulfil certain functions. In particular they hold that changes in the stock of money affect important economic variables. Keynesians, as we have seen, believe that the supply of money affects real things such as output, investment and employment whereas the Friedmanites stress the effect of the money stock on the value of money, and hence prices. They argue that real things are affected not so much by money but by supply side factors such as production and costs.

However, while Keynesians are still dubious about the causal link between the supply of money and the price level, they do not doubt that, irrespective of how and why prices rise, an increase in prices must require an increase in the money stock. If this does not happen, they argue, a shortage of bank credit will lead to rising interest rates and bankruptcies.

MONETARY POLICY AND CONTROL BEFORE 1981

In 1971 there was a radical break with previous policies. Before 1971 the chief means used were lending ceilings (quantitative) and qualitative guidance reinforced by special deposits.

From 1971 onwards there was a distinct shift towards allowing market forces, through interest rates, to allocate credit, with the use of special deposits (see below) as a government weapon if market forces did not achieve the desired effect. The policy failed, and additional measures, in particular a Supplementary Special Deposits Scheme (the "corset") had to be introduced. However, this scheme failed too as the banks found ways to avoid its potentially severe impact on their operations.

MONETARY POLICY AND CONTROL – POST 1981

One of the problems under the previous system was that the rules did not extend to all the banks. The Banking Act 1979 provided for a more equal treatment between the different kinds of banks and this has made monitoring and control somewhat easier.

Monetary control is now recognised as being of central importance though considerable difficulties have been experienced in achieving effective control. The authorities can exercise monetary control in two ways: either they can attempt to control interest rates (i.e. the price of money) or they can endeavour to control the money supply. In this connection it is important to remember the relationship between the level of credit and that of bank deposits. As we saw in Chapter 23, when a bank makes a loan this may have the effect of increasing the level of bank deposits.

The control of inflation means, in effect, that consumer expenditure must be contained but governments clearly cannot take direct action on this front. Government action can only be taken indirectly.

For many years, the authorities have been identifying a number of targets – *intermediate targets* – and to use a number of monetary instruments to tackle these targets to get at what they have seen to be the real problem, the major target – inflation.

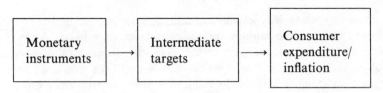

The *intermediate objectives* of monetary policy for which targets might be set, could be any of the following:

(a) Growth in the money supply

It is a vital feature of monetarist theory that the link between the money supply and prices, incomes and expenditure is reasonably predictable and stable. Thus, the velocity of circulation must remain fairly stable so that money income and money expenditure are directly determined by changes in the money supply. If this is not so, then attempts to control inflation will be made more difficult and complications can result from action taken by the authorities.

The Government has, since 1980, recognised that controlling the growth of the money supply must be a medium-term policy, and that reliable results cannot be expected within a short time: it takes time, for instance, to reduce the level of government spending or to change peoples' expectations. Experience has also shown the difficulty of having suitable monetary aggregates for measuring changes in the money supply. Indeed, a significant body of opinion questions whether controlling the growth in the money supply will result in control over the rate of inflation.

The current approach in the U.K. towards money supply growth is:

- to set targets for growth in MO "narrow money", as growth in MO shows a stable relationship with growth in "money" GDP
- to monitor growth in M4 (the measure of broad money), though not to set any targets for M4 growth.

(b) Interest rate levels

It is generally accepted that there is a connection between interest rates and business investment and consumption expenditure, though the link is not predictable and stable. Moreover, there is likely to be a time lag before interest rate changes affect expenditure levels.

Although Minimum Lending Rate (MLR) had been abolished in 1981 the authorities reserve the right to reintroduce it and it was used last in 1985 in very special circumstances. Generally, the government has wished to see market forces play a larger role again. It seeks to keep short-term rates within unpublished bands through its dealings in the discount market. The trend in interest rates can be observed day-by-day. When the discount houses are forced to borrow at a penal rate this signals a major increase in interest rates.

The U.K. Government has since 1988 used high interest rates as a means of monetary control, contending that:

    (i) this will discourage consumer borrowing

   (ii) those with existing mortgages and other loans will have less to spend on other things

  (iii) the position of sterling will be strengthened so lessening the chances of cost-push inflation from imports

  (iv) foreign investors will be attracted into buying sterling denominated securities, with the capital inflows into the U.K. helping to finance a balance of payments current account deficit.

An immediate effect of higher interest rates in the discount market is, of course, higher rates elsewhere (including mortgages) so pushing up the Retail Price Index. A bank's base rate is the published rate to which most of its lending is related. Thus an overdraft may be quoted at "base + 2%". The actual "plus factor" depends on the status of the borrower. In the wholesale markets the banks are more likely to use LIBOR (London Interbank Offered Rate) as the basis for charging interest. In setting their interest rates the banks have regard to two crucial periods:

3 months deposit rate	– the marginal cost to banks of raising deposits for lending operations.
up to 7 days	– if short-term money market rates rise above company borrowing rates *arbitrage** will occur.

In conclusion, it is true to say that the authorities are able to influence interest rates more effectively than they can influence other policy targets.

(c) Growth in the volume of credit

Higher bank lending is likely to result in higher bank deposits and

---

* Arbitrage means buying in one market and selling virtually simultaneously in another. Translated into banking terms this means borrowing cheaply on overdraft to take advantage of the better money market rates. This form of arbitrage is known as "round tripping".

thus an increase in the money supply. Furthermore, the consequence of an increase in bank lending is likely to be a rise in the level of expenditure in the economy. Therefore, the government might decide to restrict the power to grant credit. However, to be at all effective and to avoid discrimination, the control would need to be over *all* financial institutions and all means of lending money. Even then, money could come into the country from "offshore" institutions (no longer subject to exchange control).

(d) The exchange rate

When sterling is high relative to other leading currencies – notably the Yen, the Deutschmark and the U.S. dollar – it makes it difficult for U.K. exporters but eases inflation in the short-term by making imports cheaper. However, this is bad for the balance of payments, and in the long run has adverse effects on money growth and inflation. The authorities sometimes set a target for the pound sterling. This may be directed to maintaining the rate to avoid a rise in the cost of imports; conversely it may be aimed at a lowering of the rate to facilitate an increase in the volume of exports. The problem is that the exchange rate is dependent on both the domestic rate of inflation and the level of interest rates, so that any target for the exchange rate is dependent on the authorities getting to grips with domestic inflation.

Instruments of monetary policy available to the authorities towards achieving the monetary policy targets might be:

(a) Changing the level and/or structure of interest rates

U.K. Government influence over interest rates concentrates on short-term, money-market rates. The influence can be achieved through open market operations as well as through the interest rate imposed form time to time by the Bank of England in its role as lender of last resort. Interest rates are initially affected in the discount market with consequential effects in other money markets, especially the inter-bank market. This in turn influences commercial banks' base rates and lending rates.

Attempts in the 1980s to control the growth of the broad money supply (e.g. M3) through interest rate policy met with only limited success. It is now accepted that the interest rate weapon is more suitably used to control inflation or the exchange rate rather than to control broad money supply growth.

(b) Reserve requirements

All institutions in the monetary sector with eligible liabilities (broadly deposits with less than two years to maturity) are now

required to maintain 0.45% of their eligible liabilities in non-operational, non-interest-bearing deposits with the Bank. The clearing
banks keep with the Bank of England, in addition, sufficient
balances for clearing purposes.

Apart from this cash ratio there are no specific liquidity requirements laid down. However, in its supervisory role over the monetary sector, the Bank does lay down undisclosed criteria on a
bank-by-bank basis.

(c) Government funding policy

The Bank of England operates in the gilt-edged market by buying
and selling government stocks thus reducing or increasing the
banks' reserve assets and hence their ability to create credit. These
activities are known as open market operations. A sale of £1b
worth of gilts, for example, will result in bank customers drawing
cheques in favour of the Bank of England, and this will result in
reducing the banks' balances with the Bank of England (Figure
27.1). As a consequence of this interest rates would rise.

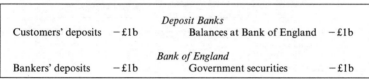

		Deposit Banks	
Customers' deposits	−£1b	Balances at Bank of England	−£1b
		Bank of England	
Bankers' deposits	−£1b	Government securities	−£1b

Figure 27.1: Open Market Operations – Reducing the Money Supply.

If, on the other hand, the Bank wished to see some expansion of
credit it would purchase government stocks thus increasing the
bank's working balances at the Bank of England and their overall
reserve assets. This traditional method of monetary control does
not, however, have the immediacy of special deposits (see below).

The Public Sector Borrowing Requirement (PSBR) is generally
expansionary and has the effect of increasing the money supply as
the Authorities issue new government shares to fund the debt. Increasing confidence in the personal sector, however, can lead to a
fall in private sector deposits and inflation. From 1987/88 the PSBR
turned positive and is known as the Public Sector Debt Repayment.
Government purchases of gilt-edged stocks from the public brought
about the first reduction in the national debt for several decades.
(As percentage of GDP it had been falling for many years however).
With fiscal pressures on the growth of the money supply gone,
bank and building society credit remains the main source of money
supply growth.

(d) Direct controls over bank lending

QUANTITATIVE controls might be imposed on the growth in *volume* of either bank lending (i.e. assets) or bank deposits.

QUALITATIVE controls may be used to influence the *type* of bank lending, e.g. favouring the business sector as against the personal sector.

(e) Special deposits

The Bank of England may require the banks to lodge non-operational special deposits to reinforce its control over credit. In the example below a bank faces a call for special deposits of 2% when its holdings of liquid assets are already quite low. It can find a quarter of this requirement by selling liquid assets but must sell investments (perhaps at a loss) and call in loans to make up the remainder of the requirement.

	Before	After
	Special Deposits(%)	
Liquid Assets	13	12.5
Special Deposits	—	2
Investments	10	9
Advances	65	64.5
Other assets	12	12
	100	100
Eligible liabilities	100	100

This little used weapon can be a sharp and effective means of affecting interest rates.

THE BROAD ASPECTS OF MONETARY POLICY

With diminished emphasis on control of the money supply has come increased emphasis on the sterling exchange rate. For a period in 1986, sterling was allowed to depreciate against most world currencies. Then, from late 1986 the official aim was to stablise the rate for sterling within a "target zone".

The four strands of current policy (1990) are:

(a) to control MO growth

(b) to use interest rates as deemed necessary

(c) to develop funding policy to affect monetary conditions (e.g. to ease inflationary pressures)

(d) to intervene as necessary to influence the exchange rate for sterling.

Governments always face the dilemma that high interest rates help to control inflation, but through retarding export growth make more difficult the elimination of a deficit on the balance of payments; whilst any major lowering of the exchange rate (to stimulate exports and discourage imports) would raise the rate of domestic inflation.

QUESTIONS

1. "The Keynesian objectives of economic policy enunciated in the Radcliffe Report of 1959 are no longer applicable today." Discuss.

2. Explain how (a) special deposits and (b) open market operations can be used to restrict monetary growth. What other means are at the disposal of the authorities?

3. What have been the aims of monetary policy since 1981?

CHAPTER 28

THE NATIONAL INCOME

So far we have been primarily concerned with individual components of the economy. We have looked for example at the behaviour of individuals and of firms and seen how they operate in different circumstances. It is now time to move from micro- to macro-economics and turn our attention to the economy as a whole. What we will now be concerned with are aggregates – for example total demand in the economy rather than the demand for particular goods.

Governments in the U.K. since World War II have attempted to achieve four main macro-economic objectives. These, it will be recalled, are:

1. A high level of employment.
2. A low rate of inflation.
3. A satisfactory balance of payments with the rest of the world.
4. A satisfactory rate of growth of income and output in the economy.

In order to evaluate progress it is essential for the economist to know how much is being produced in the country – the Gross Domestic Product (GDP). This figure will provide a guide to the standard of living, it will enable comparisons to be made over time and with other countries and it will provide detailed information about the economy, thus enabling it to be more efficiently managed.

THE NATIONAL OUTPUT

The National Output is the measurement of the total value of goods and services produced during a given period of time (usually a year) by the factors of production in an economy. One way of doing this would be to look directly at what had been produced. We would then have a list of various items ranging from vehicles to houses to squash balls and it would be difficult to use this for any further calculations or comparisons with other countries producing a different set of goods. Therefore all the goods and services produced are valued in money terms. Note that we include services, such as those provided by accountants and bankers, since what they are providing is just as much a part of the National Output as is the quantity of vehicles manufactured at Cowley.

When measuring the value of what has been produced we do not simply add up the output of all the producers in the economy since this would mean that we have included certain elements more than once and therefore overvalued the National Output. An example will illustrate this. Imagine a farmer selling wheat for 20p to a miller who turns it into flour and then sells it to a baker for 30p who in turn sells it as a loaf of bread to the customer for 60p.

Adding up the total value of each person's output would give a value of 110p – considerably in excess of the value of the one loaf of bread produced in our example. By including the farmer's output at each stage and the miller's output twice we have overstated the value of what has been produced. This is called *double-counting*.

There are two solutions. The first, *the final product method* of tackling the problem, is to consider only the sum of the values of the final products in the economy – those things not used to make others. Thus, in the example above, the final product would be the value of the bread – 60p. However in reality final products are difficult to identify. What might be classed as a final product for one person, e.g. a car for a consumer, might be an intermediate good for another, as a car is for a hire-car business. There are also further problems with this method such as accounting for the value of work in progress at the start and finish of the period and deducting for any import content of the final products since this would represent output produced in a different economy.

The second solution, known as *the value-added method*, involves considering the value added by each firm in the production process. Thus in

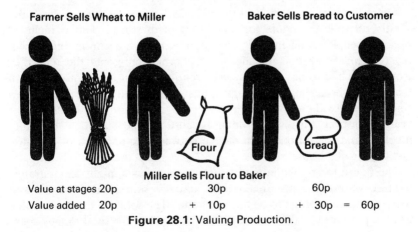

Farmer Sells Wheat to Miller   **Baker Sells Bread to Customer**

Miller Sells Flour to Baker

| Value at stages | 20p | 30p | 60p | |
| Value added | 20p | + 10p | + 30p | = 60p |

Figure 28.1: Valuing Production.

Table 28.1: Gross Domestic Product by Industry, 1988.

	£m
Agriculture, forestry and fishing	5,625
Energy and water supply	21,845
Manufacturing	93,433
Construction	25,745
Distribution; hotels and catering; repairs	55,131
Transport and communication	28,657
Banking, finance, insurance, business services and leasing	76,922
Ownership of dwellings	21,407
Public administration, national defence and compulsary social security	27,023
Education and health	35,237
Other services	25,785
	416,810
Adjustment for financial services	− 22,204
Residual error	181
Gross Domestic Product, at factor cost	394,787

Source: Annual Abstract of Statistics 1990

our example, as is shown in the following diagram, the farmer adds 20p, the miller adds 10p and the baker a further 30p, making a total of 60p, the same as the figure arrived at by the final product method.

This method automatically takes account of any work in progress and any imports since they are not counted, not being part of the value added by any firm in the economy.

Table 28.1 sets out the figures for the U.K. economy for 1988 for the *Gross Domestic Product (GDP)*. This is the name given by economists to the measure of the total value of goods and services produced in the economy in a specified period of time, in this case the year 1988.

There are various items in the Table 28.1 which require explanation. Firstly, there is the figure for ownership of dwellings. This is included because people living in their own houses receive a continuing benefit from them. The value included in the table represents the rent they would have had to pay had they been renting similar accommodation. In theory one should make a similar adjustment for all consumer durables since they provide a continuing use to the consumer over a number of years. However this is not done because of the statistical difficulty involved and the difference in degree between the duration of their use and the life of a house.

The figure for public administration and defence might seem strange because output in this area is not actually sold in the market and therefore might appear to be hard to value. The solution used is to value what is produced at the cost of providing it. Thus the total money spent on defence is the value of defence output. The adjustment for financial services is an allowance made to avoid double counting the interest paid on loans and the interest received by financial institutions. The figures given in the table include an allowance for stock appreciation. This occurs where the price of goods held in stock during the period increases owing to inflation. It is necessary to take account of the illusory increase represented by the increase in price. After this has been done, any increase in the value of stocks will represent a real increase in the quantity of goods held. There is also an attempt to allow for any goods produced and consumed without being sold, such as a farmer consuming part of his own output since, if this were not done, there would be an undervaluation of what had been produced.

The table also contains a figure for the residual error. This is included because of statistical inaccuracies in collecting the necessary data. Information is collected from a sample of companies, half concerning output and half the value of sales; however when the structure of an economy is changing and when relative prices are changing the figures from the sample become slightly inaccurate.

Finally we note that the GDP is measured at what is known as *factor cost*. This means that the figure which is used is the actual value of the output produced and does not include any indirect taxes levied or subsidies provided by the government. The inclusion of indirect taxes such as VAT would artificially increase the value of what had been produced while subsidies would reduce it. An alternative method of measuring the GDP would be to use *market prices* which includes any indirect taxes and subsidies which have been levied. We can therefore say:

GDP at factor cost =
   GDP at market prices − indirect taxes + subsidies.

THE NATIONAL EXPENDITURE

National income can also be measured as the aggregate *expenditure* of the nation. Goods (and services) can either be sold (as happens in most cases), or put into stock, which can be regarded for this purpose as the firm selling its output to itself. If output is sold, it means that someone else is buying it. Therefore the total value of the goods and services produced will equal the total value of final expenditure in the economy. We can thus measure the GDP by looking at the expenditure of an economy as well as by looking at the value of output.

Table 28.2 sets out the national expenditure and its main components for the U.K. for 1982.

Table 28.2: Gross National Product by Category of expenditure 1988

At market prices:	£m
Consumers' expenditure	241,873
General government final consumption	86,061
Gross domestic – fixed capital formation	86,125
Total domestic expenditure	414,059
Exports of goods and services	103,866
Total final expenditure	517,925
less Imports of goods and services	− 125,194
	392,731
Add Statistical adjustment	2,056
Gross domestic product at factor cost	394,787

Source: Annual Abstract of Statistics 1990

If we look at the above table, we see that the first category, consumers' expenditure, is the largest, accounting for over half of the GDP. The figures throughout the table are measured at market prices and there is then the necessary adjustment made to bring them to factor cost. The second item relates to government expenditure but excludes any expenditure on *transfer payments*. These are payments which are made without a corresponding flow of goods and services being generated. Thus expenditure on the health service is included since a service is provided but unemployment benefit, which is simply a transfer from the taxpayer to the unemployed, is not.

The third category, gross domestic fixed capital formation, refers to expenditure on the replacement of and addition to the stock of fixed capital assets such as factories and machines. The use of the word "gross" means that no deduction has been made for any wearing out of the machines during the production process. During the year, some machines would have become obsolete and others would have worn out. This is known as *capital consumption* or *depreciation* and an allowance is made later in the table to take this into account and provide the net value of the GDP. We can therefore say that:

Net Domestic Product =
Gross Domestic Product − Capital Consumption

Since the value of capital consumption is difficult to measure accurately, it is quite common to talk of the gross domestic product rather than the net domestic product.

The fourth figure represents an allowance for any increase in stocks between the start and the end of the period and also takes account of differences in the amount of work in progress at the start and the end of the period. A positive figure denotes an increase whereas a negative figure implies a decline in the level of stocks, which is known as destocking, or a fall in the amount of work in progress.

The sum of the above figures provides us with domestic expenditure – expenditure undertaken within the U.K. but we also need to take account of the expenditure made on British goods by foreigners, our exports, which increases the GDP, and of our expenditure on imports which has been included in the earlier categories but now has to be deducted because it does not increase the U.K.'s GDP, but that of some other country. We then similarly have to adjust for the interest and profits sent back to the U.K. by British firms working abroad minus any similar flows sent home by foreign companies, such as Banque Nationale de Paris, with offices in the U.K. Once we have done this we have moved from the gross domestic product to the gross national product, having taken into account *net property income from abroad*. We can therefore say that:

Gross National Product = Gross Domestic Product + Net Property Income from Abroad

What we are left with, having made all the above adjustments, is the net national product. This is generally referred to as the *National Income*, regardless of the way in which it is measured. The third method of measuring the National Income is to look directly at the incomes earned in the economy.

THE NATIONAL INCOME

This method of evaluating the output produced in an economy involves studying the flow of income generated from the production of goods and services. If we regard the National Output in terms of value added and consider the value added by one firm, it will equal the firm's revenue minus its expenditure on materials, neglecting any changes in stocks or work in progress. Out of this value added, the firm will have to pay its wages, salaries and rent with its profit being what is left after these payments have been made. All of these items are forms of income and so we have broken down the firm's value added and expressed it in terms of the income received by people or businesses in the economy. What is true for one firm is also true for all enterprises in the economy and so we can consider the GDP a third way by looking at the incomes earned in an economy in a given period.

Table 28.3: Gross National Product by Income, 1988

Factor Incomes	£m
Income From Employment	249,635
Income From Self-Employment	41,895
Gross Trading Profits of Companies	65,077
Gross Trading Surplus Of Public Corporations	7,057
Gross Trading Surplus Of General Government Enterprises	70
Rent	27,464
Imputed Charge For Consumption Of Non-Trading Capital	3,408
Total Domestic Income	394,606
Statistical adjustment	181
Net Property Income From Abroad	
	394,787
Gross Domestic Product at Factor Cost	

Source: Annual Abstract of Statistics 1990

In order to make the identity between output, expenditure and income clearer, imagine a small community where people sell their output to provide themselves with income. If they sell it, others must be buying it. Therefore expenditure equals output. However the money received by the producers will be their incomes and the incomes of people working for them and the other producers from whom they buy their inputs. Therefore expenditure is also equivalent to income. What is true for this simple economy is also true for more complex economies such as the U.K.

Table 28.3 sets out the U.K.'s National Income for 1988 measured in this last method, by considering the total value of incomes received, and Figure 28.2 shows the share of income received by the various sectors of the economy.

The first item in Table 28.3 comprises the pay in cash or kind (e.g. free food or travel provided by an employer) of all employees, plus employers' contributions to National Insurance. This latter item is regarded as part of the employee's income which is deducted at source. What is excluded from the income figure, and from those following, are any *transfer payments*; these are payments for which there is no corresponding production of goods and services. Thus a student grant is not counted as income since it will be financed by payments from individuals and businesses in tax out of income which has already been included in the statistics and does not relate to production of output. Similarly pocket money is not counted as income because it too is a transfer payment. As with the output method, double counting is again avoided. So, for example, company profits are included as income but the dividends

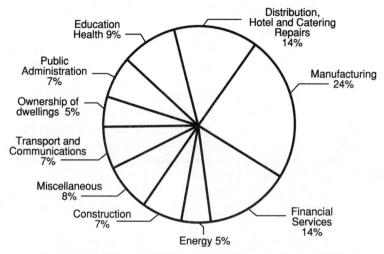

Figure 28.2: Shares of U.K. Domestic Income by Sector, 1988.

Source: Annual Abstract of Statistics, 1990.

which they pay to shareholders from these profits are not counted since, including both items, would involve double counting.

Apart from this, all forms of income are counted. Thus there are figures for the income from self-employment, the surpluses of public corporations and government enterprises. Rent is included and the figure given contains an allowance for the imputed income for owner-occupied properties and houses provided rent-free by employers. The next item, the imputed charge for consumption of non-trading capital, refers to the assumed "income" for government, individuals and private non-profit-making bodies from owner-occupied non-trading property.

After totalling these items there is again a residual error. The majority of the figures are collected from Inland Revenue information which have a tendency to understate the level of the National Income! A survey by the Inland Revenue has estimated that the "black economy" – that which is not recorded in official statistics – could be as high as $7\frac{1}{2}$ per cent of GDP. This missing $7\frac{1}{2}$ per cent would include such items as people doing jobs, such as gardening, decorating or private coaching, without disclosing the income for tax assessment not to mention tax evasion on a much larger scale.

When the residual error has been taken account of, the usual adjustments for net property income from abroad and capital consumption can be made to give a value for the National Income.

THE NATIONAL INCOME AND INFLATION

The figures so far given take no account of inflation which increases the value of the National Income without there being any actual increase in what has been produced. For example if a business produced ten million goods and sold them at £5 each, its output would be worth £50 million. However, if next year, it increased its price by 20 per cent to £6 but produced the same output, it would now be valued at £60 million, an increase of £10 million without any extra goods having been produced.

In order to eliminate the effect of rising prices and make the National Income figures more suitable for comparisons, it is often expressed in *constant price* or *real* terms instead of in *current price* or *money* terms. The last two refer to the National Income before any adjustment has been made for inflation whereas the first two mentioned include such an adjustment.

The way the adjustment is made is by using index numbers, which was mentioned previously in Chapter 21, to express the level of current prices in terms of the prices prevailing in a base year. A value of 100 is conventionally assigned to represent the level of prices in the base year and if, for example, prices had risen by 20 per cent since then, today's price index value would be 20 per cent higher, namely 120. An example will show how this figure is used.

	1972	1982 (£ billion)
National Income (Current Prices)	56	228
Price Index	100	377

It appears that the National Income rose fourfold between 1972 and 1982; however prices rose by almost as much, therefore to adjust the National Income figure, the following calculation would be performed:

1982 National Income in 1972 Prices =

$$\text{1982 National Income in Current Prices} \times \frac{\text{Index of 1972 Prices}}{\text{Index of 1982 Prices}}$$

$$= 228 \times \frac{100}{377}$$

$$= £60.5 \text{ billion, (1972 Prices)}$$

Therefore, after taking account of inflation, the National Income had risen by only 8 per cent during the period. Table 28.4 shows the effect of

Table 28.4: Purchasing power of the pound taking value as equivalent to 100p in various years

	1888	1900	1913	1928	1938	1948	1958	1968	1978	1982	1983	1984	1985	1986	1987	1988
1888	100.0															
1900	98.0	100.0														
1913	90.1	91.9	100.0													
1928	54.1	55.1	60.0	100.0												
1938	57.5	58.6	63.8	106.3	100.0											
1948	29.6	30.2	32.8	54.7	51.5	100.0										
1958	20.5	20.9	22.7	37.9	35.7	69.3	100.0									
1968	15.3	15.6	17.0	28.4	26.7	51.8	74.8	100.0								
1978	5.1	5.2	5.6	9.4	8.8	17.1	24.8	33.1	100.0							
1982	3.1	3.2	3.5	5.8	5.4	10.5	15.2	20.3	61.5	100.0						
1983	3.0	3.0	3.3	5.5	5.2	10.1	14.6	19.5	58.8	95.6	100.0					
1984	2.8	2.9	3.2	5.3	4.9	9.6	13.9	18.5	56.0	91.1	95.3	100.0				
1985	2.7	2.7	3.0	5.0	4.7	9.1	13.1	17.5	52.8	85.9	89.8	94.3	100.0			
1986	2.6	2.6	2.9	4.8	4.5	8.8	12.6	16.9	51.1	83.0	86.8	91.2	96.7	100.0		
1987	2.5	2.5	2.8	4.6	4.3	8.4	12.1	16.2	49.0	79.7	83.4	87.5	92.8	96.0	100.0	
1988	2.4	2.4	2.6	4.4	4.1	8.0	11.6	15.5	46.7	76.0	79.5	83.4	88.5	91.5	95.3	100.0

Source: Lloyds Bank Economic Bulletin

inflation on the purchasing power of the pound sterling, using various base dates. Thus £100 in 1948 was worth only £8 in 1988.

The price index used for the adjustment; the *GDP Deflator* as it is known, is calculated by government statisticians by weighting the rise in the prices of goods and services according to their relative importance in the economy on the base date. The indices are periodically updated to take account of changes in the structure of the economy. The other index widely used to measure the rate of inflation is the *Retail Price Index* (RPI). This is calculated on a monthly basis by taking note of the prices of approximately 600 goods on sale in different locations and different types of shops. In total, 130,000 readings are taken each month by the Department of Employment. The selection of goods and services included is based on the government's Family Expenditure Survey which shows the average spending pattern of households across the country. From this survey, the government is able to calculate the importance, or weight, which it should give to each of the items included. In order to adequately reflect changing spending patterns, the weights are reviewed each January and amended if necessary. Diagram 28.3 shows the weights of the main groups in 1987.

THE NATIONAL INCOME AND THE STANDARD OF LIVING

The National Income is often used to assess the standard of living, a measure of the material well-being of the population. Since the National Income is a measure of the flow of output, it is a good guide to living standards. However there are various adjustments which should be made

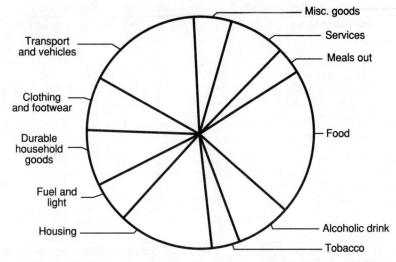

Figure 28.3: Weighting of Main Groups in the Retail Price Index, 1987.
Source: Department of Employment

to the National Income figures before attempting to use them to reflect living standards.

1. The National Income should be expressed in constant prices to remove the effects of inflation if it is intended to compare living standards over time.

2. Similarly changes in population will occur so it is therefore best to measure the National Income on a per capita basis.

3. Tax rates might change, thus affecting how much money people have to spend on goods and services. Therefore it is sometimes the case that the *disposable income*, income left after tax and national insurance contributions have been paid, is used instead. For this reason, an alternative to the RPI, known as the *Tax and Price Index* (TPI), is sometimes used. It measures not only changes in prices but also changes in income tax and national insurance contributions.

Even after making the above adjustments there are still problems with using the figures obtained as a measure of living standards. Firstly no account has been taken of the structure of the economy. It is possible that the National Income might increase but the quantity of goods available for consumption might go down if there were a shift of output towards such things as defence expenditure or capital spending. Secondly, nothing has been said regarding the distribution of income. If this becomes more uneven as the National Income increases it is possible for the average figure for the standard of living to increase but for the majority of the population to suffer a fall in their living standards while a small minority experience a very large rise. Thirdly, there might be a change in the number of people producing goods or providing services for self-consumption; such things as growing vegetables at home and working on D.I.Y. jobs around the house increase living standards but are not properly reflected in the statistics. Furthermore, we have been concentrating so far on the material aspects of people's well being but there are also non-measurable factors such as pollution and congestion which might suffer at the expense of the measurable rise in living standards. If we attempt to make comparisons with other countries, then there are additional problems. There might be different degrees of accuracy in the collection of the data, especially in less-developed countries. One will also be faced with the problem of comparing figures in different currencies and although one can convert them, this assumes that the rate of exchange used is an accurate measure of the value of each currency. The countries might value leisure differently, one preferring more leisure at the cost of a smaller quantity of consumable goods.

Therefore, although the National Income figures are the best guide to living standards, they should be used with caution especially when attempting to compare dissimilar countries or one country over a long period.

QUESTIONS

1. What is meant by the phrase "a country's National Income"?
2. How does one measure National Income?
3. Why should the three methods of measuring the National Income all give the same answer? Why do they not in practice?
4. Why is the National Income used as a measure of a country's standard of living?
5. What problems would be encountered in attempting to compare living standards in the U.K. and the U.S.A.?
6 If a country's National Income increased by 50 per cent over a twenty year period, would it follow that the standard of living had increased by the same amount? Give reasons for your answer.

CHAPTER 29

THE CIRCULAR FLOW OF INCOME

INTRODUCTION

The last chapter explained how the national income of an economy could be measured and how an estimate of the standard of living could be made, with an increasing national income being generally associated with a high standard of living. Besides being important in this respect, the national income is also important because it is closely related to the level of employment. A rising national income usually leads to people spending more money, thus causing firms to raise their output. In order to do this, in the short term, it will be necessary for them to employ more people or to persuade their existing workforce to work overtime and so it is likely that employment will rise.

In order to analyse this more closely, a model of the economy can be constructed in which all the unimportant variables have been removed and only the important elements remain. Providing such a model is carefully constructed, what can be deduced about its working is then applied to the economy as a whole. A far more complicated analysis is undertaken by the Treasury when it studies the economy as, for example, when it analyses the effects of possible changes the Chancellor of the Exchequer might make in the Budget. People, hence economies, do not always behave in a predictable fashion, however.

A SIMPLIFIED MODEL OF THE ECONOMY

The economy can be regarded as containing only two sectors, firms and households. It is a *closed* economy, i.e. there are no exports or imports. In addition we assume that there is no government sector, i.e. there are no taxes or any government spending. Later, these assumptions will be relaxed and these variables included.

In the simplified economy described above, households fulfil two functions. Firstly they purchase goods and services from the firms and secondly they provide the firm with labour. Firms similarly fulfil two functions. They produce the goods and services required by the households and they provide the households with income in exchange for their

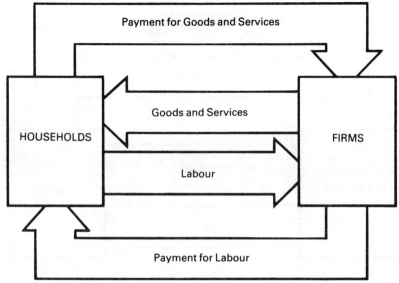

Figure 29.1: The Circular Flow of Income.

labour with which they buy goods and services. The process can be illustrated on Figure 29.1.

The above process is known as the *circular flow of income* since it describes how money flows around the economy. Households receive income for providing labour which they then spend on goods and services. This then provides the firms with the means and the desire to employ labour to produce more goods and hence provide further income.

As it is described above, the economy is in equilibrium. It will continue unchanged ad infinitum since there are no forces causing it to change. However, not all income is spent on consumption, some of it is saved. (For the economist, *saving* is defined as anything not spent on consumption out of disposable income and therefore includes items as diverse as money kept under a mattress, used to buy shares on the Stock Exchange or put into a building society account.) The act of saving will reduce the amount of money available in the economy for spending.

Firms facing a lower demand for their goods will need a smaller workforce and therefore income and employment will decrease. Saving is known as a *leakage* or *withdrawal* from the circular flow of income since it takes money out of the economy.

Besides the act of saving taking money out of the economy, there will also be an inflow of money in the form of *investment*. This is defined as

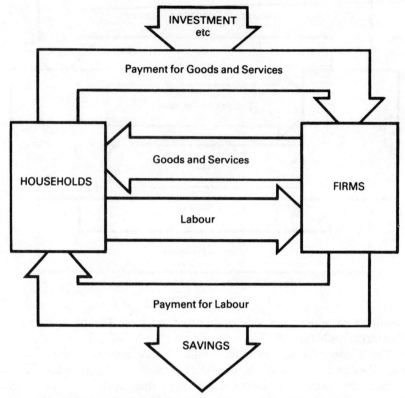

Figure 29.2: Savings and Investment in the Circular Flow of Income.

any spending on capital formation, such as factories and machines which assist in the production of future goods and services. It should be emphasised that there is a difference between the everyday use of the term "investment" which includes the purchase of shares and government bonds – counted as a form of saving by the economist – and the use of the term in this context where it refers to additions to the nation's capital stock and stocks of raw materials and finished goods.

If businessmen invest, e.g. they use past savings to build a new factory, then they are creating additional demand and putting money into the circular flow of income. Investment can thus be seen as an *injection* of money into the economy. The previous diagram can now be redrawn to include both savings and investment.

Similarly, the idea of equilibrium mentioned previously can also be reconsidered in the light of the addition of savings and investment to the circular flow of income. An economy will now be in equilibrium, i.e. the level of income will be stationary, so long as the volume of investment, putting money into the economy, equals the volume of savings taking money out. If the level of investment exceeds that of savings then there is a net inflow of money into the economy and the national income will increase. If savings exceed investment then there will be a net outflow from the economy and the national income will go down.

A CLOSER EXAMINATION OF THE RELATIONSHIP BETWEEN SAVINGS AND INVESTMENT

If one considers the national income of a country (assuming the economy is still closed i.e. without a government sector), in terms of output, then only consumer or investment goods are produced. The quantity of the latter thus equals the national output minus the quantity of consumer goods produced. Similarly, if one considers the national income, not in terms of output produced, but in terms of income received, then it can be split up into income which is spent on consumption and income which is saved, these being the only two alternatives. Thus the level of savings equals the national income minus consumption. But if investment is national output less consumption and savings is national income less consumption, then, since national output and national income are identical, *savings equals investment*.

This can be explained in mathematical notation:

$$NO = C + I$$
$$NI = C + S$$
$$\text{Therefore: } C + S = C + I$$
$$\text{Therefore: } S = I$$

where NO = National Output; NI = National Income; I = Investment; S = Savings; C = Consumption.

It might seem strange that the level of investment, based upon decisions by thousands of businessmen, will equal the level of savings which are carried out by millions of individuals. However the equality between them will become clearer if we examine what would happen if what individuals wished to save differed from what businessmen wished to invest. If savings increase, consumption will therefore decrease and businessmen will find that their stocks of unsold goods increase. But because these stocks are included as part of investment, it will have risen, preserving the equality with savings. The rise in investment which has taken place is an unplanned increase as opposed to the rise in savings which was planned. The idea of equilibrium presented above can now be modified to make use of this distinction between actual and planned savings and investment.

It is important to note that actual savings equal actual investment at all times but the economy will only be in equilibrium if planned savings equal planned investment. If not, forces will be set in motion to change the level of national income and reach a new equilibrium level.

In the previous example, with planned savings exceeding planned investment, businessmen will react to finding themselves with high stocks by reducing their output. This will lead to a fall in employment and incomes and therefore, with smaller incomes, people will save less. The process will continue, with falls in income causing falls in actual and planned savings, until equilibrium is reached when planned investment equals planned savings. Only then will there be no incentive for firms to change their level of production.

This view of the economy, whereby equilibrium is restored via changes in the level of income, was first presented by John Maynard Keynes in his *General Theory Of Employment, Interest And Money* in 1936. It formed the basis of much modern macroeconomic thinking since World War II and also explains the "Paradox of Thrift" whereby an initial increase in savings can ultimately cause a fall in savings due to a fall in income. Keynes differed strongly from the classical economists who regarded savings and investment as being brought into balance with each other by the rate of interest rather than by changes in the level of income.

A MORE REALISTIC MODEL OF THE ECONOMY

It is now time to relax the assumptions made earlier regarding the lack of a government sector and of exports and imports. Any money taken by the government in tax will reduce the amount which households can spend on consumption and which therefore will be available to generate further income. Taxes have the same effect as savings and act as a withdrawal from the circular flow of income. Similarly spending on imports will take money out of the economy and so imports are also a withdrawal.

However, any money which the government itself spends will act as an injection into the economy as will any exports sold since, in this case, there will be an inflow of money into the economy from other countries.

The idea of the economy being in equilibrium can be revised once again and we can now replace savings and investment with the terms withdrawals and injections. If withdrawals – savings, imports and taxes – equal the level of injections – investment, exports and government

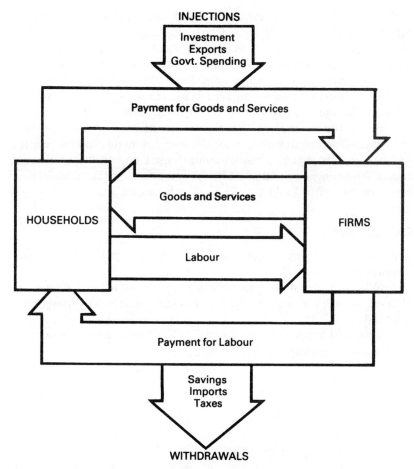

Figure 29.3: Injections and Withdrawals in the Circular Flow of Income.

spending then the economy will be in equilibrium. The equality between planned savings and investment is simply another way of stating that the level of aggregate demand in an economy must equal aggregate supply if there is to be an equilibrium situation. This is because the injections into the economy can be regarded as the addition to demand after taking account of household consumption while the withdrawals represent that part of income, and so of the national output, which is analogous with aggregate supply not needed for consumption. Provided what is being added represents what is "spare" after consumption has taken place, there will be no shortfall or excess of demand over supply. Figure 29.3 illustrates this diagrammatically.

To understand the concepts of injections and withdrawals it may be helpful to think of the economy as a bath. Imagine that there are three taps, an investment, exports and government spending tap, and three plug-holes, corresponding to the three withdrawals, savings, imports and taxes. The level of water corresponding to the level of income in the country. If injections exceed withdrawals there is more water coming in through the taps than is leaving via the plug-holes and the water level will rise. So too the national income will rise and will continue to do so until injections equal withdrawals. It does not matter in this context whether exports equal imports, savings equal investment or taxation equals government spending. What is important is the total level of injections compared to the total level of withdrawals.

QUESTIONS

1. Explain the terms "circular flow of income", "injections" and "withdrawals".

2. Why are actual savings always equal to actual investment but planned savings only equal to planned investment when the economy is in equilibrium?

3. What will happen in an economy if the level of planned investment exceeds that of planned savings?

CHAPTER 30

HOUSEHOLD CONSUMPTION

INTRODUCTION

In order to explain the idea of equilibrium, introduced in the last chapter, in more detail, it is necessary to examine the components of aggregate demand and consider what affects them. Consumption, savings and investment will be considered in this chapter and the next two chapters respectively; government spending and taxation will be discussed in Chapters 34 and 35. Exports and imports will be dealt with in Chapter 36, which assesses the role of international trade in the economy. Household consumption is considered first since it is the largest single component of aggregate demand, accounting for 64 per cent of national expenditure in 1988. (This includes spending on imports.) Although it is generally stable, because of its size even a small percentage change will have a large impact on the economy.

CONSUMPTION AND THE LEVEL OF INCOME

The major determinant of the level of consumption is, as one would expect, the level of income since, as people's incomes rise, they tend to spend more on purchasing goods and services. The relationship between consumption and income is shown by the *consumption function* which is an aggregate version of the income–expenditure curve which shows the relationship between the quantity demanded of one particular good and the consumer's income. The consumption function shows the relation between income and consumption of all goods. It can be shown diagrammatically as in Figure 30.1 below. The level of disposable income is plotted along the horizontal axis with consumption on the vertical axis. Disposable income is used because it is only what remains after tax and national insurance payments have been made that is available for consumption.

The dotted 45° line OP shows what the consumption function would look like if all income were consumed. Thus at an income of £100m, £100m would be consumed whereas, from the actual consumption function, only £70m is consumed at this level of income. Where the consump-

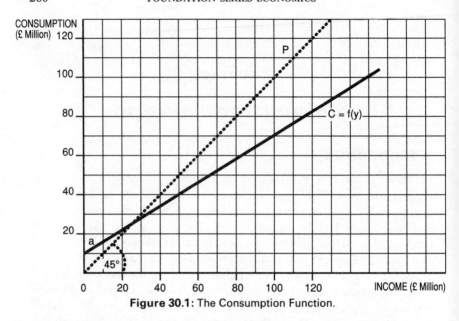

Figure 30.1: The Consumption Function.

tion function intersects with the 45° line, at an income level of £25m, all income is consumed. To the right of this point, e.g. at an income of £50m, not all income is consumed and some is saved. The distance between the 45° line and the consumption function shows the amount of savings. In this example, with an income of £50m, the level of consumption is £40m and savings are £10m. When, at low income levels, the consumption function is above the 45° line, at income levels below £25m in the diagram, this implies that the level of consumption exceeds the level of income. Although this might appear strange, it is made possible by people using their past savings or by borrowing. Indeed, even when the level of income is zero, there will still be some consumption, at the level of "a" in the diagram. This is known as *autonomous consumption* since it is not influenced by the level of income.

The consumption function can also be expressed in terms of an equation similar, in this example, to the equation for any straight line, where:

$$C = a + bY$$

"C" and "Y" represent the level of consumption and income respectively. The volume of autonomous consumption is shown by "a". That proportion of income which is spent on consumption if there is a small change in income is represented by "b". It is known as the *marginal propensity to consume* (m.p.c.) and is defined as the change in consumption induced by a change in income. The value of the m.p.c. is usually less than unity since some part of a rise in income is likely to be saved. A marginal propensity to consume of unity would imply that all income received were spent on consumption while one with a value of zero would mean that none of any extra income was spent on consumption. The majority of the population will be in between these two extremes although, for people on low incomes, any additional income might all be consumed. However, for those on higher incomes, some will be saved or will be removed in tax. The m.p.c. is similar to such concepts as marginal utility and marginal cost, being concerned with changes in income rather than the level of income itself.

The measure of total consumption compared to total income is known as the *average propensity to consume* (a.p.c.) and is defined as the proportion of income which is used for consumption, i.e. total consumption divided by income. It is generally higher than the m.p.c. since it is concerned with all of one's income whereas the m.p.c. is only concerned with the last portion received, out of which a higher amount of saving will take place than before, because immediate consumption needs will have been satisfied.

Both the a.p.c. and the m.p.c. can be considered in the case of the consumption function in Figure 30.1. The equation of this line is:

$$C = 10 + 0 \cdot 6Y$$

Autonomous consumption, represented by the point where the consumption function cuts the vertical axis, is 10 and the m.p.c. is 0·6. Thus if income were to go up by £10m, consumption would go up by £6m. An example shows this:

$$
\begin{aligned}
\text{With income of £50m: } C &= 10 + 0 \cdot 6 \times 50 \\
&= 10 + 30 \\
&= 40 \\
\text{With income of £60m: } C &= 10 + 0 \cdot 6 \times 60 \\
&= 10 + 36 \\
&= 46
\end{aligned}
$$

The a.p.c. at the first level of income would be 0·8 (40/50) and at the second level it would be approximately 0·77 (46/60).

In the above example the m.p.c. was assumed to remain constant at 0·6 as income changed. A more realistic situation would be where, as income rises, the m.p.c. decreases. This implies that as income increases,

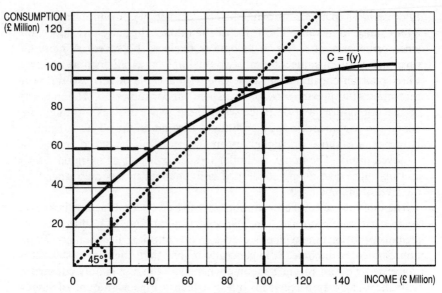

Figure 30.2: A More Realistic Consumption Function.

so does consumption but at a slower rate. This is because, as income rises, once one's immediate desires have been satisfied, one has more resources available to devote to savings. Figure 30.2 shows this.

As income rises from £20m to £40m, consumption rises from £42m to £60m but as income rises from £100m to £120m, consumption rose by only £6m. In practice, if one were to plot the relevant figures for the U.K. economy over a period of time, there would not be a smooth line but a series of points. The consumption function drawn would be the line which fits these points best.

OTHER FACTORS AFFECTING CONSUMPTION

Besides the level of disposable income, there are a number of other factors which will affect consumption. These are also concerned with the income earned by consumers and will be considered first.

The Distribution of Income: Because different sectors of the economy have a different propensity to consume, any redistribution of income will affect the level of consumption. This could be caused, for example, by the government raising the level of taxation on upper-income earners and lowering it on lower-income earners. Thus if £1m is taken from the former group with an m.p.c. of 0·25, the effect is to reduce consumption by £250,000. If the money is then redistributed to pensioners with a m.p.c. of 0·8, they will spend £800,000 and the net effect is to increase consumption by £550,000. This effect is one of the reasons why world consumption dropped in 1974/5 after the first OPEC oil price rises. Spending power, in the form of higher oil revenue, was transferred initially to the wealthier sectors of the OPEC countries with a lower m.p.c. than consumers in Western Europe and the U.S.A.

Previous Income: If one's income changes then consumption does not alter immediately. It is more likely that this month's consumption will be affected by what was earned last month than by what is currently being earned. Therefore any change in income will have a lagged, or delayed, effect on consumption.

Permanent Income: Milton Friedman, in his permanent income hypothesis, carries the above argument further and suggests that consumption is determined by expectations of long-term income rather than by short-term fluctuations, The former is based upon such things as promotion prospects and the salary structure of one's occupation. If a person's income were to increase, he would wait to see whether it was a permanent rise in income before substantially changing his consumption pattern. Using the microeconomic idea of income elasticity, we can conclude that the long-term income elasticity of consumption is substantially higher than its short-term value.

Changes In the Value of Assets: Besides income, consumption is affected by one's wealth although, for the majority of the population, this factor is far less significant than income. If, for example, share prices were to increase, people holding shares might feel themselves to be better off and would therefore increase their consumption financed out of current income because they now have less need to save for the future. Conversely, if rapid inflation reduces the value of one's assets then present consumption might be sacrificed in order to build up assets for the future.

Savings: Consumption and savings can be regarded as inverses since anything remaining out of disposable income after consumption has taken place will be saved. Therefore factors which affect saving will also influence consumption in the opposite way. These will be considered in the next chapter.

Expected Price Changes: If prices are expected to rise in the future, or, in times of inflation, to increase substantially more rapidly than previously, consumers might be encouraged to purchase goods, especially consumer durables, now rather than waiting until the price has risen in the future.

The Availability of Credit: Many purchases of large items, e.g. cars or video recorders, are not paid for out of current or past income but by using borrowed finance. If credit for hire purchase contracts or borrowing from banks is expensive, i.e. the rate of interest is high, then such consumption might be deterred.

QUESTIONS

1. Explain the meaning of the following terms:
   a. autonomous consumption
   b. consumption function
   c. marginal propensity to consume
   d. permanent income.

2. "Income is the main determinant of consumption yet the level of consumption affects the level of future incomes in an economy." Explain.

3. What will be the effect of (a) a fall in share prices and (b) a fall in income tax on the level of consumption in an economy. Which of the two will have the greater effect? (Give reasons.)

4. If income is £100m, consumption is £70m; and if income is £200m, consumption is £110m. Sketch the above consumption function and calculate the value of autonomous consumption and the m.p.c. What will the level of consumption be if income is (a) £400m (b) £50m.

CHAPTER 31

SAVINGS

INTRODUCTION

As suggested in the last chapter, there is a strong link between the factors affecting savings and those affecting consumption since any disposable income not consumed will be saved. Any changes in consumption therefore will affect savings in the opposite direction, assuming income is unchanged. However, when the assumption concerning income is relaxed, savings are generally thought to be more unstable than consumption since, as income changes, it is usual for consumption to be maintained in the short term and for savings to change to accommodate this.

SAVINGS AND INCOME

The savings function, the relationship between savings and income, can be presented in a form similar to the consumption function, as in the last chapter, as the following diagram shows.

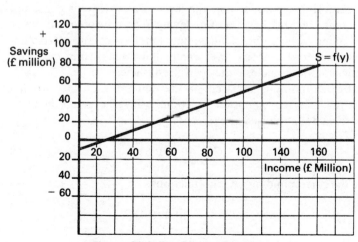

Figure 31.1: The Savings Function.

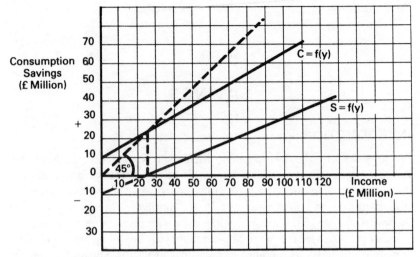

Figure 31.2: The Consumption and Savings Functions.

At low income levels, below £25m in the diagram, savings are negative. This is because income is insufficient to finance consumption and dissaving – using past savings or borrowing – is necessary. As income rises, the level of dissaving falls and saving starts to occur. However, for an industrialised country such as the U.K., the negative part of the savings function is of little concern since the level of national income is sufficiently high to allow saving to take place.

If both savings and consumption are plotted on the same diagram, as in Figure 31.2, we notice that the level of autonomous consumption is exactly matched by the level of dissaving at zero income and the point of zero saving, where the savings function crosses the horizontal axis, corresponds to the income level where all income is consumed, i.e. where the consumption function intersects the 45° line.

A further point is apparent if the equations of the two lines are compared. The consumption function, using the equation in the last chapter, and that plotted above, is:

$$C = 10 + 0 \cdot 6Y$$

while the corresponding savings function is:

$$S = -10 + 0 \cdot 4Y$$

0·4 in the equation represents the marginal propensity to save (m.p.s.), the proportion of a change in disposable income which is saved. The m.p.c. (0·6) plus the m.p.s. (0·4) together sum to unity as is expected since any change in disposable income must either be consumed or saved.

As with the m.p.c., it is more realistic to suggest that the proportion of income which is saved will rise at an increasing amount as income increases and therefore the savings function will not be a straight line, but a steepening upward-sloping curve, in the same way that the consumption function in the previous chapter flattened out at higher income levels.

INCOME-RELATED DETERMINANTS OF SAVINGS

As with consumption, the major determinant of savings is income. Also important are such things as the distribution of income, with different sections of the population having different propensities to save, and the consumer's expected income. These factors, discussed with respect to consumption in the last chapter, will not be considered again here.

SAVINGS AND THE RATE OF INTEREST

It used to be thought by the pre-Keynesian economists that *the rate of interest* was the most important determinant of savings and investment. With a high rate of interest, the reward for not spending was high and therefore an increased number of people would be willing to defer their present consumption. However, modern economists, although not totally rejecting the rate of interest as a factor, regard income as being of greater importance and suggest a number of other reasons for saving, not influenced by the rate of interest.

OTHER DETERMINANTS OF SAVINGS

Firstly, much saving is done for *psychological reasons*. It might be habitual, e.g. £10 per week put aside "for a rainy day" or it might be because of quasi-Victorian ideas about savings being "a good thing". Secondly some saving is undertaken on a *long-term, contractual basis* where an agreement, which might last for a number of years, is reached to save money. This would include for example the person who saves with a life assurance company or one who signs a standing order to pay a regular amount into a building society account each month. These people, like those saving for the previous reason, are not going to be affected by short-term fluctuations in the rate of interest.

Thirdly, some people are *target savers*. This means that they save a certain amount regularly, irrespective of the rate of interest, for a particular objective, e.g. a new car or a summer holiday. Indeed, for these people, there might even be an inverse relationship with the rate of interest since increased interest payments will mean that less need be saved to reach a certain target.

Fourthly, there is a relationship between the amount that people save and the stage they are at during their working life; this idea, proposed by Modigliani and Brumberg, is known as the *life-cycle hypothesis*. Initially, when one starts to work, income is relatively low and savings will also be low, especially if one has commitments in the form of a young family. During middle age, one's income rises, especially for salaried workers, and commitments tend to fall as children leave home and the mortgage is paid off and as a result savings increase and continue at a relatively high level until retirement when, for many people, income falls below expenditure and dissaving occurs.

In less-developed countries another determinant of saving is the *availability of suitable savings institutions* into which people can safely deposit their money.

TRENDS IN PERSONAL SAVINGS

The last twelve years have seen considerable changes in the *savings ratio*, savings as a percentage of disposable income. In the years up to and including 1972, a single figure savings ratio was the norm with the figure for 1972 being 9·5 per cent. However, during the remainder of the 1970s the proportion of personal disposable income which was saved rose, peaking at 15·5 per cent in the second half of 1980 and falling to 9·8 per cent by 1983. This has had a substantial impact on the level of activity in the economy and is one factor explaining the severity of the recession in the U.K. following the O.P.E.C. oil price rise in 1973/4. The fall in the ratio contributed to the upturn in the economy in 1983/4.

In the later 1980s there was a significant fall in personal savings suggesting a high level of consumer confidence. Fortunately this was offset with growing profitability, by a rise in the level of company savings (see Figure 31.3).

However, the changes in the savings and consumption ratios which have occurred were largely unanticipated. This is because there were strong reasons for expecting opposite movements to occur because of the changes in the rate of inflation which were taking place at the same time. Inflation accelerated during the 1970s at the same time as savings increased whereas one might have thought that with a negative real rate

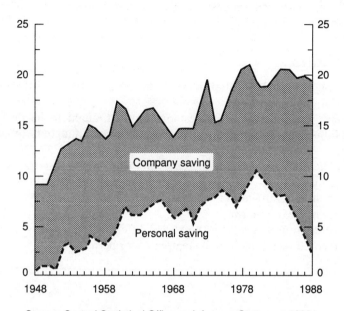

Source: Central Statistical Office and *Autumn Statement 1988*

Figure 31.3: Total Private Saving

of interest (the rate of interest adjusted for the rate of inflation), savings would be discouraged. This suggests a final determinant of savings which would explain both the rise in the 1970s and the fall in the 1980s. This is that people are influenced by *the state of the economy*. If they see a serious recession then they might start to save more, for fear of being made redundant, yet when the economy starts to improve, this motive becomes less important. Furthermore, with high inflation, it is often necessary to save substantially to preserve the real value of one's wealth.

The savings ratio continued to fall in the later 1980s. Consumption

Table 31.1: Personal Income and Saving.

Annual Percentage Changes	1985	1986	1987	1988	1989 estimate
Real personal disposal income	2·9	4·0	3·4	5·4	5·2
Real post-tax wages & salaries	3·4	6·3	5·6	8·2	3·7
Real consumers' expenditure	3·7	5·5	6·1	6·9	4·3
Official saving ratio (%)	9·5	8·2	5·7	4·3	5·2

Source: Banking World.

was at a high level. It also seems that as house prices soared, home owners became less sensitive to rising interest costs and less likely to save. It appears that interest rates must sometimes reach quite penal levels for any monetary squeeze to start to bite.

QUESTIONS

1. Explain the relationship between the consumption and the savings ratio.

2. Why was the rate of interest previously thought to be the major factor influencing the level of savings? Why is it now thought to be less important?

3. What effect would an increase in income have on the level of savings:
    a. in the short-term
    b. in the long-term.

How would your answers to the above differ according to whether the rise in income was thought to be temporary or permanent?

CHAPTER 32

INVESTMENT

INTRODUCTION

Investment was defined in Chapter 29 as any spending on capital formation, those items such as factories and machines which are not consumed in the production process but are available over a long period to produce more goods. Also included as investment are any holdings of stocks of raw materials and finished goods since these too, are not used up initially in the production process, but are available for use in the future.

Although the level of investment in the U.K. is significantly lower than the level of consumption, it is more volatile. Because of this, it has a far greater effect than consumption on the economy.

Table 32.1: Gross domestic fixed capital formation plus changes in stocks as a percentage of GDP at market prices.

	%
1980	15·5
1981	14·1
1982	15·3
1983	16·3
1984	17·2
1985	17·1
1986	16·9
1987	17·6
1988	19·8

Source: Annual Abstract of Statistics 1990.

In order to determine what influences the level of investment in the economy and the factors causing it to change, one has to remember that

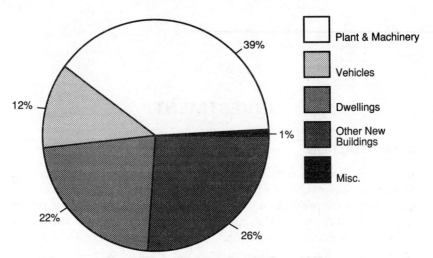

Figure 32.1: U.K. Investment by Type, 1988.

Source: Annual Abstract of Statistics, 1990.

there are a large number of different types of investment and of investor. The composition of investment by type, excluding inventory investment, is shown in the following diagram for 1988.

Of the total investment of £69 billion in 1987*, the manufacturing sector accounted for 14 per cent and the energy sector, which includes investment necessary for the production of North Sea Oil, for 9 per cent. In 1982, the latter amounted to 16 per cent.

BUSINESS INVESTMENT IN PLANT AND MACHINERY

This is the most important type of investment, accounting for 39 per cent of investment in 1988. However, it is significant, not only because of its size, but also because of its impact on the long-term rate of growth of the country. This is because it has a direct effect on firms' ability to expand and produce more and better goods in the future. Companies which fail to modernise and invest in new machinery will find that they are losing their markets to their competitors.

In this section, we are therefore concerned with the factors which might influence an enterpreneur in deciding whether to buy new machines or introduce a more modern production technique. (Although separated in the government's statistics, the arguments in this section will also apply to the producer's investment in new factories.) Whether the initial

* The latest figures officially available in April 1990.

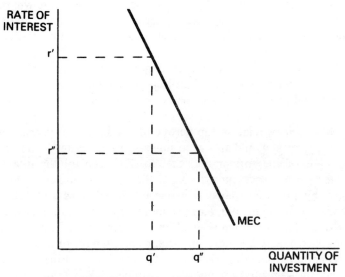

Figure 32.2: The Marginal Efficiency of Capital Curve.

aim is to raise quality, reduce the average cost of production, introduce a new product or increase sales of an existing good, the ultimate objective for the businessman when investing is almost always to increase profits or, in the case of a business investing to keep up with its competitors, to maintain profits at their present level and to prevent them from falling.

The following discussion will examine the factors which will determine the level of this investment. It will be concerned with new, or net investment, rather than with investment purely to replace machines which have depreciated. In terms of the effect which investment has on the level of activity in the economy, it is the gross figure which is important but in terms of the ability of the economy to increase its future output, net investment is the relevant concept.

When assessing the viability of an investment project, the firm will compare its expected rate of return – known as the Marginal Efficiency of Capital (MEC) – with the rate of interest it will have to pay if it borrows money or that which it could earn if it were to lend out its own funds. If the rate of interest is greater than the expected rate of return on a project, then it will not be viable to adopt it. Figure 32.2 shows this diagrammatically. The MEC curve can be regarded as being the demand curve for investment and is similar to any other demand curve. In this case, the price is the rate of interest which would be paid on borrowed money and the quantity is the quantity of investment undertaken. When the rate of interest is high, e.g. r' on the diagram, then there will only be a small number of projects which generate a higher rate of return and are therefore viable, namely q', which is all the investment which will occur.

If the rate of interest in the above diagram were to fall to r" then there will be an increased number of projects which will now be worthwhile, the additional projects being those between q' and q" on the horizontal axis.

The MEC curve relationship between the quantity of investment and the rate of interest would appear to suggest that the latter is an important determinant of the former and therefore, to control the quantity of investment, one needs only to vary the rate of interest. This view, accepted by pre-Keynesians, was rejected by Keynes and subsequent economists as being invalid. Keynes pointed to the situation in the Great Depression when, although rates of interest were low, so was investment. He suggested that a far more important determinant of investment was the *level of businessmen's expectations*. If they think that future prospects, and hence future profits, are poor, they will be unlikely to invest whatever the rate of interest. Thus Keynes argued that the MEC curve was likely to be interest inelastic and that changes in the rate of interest might be outweighed by changes in expectations which would cause the MEC curve to shift. An improvement in prospects would, for example, raise the expected level of profit and hence move the MEC curve to the right. A further reason for the relative unimportance of interest rates is that short-term changes are unlikely to have great effects on long-term projects, where the relevant variable is the long-term rate of interest over the project's life. Furthermore, because of the risks involved in some projects, e.g. where a product might become obsolete because of a new invention, some businesses prefer to use the idea of a pay-back period where they might, for example, require a project to repay its cost over a specified period, e.g. five years, irrespective of the rate of interest.

Another determinant of the quantity of investment is the *level of past profits* in the economy. This has two effects. Firstly, future expectations are often based upon what is happening today and profits are a good measure of this. Secondly, retained profits are an important means of financing investment projects. This is likely to be especially important for the smaller business which might find difficulty in obtaining adequate funds elsewhere.

A final explanation of investment is known as the *accelerator hypothesis*. This attempts to provide an explanation of firms' investment by considering changes in the level of output and suggests that small changes in consumer spending will cause much larger changes in the level of investment. An example will show how this works. Imagine a firm producing 100,000 units per annum for which it needs twenty identical machines, each producing 5,000 goods. Depreciation is 10 per cent, i.e. two machines wear out and are replaced each year. If the demand for the firm's product were to rise by 5 per cent – an extra 5,000 goods – it will need to purchase an additional machine, making a total of three (one additional one plus two to cover depreciation). Therefore a 5 per cent rise in demands has led to a 50 per cent rise in investment. The process will not work as smoothly as suggested in the example since firms will wait to see if changes in demand are permanent, they might work overtime, use past stocks, raise prices or use any combination of these measures. Nevertheless, the accelerator is an important explanation of investment in new, expanding sectors of the economy.

INVESTMENT IN STOCKS

The second type of investment is business investment in stocks of finished goods and raw materials; this is known as *inventory investment*. In the short-term, this can be extremely volatile, as the following diagram, showing the value of the changes in stocks in the U.K. from 1978 to 1988 reveals.

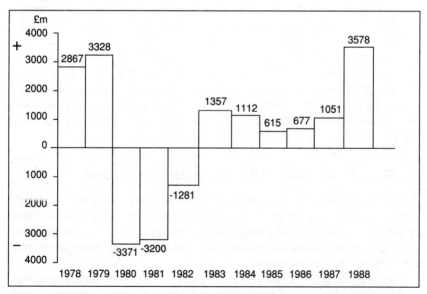

Figure 32.3: The Value of the Physical Increase/Decrease in Stocks and Work in Progress, 1978–1988.

Source: Annual Abstract of Statistics.

It can be seen from the above diagram that this type of investment can be negative, as it was in 1980–82, when industries engaged in *destocking* – running down the level of their stock-holdings. This can have a substantial effect on the economy since demand is being met partly out of stocks rather than by current production and therefore it is possible to reduce the labour force, with a downward impact on the national income. Unlike other types of investment, changes in stocks can occur for short periods unplanned by the businessman. This will happen, for example, if consumption falls. Stocks will rise at least briefly until decisions about the level of production can be changed.

The level of stocks will be largely influenced, apart from temporary fluctuations, by the producer's expectations of future demand. If they are poor, he will be willing to allow his stocks to decline. Since holding stocks involves tying up money without earning any return, another factor affecting the level of stocks will be the rate of interest. A high rate of interest increases the opportunity cost of holding stocks and acts as a discouragement to firms to hold large stocks.

INVESTMENT IN HOUSING

Unlike investment in plant and machinery and in stocks which is carried out by public corporations, public companies and other businesses, investment in housing is undertaken by individuals and by local authorities. Long-term determinants, common to both groups, concern the population, its size and age-structure and the rate of formation of new households. Local authorities, viewing housing primarily as a social service rather than a commercial enterprise, will be additionally influenced by political considerations. Private housebuilding is also affected by the availability of finance, and in particular mortgage waiting lists, the rate of interest and the level of long-term income.

PUBLIC INVESTMENT IN THE INFRASTRUCTURE

Lastly we consider the capital expenditure of central and local government in the infrastructure – the capital of a society. This includes such things as the building of schools, hospitals and roads. It is undertaken, as is government investment in housing, on the basis of perceived social need, rather than to gain profit.

Like the previous category, it is long-term and cannot be easily halted once started. A project like the Channel Tunnel, once undertaken, will take several years to complete and several more years to break even financially. All that can be done is to partially delay or accelerate it. The problem which this poses for a government attempting to regulate the economy by affecting the level of investment will be considered in the next chapter.

QUESTIONS

1. Define investment and explain how changes in the level of investment will affect the economy.

2. What is the MEC curve? What will be the effect on investment of a fall in the rate of interest combined with a C.B.I. survey which suggests future prospects are poor?

3. Why is inventory investment so volatile?

4. Of the four types of investment, which is the government likely to be most able to affect if it wished to stimulate the economy? Explain whether your answer would be different if the government wished to reduce the level of activity in the economy.

MULTIPLE CHOICE Test No. 2

Answers are on page 371.

1. In the marginal productivity theory of distribution
   (a) the MRP curve will always be downwards sloping from left to right
   (b) due regard is paid to differences in the factors of production
   (c) the price elasticity of demand for the final product is of critical importance
   (d) the ease of substitution of other factors is of only limited importance

2. Two companies, X PLC and Y PLC, using similar techniques but producing different yet related products, are about to merge. This is an example of
   (a) diversification
   (b) lateral integration
   (c) vertical integration
   (d) horizontal integration

3. Successful price discrimination will not be possible where
   (a) equal price elasticities exist in each market
   (b) supply is in the control of a monopolist
   (c) there is an absence of arbitrage between markets
   (d) different price elasticities apply and arbitrage is not practised

4. In determining the composition and balance of their assets, the commercial banks are fundamentally concerned with
   (a) prudence
   (b) outwitting the actions of their competitors
   (c) risks and rewards
   (d) always meeting customer needs

5. LIBOR refers to
   (a) the sterling exchange rate
   (b) the average rate of interest charged between banks for three month loans
   (c) bank base rates
   (d) the rate at which the Bank of England will lend to the money markets

6. A rise in the Retail Price Index
   (a) signifies a fall in the standard of living
   (b) will be reflected in a rise in National Income expressed in current prices
   (c) will affect all members of the community equally
   (d) will stimulate the level of bank lending

7. Certificates of deposit
   (a) are issued for periods ranging from two months to three years
   (b) always carry a fixed rate of interest
   (c) are held predominantly by non-bank investors
   (d) are noticeably different from Treasury Bills

8. Given that MV = PT, P will rise if otherwise
   (a) T rises and MV remains constant
   (b) MV falls and T rises
   (c) M rises, V is constant and T falls
   (d) M is constant and V and T rise in the same proportion

9. The value of national output
   (a) is the sum of the output of all businesses
   (b) is the aggregate of output of employed persons
   (c) is synonymous with aggregate manufacturing output
   (d) utilises the "added value" concept

10. Quasi-money includes
    (a) National Savings Bank deposits
    (b) National Savings Certificates
    (c) Treasury bills
    (d) bank notes issued by Scottish banks

11. Treasury bills
    (a) are issued at a variable price
    (b) are redeemable 60 days after issue
    (c) are bid for weekly by the clearing banks
    (d) carry no guarantee of repayment

12. An increase of £1,000m in bank deposits will
    (a) result in a higher level of inflation
    (b) mean proportionately increased bank profits
    (c) facilitate the credit creation process
    (d) bring about government intervention in the working of the banking system

CHAPTER 33

MANAGING THE ECONOMY

INTRODUCTION

In previous chapters we have looked at the various components of the economy and seen what the main forces are which affect them. However they have, so far, all been considered in isolation. In this chapter we see how they interact to affect the level of output in the economy. Using the idea of injections and withdrawals, considered when looking at the circular flow of income, one can see what the impact of, for example, a change in the level of investment will be on the national income, employment and consumption. We then go on to analyse the role which the government can play in controlling the economy with particular reference to the problem of unemployment.

ECONOMICS BEFORE KEYNES

The publication of Keynes's *General Theory of Employment, Interest and Money* in 1936 marked a turning point in economics. The classical economists believed that the economy would, if left to itself, automatically tend towards full employment and therefore there was no need for the government to intervene in its management. There would be periods of temporary unemployment as consumers' tastes changed and demand shifted from one good to another and also during the troughs of a trade cycle. This latter phenomenon would be balanced by periods of inflation when output was at a higher level. When demand was low, with the quantity of savings exceeding the amount businessmen wished to invest, there would be a surplus of funds available and so the rate of interest would fall. This would encourage firms to invest, thereby causing an increase in the demand for labour. Simultaneously, the low demand for goods and factors of production would lead to a fall in prices, accompanied by a drop in wages and other costs and, economists argued, this would also tend to stimulate demand and restore full employment.

When faced with the Great Depression of the 1930s, economists still followed the same basic ideas but argued that the adjustment process was prevented from working smoothly because of imperfections in the economy – namely downward wage and price rigidity – and it was these which prevented the movement back towards the usual full employment position.

KEYNESIAN ECONOMICS

Keynes's views differed from the previous economists in a number of important ways. First he argued that what was important in determining the level of output, and hence employment, was the level of aggregate demand. This comprised consumer demand and the injections into the economy in the form of investment, government spending and exports. An increase in the level of aggregate demand would cause firms to raise their output and, in the short run, with fixed factors of production unchangeable, would lead to an increase in employment. Conversely, a fall in aggregate demand would lead to firms reducing their labour force and laying off workers. If the level of aggregate demand were to remain low then, according to Keynes, there would be no automatic movement back towards full employment as predicted by the classical economists. The economy would simply remain with a degree of unemployment until something happened to change the level of aggregate demand. This was what occurred in the 1930s. Because the level of aggregate demand was too low, firms reduced their output and their labour force and had no need or incentive to invest in new machinery since output was so low. It was up to the government, argued Keynes, to intervene and regulate the level of aggregate demand by varying its own spending and taxation. These ideas were accepted by the government in a White Paper on Employment Policy, published in 1944, and the story of economics for the next two decades is very largely concerned with the extent to which successive governments used (and abused) Keynes's ideas.

EQUILIBRIUM IN THE ECONOMY

Keynes's view that the economy could remain in equilibrium, i.e. stationary, at any level of employment and would not automatically return to full employment was a highly significant departure from the views of the economists who preceeded him and it had considerable implications for the government, causing them to move from a non-interventionist to an active policy of economic management. So significant were Keynes's ideas that later economists talked of the "Keynesian Revolution" in economics. This section considers his ideas in greater detail.

The idea of equilibrium which we have already mentioned, is similar

282FOUNDATION SERIES ECONOMICS

to that used in the natural sciences where something is said to be in equilibrium if there are no forces acting upon it, causing it to change. In terms of the economy, equilibrium exists when the level of the national income is stable. This will occur when the injections into it are exactly matched, as suggested in Chapter 29, by the withdrawals from it. If this is not the case and, for example, injections exceed the level of withdrawals, then the level of the national income will increase.

An alternative way of considering the equilibrium level of national income is to regard it as being that level which generates sufficient demand (people and firms spending from out of their incomes), to match the output which has been produced. If this is the case, there will be no unwanted stocks of goods piling up and nothing therefore to cause firms to change their production decisions. Planned expenditure will be generating exactly enough income in the economy to keep the level of national income unchanged and thus, in equilibrium.

THE 45° DIAGRAM

The ideas expounded in the last section can be illustrated graphically in the following diagram which provides a means of illustrating the various policies which the government can pursue.

From Chapter 28 we know that the national income and national expenditure are simply two different ways of measuring the same concept

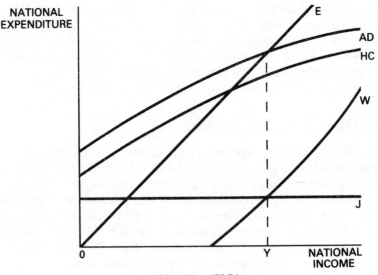

Figure 33.1: The 45° Diagram.

and therefore are equal. The points where this is so are represented on the line OE, drawn at 45° to the horizontal axis. It can also therefore be regarded as the line showing the set of possible equilibrium points for the economy. The line marked HC (Household Consumption) is simply the consumption function as drawn in Chapter 30, showing the relationship between consumption and income, but in this case and subsequently, it refers only to consumption of domestically-produced goods; imports are not included in it. The line J (Injections) refers to the addition to aggregate demand from the injections into the economy, namely investment, exports and government spending. It is drawn parallel to the horizontal axis, implying that as income changes, there is no corresponding change in the level of injections. This can be seen by considering their primary determinants. Investment is determined largely by businessmen's expectations, exports by the level of income in other countries and the relative prices of the exporting country's goods and government spending by long-term political decisions. Thus all three are independent of income in the short term. The line W (Withdrawals) refers to the leakages from the circular flow of income, namely savings, imports and taxation. This line is drawn upward-sloping since all the above are affected by the level of income and increase as income increases.

By adding consumers' demand, HC, to injections, J, one obtains the level of aggregate demand in the economy, AD. Because injections are constant, the aggregate demand line is parallel to household consumption but exceeds it by the extent of the level of injections into the economy. At the point where the aggregate demand line intersects the 45° line spending is just sufficient to generate enough income to keep the level of national income stable. Hence the equilibrium level of the national income will be Y. This level of income also corresponds to the level of income at which injections equal withdrawals – where the J and W lines intersect.

As happened in the 1930s and during much of the 1980s, the equilibrium level of national income was below that required to maintain full employment. Figure 33.2 illustrates this situation. Y is again the equilibrium level of income but Y^f is the level of national income necessary to maintain full employment. In order to attain this it is necessary to raise the level of aggregate demand by the distance "d" to AD'.*

This distance "d" is known as *the deflationary gap*, the amount by

* To simplify the diagram, it has been assumed that the m.p.c., the slope of the HC line is constant.

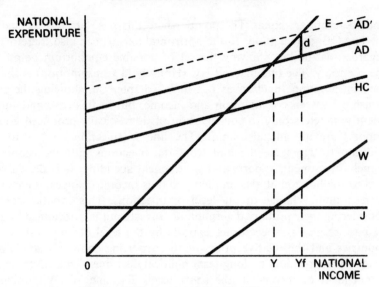

Figure 33.2: An Unemployment Situation.

which aggregate demand is below that required for full employment. In order to remedy this situation, the government has two options. First it can increase its own spending which will have the effect of increasing

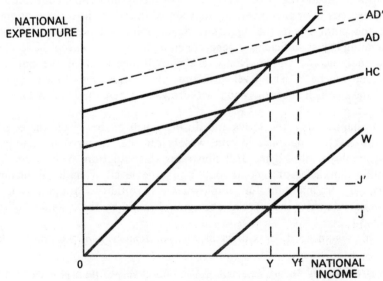

Figure 33.3: Increasing Injections to Cure a Deflationary Gap.

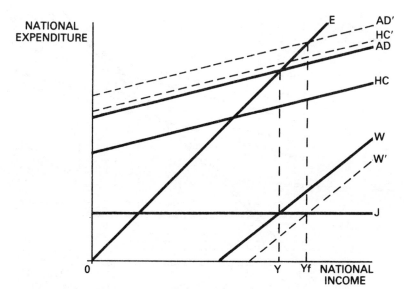

Figure 33.4: Reducing Withdrawals to Cure a Deflationary Gap.

injections as illustrated in Figure 33.3. J rises to J′ and the AD line to AD′, giving a new equilibrium point Y^f. Withdrawals are again equal to injections but both are now at a higher level.

Alternatively the government could reduce the money it takes out of the economy in the form of taxation. This would lead to an increase in household consumption and a reduction in withdrawals as shown in Figure 33.4. Again, equilibrium would be reached at the required level of national income, but this time with injections unchanged and withdrawals reduced.

It is also possible for the level of aggregate demand to exceed that required to attain full employment. If this happens, possibly because of excessive government spending or too little taxation, a high demand for exports or low demand for imports, high investment or low savings, or finally, any combination of these conditions, then aggregate demand will exceed the quantity of goods which can be produced and therefore prices will rise. The subsequent increase in the national income will be a "money", rather than a "real" one. There will be no increase in the quantity of goods and services available, only in prices; indeed output cannot rise in the short term if the economy is already at full employment. In such a situation, an *inflationary gap* is said to exist, as shown in Figure 33.5 by the distance "i", this being the amount by which the government will have to reduce aggregate demand either by raising taxes

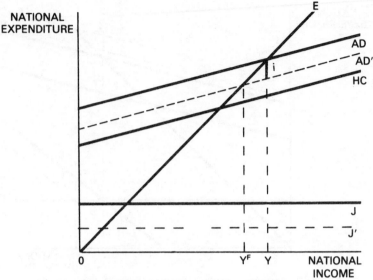

Figure 33.5: An Inflationary Gap Situation.

or reducing government spending, the latter option being illustrated on the diagram.

Examination of Figure 33.5 reveals that the change in the level of injections required to reduce aggregate demand is smaller than the eventual drop in the national income from Y to Y^f. This is because of what is known as the multiplier process and it will be considered in the next section.

THE MULTIPLIER PROCESS

If a person experiences a rise in his income, possibly because he was previously unemployed and now has a job, it is likely that he will spend some of his additional income. The amount he spends will depend upon his marginal propensity to consume (m.p.c.). The only difference between our use of this term now as compared to Chapter 30 is that henceforth it will only include the amount spent on home-produced goods, not total consumer spending.

It is necessary to consider what will be the effect of the extra spending on the economy. It will, when spent, provide additional income for another person who will in turn spend only a part of what he receives. This will continue, with smaller and smaller amounts being passed on each time. A similar process operates if the increase in income is more

Table 33.1

Stage	New Income Created		Amount of New Income Spent
1	160		120
2	120		90
3	90		67·5
4	67·5		50·6
⋮	⋮	and so on	⋮
Finally	640		480

widespread. Imagine that the government carries out major widening of the M25 motorway; those employed to do the construction, assuming that they were previously unemployed, will spend part of this income, businesses receiving additional income will do likewise and so income will be generated in other parts of the economy. The amount generated will depend upon the m.p.c. of those receiving it initially. *Example*: Assume that the m.p.c. for the economy average 0·75 and £160m is spent by the government on the motorway. Of this £120m (£160m × 0·75), will be respent and then a further £90m of this (£120m × 0·75), and so on. The process is illustrated in Table 33.1

One can see that the increase in spending of £160m has been passed on and has eventually created a further £480m, giving a total rise in the national income of £640m. The process, whereby the economic system magnifies any change in the level of income, is known as *the multiplier process*. The size of the process is determined by the amount of any change in income which is spent by the recipients, i.e. by their m.p.c., or, looked at the other way round, by the amount which gets withdrawn from the system in taxation, savings and imports. The larger is the m.p.c., the greater the amount which is passed on, and so the final change in the economy will be greater. If hypothetically, everything were passed on, i.e. the m.p.c. were one, then the process would continue indefinitely and the national income would not stop increasing. The value of the multiplier, the number of times an initial increase or decrease is multiplied, is given by the following formula:

$$\text{Multiplier} = \frac{1}{1 - \text{m.p.c.}}$$

Thus, in the above example, the m.p.c. was 0·75 and therefore the multiplier was 4, (1/(1 − 0·75)). The initial spending was £160m and so total additional spending was four times as large.

An alternative formula, used to calculate the multiplier retrospectively, is:

$$\text{Multiplier} = \frac{\text{Final Change In National Income}}{\text{Initial Change In National Income}}$$

Using the above example once again, the initial change in national income, the spending on the road, was £160m with a final change of £640m, giving, as before, a multiplier of 4. In Figure 33.5, the final change is the distance Y to Y^f and the initial change is the change in injections from J to J'. In the U.K. the value of the m.p.c. is approximately 0·25, giving the multiplier a value of 1·33; thus every £100 spent in the economy by the government would result in a final change of £133. Although this might seem small, this is after taking into account direct and indirect taxes, national insurance contributions, imports, savings and any income not passed on and retained by companies.

The process is not quite as simple as suggested above. It was assumed that unemployed workers were used to produce the additional output and previously had no income. This is not strictly accurate since some income, in the form of unemployment benefits, would have been received. The multiplier process will therefore only operate on the additional income which has been received. Furthermore, an average value for the m.p.c. was used. In practice, it will differ depending upon who the recipients of the income are and this can sometimes make it difficult for the government to predict the size of the final increase or decrease in the national income. The process takes a considerable length of time to complete, although after about thirty months the stages become insignificant. Thus, if the government is to regulate the level of demand in the economy accurately, they must be able to forecast with a degree of certainty what will happen in the future. This is difficult since the information needed, e.g. national income and unemployment figures, are not always accurate and frequently have to be revised in the light of new information. If the government were to overstimulate the economy in attempting to deal with unemployment then it is likely that, although the initial effect would be to increase output and employment, once full employment was approached, the main additional effect would be to increase prices since output would be reaching its short term maximum.

REACHING FULL EMPLOYMENT

The previous section illustrated how the government, using the multiplier

Table 33.2: Unemployment in Great Britain
1978–1988.

Year	Unemployment Rate (per cent) *
1978	4·3
1979	3·9
1980	5·0
1981	8·0
1982	9·4
1983	10·4
1984	10·6
1985	10·8
1986	10·9
1987	9·8
1988	7·8

* Seasonally adjusted and excluding persons under 18 years.
Source: Annual Abstract of Statistics.

process, could regulate the level of aggregate demand in the economy and, by doing this, increase the level of employment. However it is important to note that when one talks of "curing unemployment" and "returning to full employment", one does not mean that everyone in the working population will have a job and that there will be no one unemployed. It used to be thought, after World War II, that the lowest level of unemployment which was realistically achievable was 3 per cent. This figure was arrived at by considering that there would always be some people who were unable to work through disability, some who were unwilling to work and some who were changing jobs and therefore temporarily unemployed. During the 1950s the unemployment level fell below this figure and 2 per cent was considered to be an acceptable target level of unemployment. Since then, with the number of unemployed over three million in the early 1980s, discussion of the exact level of unemployment which corresponds to full employment has ceased to be so important. Table 33.2 shows what has happened to unemployment since 1978.

TYPES OF UNEMPLOYMENT

1. General Unemployment: The type of unemployment alluded to above is known as general, demand or Keynesian unemployment and is caused by an inadequate level of aggregate demand in the economy. Its cure, as outlined above, is for the government to increase the level of demand, i.e. to *reflate* the economy. This can be done directly by manipulating its own spending or income from taxation, known as *fiscal policy*, or indirectly, by varying the rate of interest and influencing the level of bank lending in the economy. These latter measures, known as *monetary policy*, were explained in Chapters 24 and 27.

2. Cyclical Unemployment: This is a special type of general unemployment and occurs when, over a number of years, the average level of demand is satisfactory, but fluctuates about the average so that there are periods of both excess and low demand, the latter causing unemployment. The cure for this type of unemployment is to attempt to remove the fluctuations which occur in the level of aggregate demand. To do this, the government has to operate on its own income and expenditure counter-cyclically (in the opposite direction to the private sector changes which are occurring). Various items of government expenditure and income will do this automatically. These are known as *built-in stabilisers*. Two examples are unemployment benefit and income tax receipts. When the level of unemployment starts to increase because of a fall in the private sector's spending, government expenditure automatically starts to increase because of the need to pay the additional unemployed their benefit. Similarly, as incomes fall, the amount that the government takes out of the economy in the form of income tax will also fall, thereby reducing the drop in aggregate demand. Where the operation of built-in stabilisers is not sufficient to eliminate cyclical unemployment, it is necessary for the government to intervene more actively to vary its income and expenditure.

3. Structural Unemployment: If there is a change in the structure of the economy, caused for example by long term changes in consumers' tastes or, as in the case of shipbuilding, by the rise of more efficient industries in other countries, then there will be an increase in unemployment as the domestic industries decline. This type of unemployment is known as structural unemployment. Its cure is not, as with general unemployment, to raise the level of aggregate demand – shipbuilders would not be affected by a cut in income tax of 1p – but to retrain the workers made redundant in skills which will be needed by new industries and to encourage these new industries to move into the areas previously heavily dependent upon the traditional industries. As a temporary measure, it is also possible to subsidise the declining industries to enable them to remain operative.

4. Regional Unemployment: If structural unemployment starts to occur and the industry in question is heavily concentrated in a particular area then that area might start to suffer from regional unemployment. This is when the average unemployment in a region is substantially above the national average. If an industry declines then the firms supplying it will suffer, workers will be made redundant, incomes will fall and there will be a localised multiplier effect depressing demand in the region. Government attempts to cure regional unemployment by encouraging new firms to set up in the declining areas by providing grants for capital expenditure, attractive tax allowances, cheap factories and other incentives. Alternatively subsidies could be given to firms if they increase their labour force.

5. Technological Unemployment: If the introduction of new machinery and new techniques of production enable firms to economise on their use of labour, the result will possibly be an increase in unemployment, as happened when containerisation was introduced into the docks. This is known as technological unemployment. The only ways to cure it, apart from deliberately failing to modernise which will have serious long-term consequences for the economy, are firstly to provide retraining facilities for workers made redundant and secondly to ensure that the level of aggregate demand in the economy is high enough to ensure that there will be jobs for them in other sectors of the economy.

6. Frictional Unemployment: This is the name given to the temporary unemployment which arises when people move from one job to another. There is often a time-lag between leaving one job and starting another which arises because of the time it takes to find alternative employment, be interviewed and start work. One way that this can be alleviated – it cannot ever be totally eliminated – is for the government to provide more Job Centres and generally to make available more information for workers about vacancies which exist and more for businesses about people who are looking for work.

7. Seasonal Unemployment: Because of the nature of some jobs, e.g. construction work, tourism and agriculture, there tends to be an increase in unemployment during the winter months. This is known as seasonal unemployment and, like the previous type of unemployment, can never be totally eliminated.

QUESTIONS

1. What is the multiplier process? Explain how it would operate if the government injected money into the economy by building a new hospital.

2. In what ways would your answer to the above question change depending upon whether there were unemployed resources or full employment in the economy at the time of the initial increase?

3. Why will a policy of raising the level of aggregate demand in an economy not be totally successful in eliminating unemployment?

4. What are built-in stabilisers? What is their importance in the economy?

5. Using the 45° diagram, explain how a government can reduce general unemployment.

CHAPTER 34

TAXATION

INTRODUCTION

In the previous chapter we considered the role of the government in the economy and the way in which it can intervene either to stimulate or to reduce the level of aggregate demand. This chapter considers taxation, one of the instruments available to it for this purpose. It considers this and the other reasons for taxation, the types of tax in use in the U.K. and the criteria by which different taxes can be assessed.

REASONS FOR TAXATION:

1. Raising Revenue: Governments find it necessary to levy taxes to provide revenue to finance the expenditure which they make on the behalf of the community. This comprises such diverse items as expenditure on defence, the health service, education and the civil service. Revenue will be needed for all the government's output which is provided either free or at a price below the cost of production.

2. Discouraging Consumption: Besides wishing to raise revenue, governments often seek to discourage the consumption of certain goods, known as demerit goods, which have harmful or unpleasant effects either to the consumer or to other members of the community. Cigarettes and alcoholic drink fall into this category.

3. Redistribution Of Income And Wealth: Taxation can also be used as a means of redistributing income and wealth in an economy. This will happen when those with higher incomes and greater wealth are taxed more heavily than those who are less well-off.

4. Taxation As An Economic Weapon: Taxation is a major weapon in the government's economic armoury. By varying the rates of tax and tax allowances, it is possible to determine the level of spending in an economy and also its composition. So, for example, by giving tax allowances to businesses who operate in certain areas, regional unemployment can be affected. Similarly, governments wish to encourage investment and so allow firms to offset part of the cost of investment against tax. If the government wished to change aggregate consumer spending it could simply change the levels of income tax.

5. Discouraging Imports: It is possible, although difficult because of the U.K.'s membership of the European Community and GATT (the General Agreement on Tariffs and Trade), for the government to levy high taxes on imports. This will have the effect of discouraging consumption of imports and will, ceteris paribus, lead to an improvement in the balance of payments.

TYPES OF TAXES

Taxes can be classified in a number of ways. First, according to how they affect people at different income levels. One can distinguish between three types of tax: those which are progressive, proportional or regressive.

A *progressive tax* is one where high income earners not only pay more tax in absolute terms but also pay a higher proportion of their marginal income in tax. Any tax where the marginal rate exceeds the average will be a progressive tax. In the U.K. income tax is progressive with 25% and 40% rates. At one time the progression was much steeper – with rates up to 98% including an investment income surcharge.

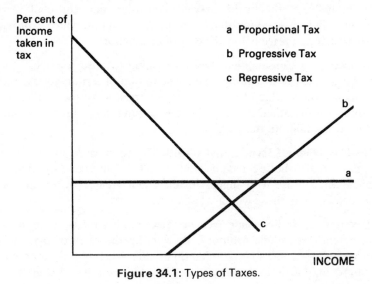

Figure 34.1: Types of Taxes.

A *proportional tax* is one where the same proportion is taken regardless of the income of the taxpayer. Thus if a worker earned £1,000 and had to pay £100, someone earning £10,000 would have to pay £1,000 if the tax were to be proportional.

Regressive taxation occurs when, as income rises, the proportion taken in tax actually falls. For example, a flat rate tax of £100 per head would be regressive since it represents a higher proportion of a low income earner's wage than that of an upper income earner. Excise duties on tobacco and alcohol are regressive in effect and so is the community charge (poll tax).

These three types of tax can be illustrated diagrammatically, as in Figure 34.1

An alternative method of classifying taxes is as to how they are levied. One can distinguish between direct and indirect taxes. *Direct taxes* are those where payment cannot be shifted onto other people or businesses in the economy. These generally relate to income or wealth. In the case of income tax, the tax is levied directly upon an individual.

Indirect taxes are those taxes where the burden can be shifted away from the person or business upon whom it is levied. These are generally imposed on goods and services and the process of producing them. So a producer can pass the tax onto a retailer by raising the price he charges and the latter, in turn, can if he wishes, pass it on to the consumer by increasing the final price of the product. Whether or not he chooses to do so will be affected by what his competitors are doing and by the elasticity of demand for the good.

TAXES IN THE U.K.

Table 34.1 shows the main taxes levied in the U.K. Figure 34.2 provides a comparison of tax revenues between 1978/79 and 1988/89.

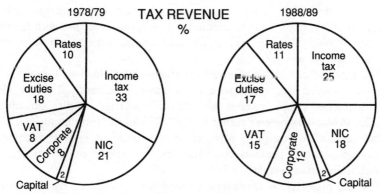

Figure 34.2: Analysis of Tax Revenue 1978/79 and 1988/89.

Table 34.1: Pence in every £ raised 1989/90.

Income tax	23
National insurance contributions	16
Value added tax	14
Local authority rates *	10
Road, fuel, alcohol and tobacco duties	9
Corporation tax	11
Capital taxes	2
Interest, dividend taxes	3
Petroleum revenue tax and oil royalties	1
Other expenditure taxes	6
Other	5
	100

* Community charge ("Poll tax") from 1.4.1990.
Source: The Treasury.

DIRECT TAXES

1. Income Tax And National Insurance Contributions: The main tax in the U.K. is income tax which accounts for approximately one-quarter of the total revenue raised from taxation. It is a progressive tax and is levied upon personal income received from all sources, whether the individual is employed or self-employed and irrespective of the nature of the income so that tax is payable on wages, salaries, royalties, rent, interest, dividends, etc. Each person is allowed a certain amount of money tax-free – a personal allowance – and then tax is paid on the income remaining, known as taxable income. The rate of tax for 1990/91 starts at 25 per cent for taxable income up to £20,700 and rises to 40 per cent thereafter. The tax is progressive because, the higher a person's income, the higher is the marginal rate of tax – the rate on the last part of income received. The higher rate of tax is only imposed on the income falling within that band, not on the whole income. Thus someone with taxable income of £60,000 would pay 40 per cent on the last £39,300 of taxable income, not the whole £60,000.

The amount of income received tax-free is determined by a number of factors. Everyone receives a personal allowance, currently £3,005 (1990/91). A married couple receive, in addition, a married couples allowance, £1,720. Pensioners receive rather higher allowances. Individuals can also offset certain outgoings in arriving at the figure of taxable income – mortgage interest, pension contributions and subscriptions to professional bodies for example.

For the majority of taxpayers, income tax is collected by the PAYE (Pay As You Earn) system whereby an amount is deducted directly from pay by the employer and sent direct to the Inland Revenue. Those people whose income comes from a number of sources, e.g. employment, dividends, interest and those who are self-employed or receive rent as all or part of their income cannot be assessed in this way and have to fill in details of their income on a tax return, setting out all forms of income received and tax already paid and their tax liability is calculated individually. Because over 90 cent of tax is collected through PAYE, income tax is a relatively cheap tax for the government to collect.

National Insurance contributions should really be regarded as income tax under a different name but with a strangely regressive effect. In 1990/91 Class 1 Contributions (i.e. those payable by employees) were effectively 9 per cent on incomes between £46 and £350 per week, the upper limit. Thus the rates of tax are not really 25 per cent and 40 per cent but 34 per cent, falling to 25 per cent, and then rising to 40 per cent, an anomalous state of affairs which successive governments have found difficult to correct.

2. Corporation Tax: Corporation tax is a broadly proportional tax which is levied upon company profits after various allowances have been made. It accounts for 11 per cent of all tax revenue and is currently (fiscal 1990/91) levied at the rate of 35 per cent for large companies and 25 per cent for small companies, i.e. those with profits of less than £200,000. There is a sliding scale for companies with profits of between £200,000 and £1 million, bringing the rate of tax up to that paid by large companies. Allowances against corporation tax are available in respect of certain projects operating in development and special development areas (areas with high regional unemployment which qualify for special assistance). This is an example of the way in which taxation can be used to direct resources to certain areas and, through doing this, affect the level of regional unemployment.

3. Capital Gains Tax: This is a tax levied on the gains made through buying and selling assets such as shares. Currently (1990/91), £5,000 of capital gains per annum can be taken tax-free. Everything earned in excess of this is taxed at the individual's marginal rate of income tax but gains arising since 1982 are index-linked. However excluded from the calculations are gains made from selling one's principal residence, private cars, National Savings Certificates, life-assurance policies and fixed interest stocks. The major argument in favour of capital gains tax is that it preserves a balance between someone who buys shares and receives a dividend from them, on which income tax has to be paid, and another who profits merely by buying and selling such assets.

4. Inheritance Tax (IHT): Introduced in 1986, IHT replaced Capital

Transfer Tax which itself replaced Estate Duty. Virtually all property held at date of death is subject to IHT and so is any property disposed of by way of gift during the seven years prior to death.

The tax is at the single rate of 40 per cent (1990/91), though not being applied until the cumulative total of "chargeable transfers" exceeds £128,000. As a general rule lifetime gifts will be free of IHT if the donor lives a further seven years but where tax is payable the rate is only 20 per cent. Fully exempt are gifts to the spouse; certain other gifts are exempt within limits. There is an annual exemption of £3,000.

INDIRECT TAXES

These, like direct taxes, can be classified in theory according to whether they are progressive, proportional or regressive. However, unlike direct taxes, it is often difficult to determine, in reality, into which category the taxes fall. This is because it is necessary to know how much of a person's income is spent on a good and how this amount changes as income rises in order to determine whether the tax is progressive or not. For example, if the government were to impose a tax on 12 year old malt whisky, this would be progressive since this is a luxury good consumed by upper-income earners. A tax on beer however would generally be regarded as regressive since lower-income earners spend proportionately more of their income on beer than upper-income earners and therefore pay proportionately more tax. Nevertheless the majority of goods are far less easy to categorise in this way.

One can also categorise indirect taxes according to whether they are *flat rate* (specific) or *percentage* (ad valorem) taxes. A flat rate tax would be where the government levies a tax of a fixed or specific amount on a good and this amount does not change if the item becomes more expensive. An example of this would be if there were an additional tax of 20p on a bottle of wine, irrespective of whether the wine were a £3 vin ordinaire or a £10 bottle of claret. An ad valorem tax is where the government takes a percentage of the value of the good and therefore a greater amount is taken from more expensive goods.

INDIRECT TAXES IN THE U.K.

1. Value Added Tax: As Table 34.1 showed, value added tax (VAT) is the third most important tax in the U.K., raising 14 per cent of all tax revenue. The tax is levied on the value added at each stage of the production process and differs from retail sales taxes because it is collected at each stage of production and not from the retailer at the final stage. The value added at each stage of production is calculated by taxing the value of the good when sold by a firm and deducting any tax already paid by producers in the previous stages of production. An example will illustrate how this works:

Example: Consider the production of a woollen jumper, assuming that VAT is levied at 15 per cent, the rate currently in use in the U.K.

Stage 1: A farmer sells wool to a weaver for £100 plus 15 per cent tax so the weaver pays £115.

Stage 2: The wool is then treated and sold to a manufacturer for an additional £50, i.e. the value of the product is now £150 and the tax due at this stage is 15 per cent of £150 − £22·50. Therefore the weaver has to pay VAT £7·50 (£22·50 − £15), this being the tax on the value which he has added during his stage of the production process.

Stage 3: The manufacturer sells the finished garments to a retailer for £350 plus tax of £52·50 − a total of £402·50. From the manufacturer's viewpoint, his tax liability is £52·50 less £22·50, the tax which has already been paid, making a tax bill for him of £30.

Stage 4: The jumpers are then sold to consumers by the retailer who adds £100 in value. Therefore the final value of the goods is £450 plus tax of £67·50 of which the retailer is due for £15, the remaining £52·50 having already been paid.

The above example can be represented diagrammatically (Figure 34.3).

At each stage the tax has been paid by the producer and then, depending upon the competitive conditions, passed on to the next stage of production. As a result sales are likely to be lower and so less money is made than would have been without the tax.

When VAT was introduced in 1973 to replace Purchase Tax and the Selective Employment Tax, one of its advantages was claimed to be its wide coverage of all the goods and services consumed, unlike the taxes which it replaced. There are only two major categories of goods and services which do not pay VAT. The first of these are classified as zero-rated; goods generally regarded as necessities, such as food, public transport fares, children's clothing and drugs supplied on prescription. Also included are books, newspapers and exports. Producers are sellers of these goods are able to claim back any tax which has been paid on them earlier. Zero-rating serves to eliminate the regressive effects which the tax, by taking consumption, would otherwise have. However, VAT is imposed on commercial users of utilities such as gas and electricity and so affects individual users indirectly. Furthermore, the tax can also be

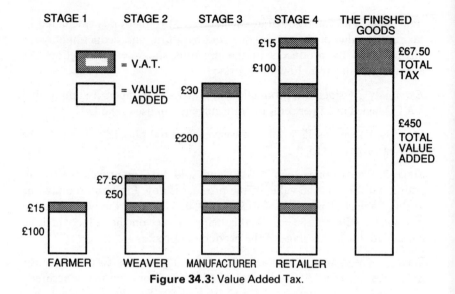

Figure 34.3: Value Added Tax.

seen as helping the balance of payments in the treatment of exports, although, of course, they will be subject to tax in the country to which they are sold.

The second category, exempt goods and services, pay no VAT but it is not possible to claim back any tax which has already been paid on these goods. In this category one has small businesses, i.e. those with a turnover of less than £25,400 (1990/91) per annum, most bank services and interest, insurance, education and health care. It should be noted that, because of the way in which VAT liability is calculated, with respect to the tax which has already been paid, it is a comparatively difficult tax to evade since it is never in someone's interest to minimise the tax which has already been paid by previous producers.

2. Excise Duties: These are duties which are imposed by the government on various goods in order to raise revenue and, in some cases, to discourage consumption. The revenue from these taxes accrues from three main areas, smoking, drinking and motoring. Thus the tax on a packet of twenty cigarettes (excluding VAT) is £1·07 making up a significant portion of the price. A similar situation applies for alcohol. Motoring is taxed in a number of ways. There is the tax on petrol and oil (plus VAT), a tax on the purchase of new cars and also vehicle excise duty, or road tax as it is more commonly known, of £100 per annum for cars and light commercial vehicles. One feature which the types of goods mentioned above have in common is their relative inelasticity of demand.

This makes it possible for the government to increase their price through taxation without causing a significant drop in sales and hence in tax revenue.

3. Protective Duties: These are duties, previously known as customs duties, which are imposed on goods imported into the U.K. from outside the European Community. As a result of its membership of this body the U.K. allows into the country tax free, goods from the other members of the Community but, in common with them, imposes a common external tariff on goods imported from outside the Community.

CRITERIA FOR ASSESSING TAXES

In deciding what sorts of taxes to impose and which goods to tax, governments consider various criteria by which taxes can be evaluated and compared to each other.

1. Equity: Adam Smith, in his *Wealth of Nations* published in 1776, suggested that taxes should be based upon people's ability to pay. Therefore the richer the person, the more tax he should pay. This is known as vertical equity (or fairness) and can be used as an argument for progressive taxes. The other type of equity is horizontal equity and the concept involved here is that people with the same income and in the same circumstances, e.g. married with two children, should pay the same tax.

2. Efficiency: This refers to the cost to the government, via the Inland Revenue or the Customs and Excise Department, to collect the tax compared to the amount of money which the tax brings in. Income tax is particularly good in this respect because of the widespread use of the PAYE system, enabling most tax to be collected automatically. VAT, however, involving over a million collection points is less efficient and the very complex capital gains tax brings in little revenue. A Wealth Tax, levied annually on assets above a certain value, if it were ever to be introduced in the U.K. could only be efficient if the threshold were relatively high.

3. Ease Of Calculation: Besides being convenient for the government, taxes should also be easy to assess by the individual taxpayer or firm. Above all, they should be able to assess their tax liability in advance of undertaking an activity or embarking upon a project, in order to know whether it will be worthwhile.

4. The Effect On The Allocation Of Resources: Ideally, taxes should have no effect upon the spending patterns of the consumer who should buy goods in the same proportion after taxes have been levied as he would before. If the government were to tax a certain type of good excessively, e.g. electrical goods, this would discourage consumption of these goods and cause people to change their spending patterns. Such a tax would therefore be unsatisfactory. VAT was therefore preferred to the taxes it replaced because of its wide coverage. The only exception to this is where there are high taxes placed upon certain types of good, deliberately to discourage people from consuming them.

5. The Effect Of The Tax As An Economic Weapon: Besides their role in raising revenue, taxes are also important instruments for the government in attempting to regulate the level of activity in the economy. It is therefore helpful if taxes have an automatic stabilising effect without having to be constantly varied by the government. The role of built-in stabilisers was considered in the last chapter and will not therefore be reconsidered here. However one power which the Chancellor of the Exchequer has, which has not yet been mentioned, is the indirect tax regulator. This is the power to vary indirect tax rates by up to 10 per cent in either direction without the necessity for seeking prior approval by Parliament. Generally however, indirect taxes are a less attractive option in this context than direct taxes. This is because of their effect on inflation when they are increased and also because of the tendency for consumption to remain more stable than income. Thus, if income falls, consumption will fall by less and so the amount of indirect tax paid will tend to increase as a proportion of income. This is the opposite effect to that desired for economic stability.

6. The Effect Of The Tax On Incentives: Much attention has been devoted by politicians to the effects which taxes have on people's desire to work. Two main areas of discussion have emerged. Firstly there is the effect of having high tax rates on upper income earners and secondly, the effects of taxes on low income earners. With regard to the former group, it is sometimes argued that high rates of tax discourage businessmen from taking risks and therefore from expanding their activities. This will have the effect of restricting the rate of growth of the economy and so future levels of income will be lower than if tax rates had been lower. Furthermore, businessmen might be unwilling to accept promotion or to work harder if they know that a high proportion of their extra earnings would be taken in tax. However evidence, collected by such bodies as the Institute for Fiscal Studies, has proved inconclusive. There is much more agreement on the effects of taxation on low income earners where the combination of high taxes and the loss of benefits such as free school meals and rent rebates can actually make people worse off if their income increases. This is known as the *poverty trap* and is especially likely to occur at the point where people start paying tax for the first time, i.e. when their income exceeds their tax-free allowances. There is also an *unemployment trap* which applies to people who are unemployed and receiving unemployment benefit. In their case, what is important is a comparison of their likely income if working, after all the deductions have been made, with their income from government benefits. The evidence shows that there are a small number of people who might be better off unemployed but this does not imply that they would, even so, prefer not to work since there is a stigma about being unemployed. It is to try to alleviate this problem that the government annually raises the level of tax-free allowances people receive before starting to pay income tax.

QUESTIONS

1. What would be the impact on the economy if the government were to:
   a. reduce the minimum rate of income tax to 20 per cent
   b. cut the rate of corporation tax to 20 per cent?
2. What is the "poverty trap"? How is it affected by:
   a. the level of income at which one starts to pay tax
   b. the steepness of the rate at which tax rates increase?
3. Analyse the taxes currently in use in the U.K. in the light of the criteria set out in the chapter.
4. What evidence does Figure 34.2 provide in support of the hypothesis that taxation in the U.K. became more regressive during the 1980s.

CHAPTER 35

PUBLIC EXPENDITURE

INTRODUCTION

The last chapter examined the methods used by the government to obtain finance by taxation. This chapter considers the various ways in which it spends its revenue, the reasons why such expenditure is necessary and the effects which it has on the economy.

THE REASONS FOR GOVERNMENT EXPENDITURE

1. Public Goods: The first type of goods provided by the government are public goods. These are goods where consumption by one person does not reduce the amount which is available for consumption by others. Examples of this type of good include the maintenance of law and order by the police, the provision of street lighting and the broadcasting of television signals. If a person watches the television or benefits from street lighting, it does not mean that someone else is therefore unable to receive the television signal or cannot also benefit from the lit street. With these goods, which are essentially non-excludable (i.e. it is difficult to prevent people from consuming them), it is often very costly to devise and implement a system of charging and a means of excluding people from consuming them if they have not paid, television licences being the only major exception to this. This, known as the "free-rider problem", means that it is very difficult for private firms to provide these services via the price mechanism. Therefore they are frequently provided by the government and financed with money collected from taxation.

2. Merit Goods: There are some goods, known as merit goods, which benefit not only the person consuming them directly, but also other members of society. An individual example would be if I spent time and resources creating an attractive garden. Not only do I benefit from it but, in addition, I provide benefit for all those people who walk past it. For society as a whole, there are gains from having a healthy, well-educated population which are in addition to the benefits experienced by the individual himself. For example, vaccination against a disease is not only of advantage to the person vaccinated, who is less likely to catch the disease, but also to everyone with whom he comes into contact since they, in turn, are less likely to catch the disease. The extension of the London Underground system by the building of the Victoria Line benefited not only users of the line but also other travellers through the decline in congestion. Because of these benefits, known as positive externalities, the government wishes to encourage the consumption of these goods. It may do this by subsidising them or even, where the externalities are large, provide them free of charge.

3. Economies Of Scale: In some sectors of the economy there are substantial benefits in the form of reduced average costs which occur when operating on a large scale. If this scale is beyond the resources available in the private sector, it is necessary for the government to provide these goods or at least to provide subsidies or grants to the private sector to persuade them to expand. An example of the former case would be the provision of electricity where there is a minimum efficient size for a reactor, with average costs falling sharply until this point is reached. In addition, it is often argued that, in some circumstances, the private sector is too short-sighted and is therefore unwilling to invest in long-term projects such as the European Space Programme. So, if such ventures are to go ahead, it is often necessary for the government to provide some or all of the finance.

4. Monopolies: There are often circumstances where there are benefits to be gained from having goods or services supplied by a monopolist in order to ensure minimum standards or, as with British Rail, to provide an integrated service across the country. If the item involved is a necessity and were to be provided by a firm in the private sector, the firm would be able to raise the price, exploit the consumer and earn excess profits. Therefore such industries are often nationalised and the goods or services supplied with a degree of government control.

5. The Redistribution Of Income: A large proportion of the government's expenditure is devoted to providing transfer payments which redistribute income towards the lower income earners. These include items such as pensions, unemployment benefit and disability allowances and, along with the other types of government expenditure, will be considered in the next section.

PUBLIC EXPENDITURE IN THE U.K.

Table 35.1 shows the estimated total public expenditure for 1989–90, together with planned figures for 1990/91.

Table 35.1: Total public expenditure by programme (£ millions).

	1989–90 outturn	1990–91 plans
Defence	20,310	21,200
Overseas aid and other overseas services:		
Overseas aid	1,570	1,680
Net payments to E.C. institutions	2,030	1,870
Other overseas services	840	890
Agriculture, fisheries, food and forestry	1,560	1,910
Trade, industry, energy and employment	5,200	5,130
Arts and libraries	440	490
Transport	1,970	2,310
Housing	1,540	2,250
Other environmental services	550	670
Education and science *	4,310	4,580
Health & personal social services	20,010	22,040
Social security	47,200	52,000
Scotland	4,010	4,420
Wales	1,890	2,120
Northern Ireland	5,520	5,750
Various departments including law and protective services	7,610	8,410
Central government support to local authorities	38,100	41,800
Financing requirements of public corporations	1,540	1,390
Reserve		3,000
Privatisation proceeds	–4,250	– 5,000
Adjustment	– 200	
Planning total	161,750	178,910

Economic Progress Report, December 1989.
* Most education spending is provided through government support to local authorities.

By far the most important single item is social security spending which accounts for 29 per cent of the total for 1989/90. Almost all of this is spent on benefits which range from unemployment benefits, payment to one-parent families and payment to those over retirement age. This element of government spending, known as "demand-led spending", is difficult to control exactly because, once the rates of payment have been fixed by the government, the level of expenditure is determined by the number of people able to apply for benefit. Such changes are very largely outside government control in the short term. The only influence which the government has is in the rate of benefit. The general procedure for fixing most of these benefits is to increase them in November based on the rise in prices in the year finishing in the previous May.

Defence expenditure and health and personal social services are two other outstanding areas of expenditure. Defence spending has been affected by the U.K.'s commitment to NATO to raise the level of spending in real terms, as well as to the defence force in the Falklands.

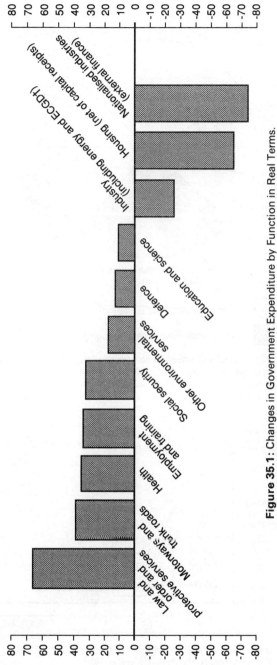

Figure 35.1: Changes in Government Expenditure by Function in Real Terms.
† Export Credit Guarantee Department.
Source: Economic Progress Report, February 1990.

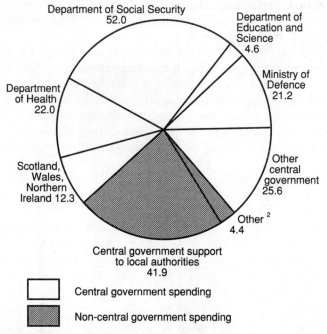

Figure 35.2: General Government Expenditure Plans, 1990–91[1] (£ billion).
[1] Excluding privatisation proceeds.
[2] Reserve and financing requirements of public corporations.
Source: *Autumn Statement 1989.*

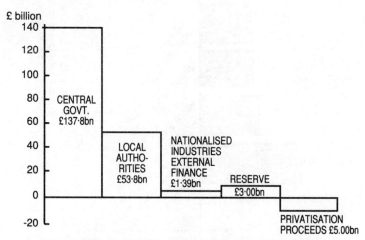

Figure 35.3: Public Expenditure by Type 1990–91 Plans.
Source: Economic Progress Report No. 205 – December 1989.

The political changes in central and eastern Europe might well facilitate a reduction in Defence expenditure. Expenditure on personal social services seems certain to increase during the 1990s with the increased numbers of elderly people.

Expenditure on the nationalised industries, although planned to increase is noticeably less in real terms than in the early 1980s. The policy of the Conservative Government has been to ensure that subsidies to loss-making sectors are reduced and also that an increasing amount of their investment is financed from internally-generated funds. This policy has also been pursued in the preparations for privatisation of public corporations: the increased electricity charges planned for 1990/91 are a case in point.

The item "Central government support to local authorities" includes expenditure on education which is the single biggest item of expenditure of local authorities.

When public expenditure plans are published, they include an item known as the contingency reserve. This is intended to cover all contingencies, including any unexpected changes in demand-led expenditure, such as social security payments, as well as any change in government policy which might occur during the period.

Figure 35.2 shows public expenditure for 1990/91 in departmental terms.

Another way of categorising public expenditure is according to who is responsible for spending it. Central government is the largest spender, accounting for approximately 72 per cent of total expenditure. Of this, slightly less than half is on goods and services, mainly for defence and the National Health Service; just under 30 per cent is on social security benefits and the remainder is accounted for by the costs of operating the civil service and miscellaneous transfer payments, e.g. housing subsidies and industrial support. The other major spenders are the local authorities who account for 28 per cent of total spending and their expenditure and income will be examined in the next section. Figure 35.3 shows the main types of public expenditure planned for 1990/91. (The figure for privatisation proceeds is shown as being negative since this item reduces the government's need to borrow or raise taxes to finance its expenditure.)

THE LOCAL AUTHORITIES

So far, nothing has been said concerning the income and expenditure of the local authorities as distinct from those of the central government. Their finance comes from three main areas. Firstly they receive grants

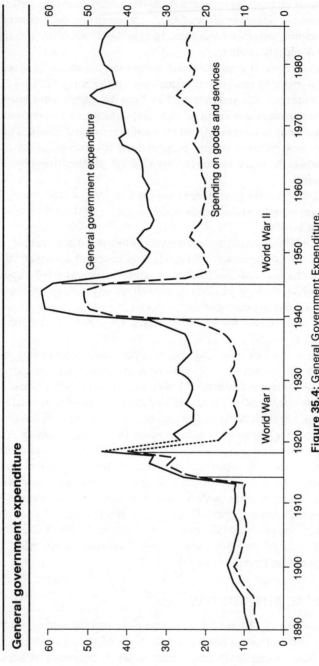

Figure 35.4: General Government Expenditure.

Economic Progress Report, December 1988.

from the central government and these amount to approximately half of their revenue. Secondly they also levy the Community Charge upon individuals and rates on businesses, which provides them with approximately one-third of their revenue. The local authorities also receive income from the rent from council properties and from charges levied for the provision of services, e.g. swimming pool charges.

Local authority expenditure can be split up into that related to the provision of goods and services and that concerned with other matters e.g. the paying or grants, subsidies and interest on money which they have borrowed. The major category of goods and services provided is education which accounts for a third of all local authority spending. Other items include spending on housing, roads and public lighting, the police, fire and ambulance services and environmental services. The amount of discretion which local authorities have in some of these areas is limited since the central government lays down the general pattern to which much spending must conform. However, the recent trend has been for the level of spending by local authorities to increase faster than that by the central government. This has been partly because of the increased provision of services by the local authorities and partly, it is felt by some people, because of the relatively lower level of efficiency in their activities.

As a result of this and of the government's desire to reduce government spending in general, local authorities' spending and their ability to raise revenue have become subject to increasing control by the central government. From 1980, the government was empowered to reduce the rate support grant for any council spending more than the government's prescribed guidelines. From 1982, the government announced that it would reduce the proportion of local authority expenditure funded by the central government and also that the power of the local authorities to levy supplementary rate increases would be removed.

THE PLANNING AND CONTROL OF PUBLIC EXPENDITURE

Figure 35.4 above shows the long-term upward trend in general government expenditure as a percentage of GDP.

During the 1970s and early 1980s, the level of public expenditure increased noticeably as a percentage of GDP, and in 1975/76 it reached over 49 per cent. Tighter control of public expenditure and greater growth in GDP in the later 1980s combined to reduce the percentage to approximately 39 per cent in 1989/90.

There have been five main reasons for the high levels of public

spending seen in the 1970s and 1980s. First, there was a long-term desire
to expand the level of care and the services provided by the state to
enable the sections of the population on low incomes to obtain living
standards nearer to the average for the nation as a whole. As the average
standard of living has risen, this objective has become more expensive.
Secondly, as society became more affluent there has been an increasing
demand for government services. Thus, for example, as more people are
able to afford cars, there has been an increased need to spend money on
roads. Thirdly, many of the services provided, especially with regard to
health, have become more expensive. New technology has led to the
development of new drugs and methods of treatment which are generally
more expensive than those they replaced, or are in fact totally new, thus
adding to the cost of public expenditure. Furthermore, these techniques,
combined with an increase in the general level of affluence, have raised
life expectancy, thereby increasing the cost of pensions. Fourthly, there
has, in the past, been a tendency for governments to use the level of
public expenditure as an economic weapon to expand the economy when
it was depressed. This had a ratchet effect since, once a department had
been expanded, it was very difficult to reduce it when the economy
started to improve. Furthermore large wage rises paid to many groups of
public sector workers exacerbated this. Finally, governments based their
plans for public spending on their estimates for the rate of growth of the
economy. These estimates, especially at the start of the recession in the
early seventies, were over-optimistic. However, there was no attempt to
reduce the growth in public spending once the forecasts for the rate of
growth of GDP were shown to be incorrect. Therefore the more rapid
rises in public spending cause it to increase as a percentage of the
GDP.

Governments have therefore taken increasing steps to control the rises
in public spending which have occurred. In 1961, following the Plowden
Report, annual surveys of public spending were introduced combined
with a five year plan which was rolled forward each year. These original
plans were in volume terms, i.e. in terms of the number of teachers
employed and the number of hospitals built, rather than their cost. This
did not matter when the rate of inflation was low but became a serious
problem with the higher rates of inflation in the late sixties. So, in 1969,
the government introduced the publication of an annual white paper on
public spending which incorporated a relative price effect which was
intended to take account of the different, and generally faster, rate of
increase in the price of items of government spending than in the
remainder of the economy. Because of the continuing tendency for
spending to rise and the increased recognition of the need to control it a

further major change was introduced which was to impose cash limits on spending departments. Thus if a project turned out to be more expensive than was originally forecast it would mean that spending elsewhere had to be correspondingly reduced or that the department had to argue its case for an increased allowance against other departments in similar circumstances. This procedure has meant that control over public spending is now far tighter than it was and, additionally, it has introduced into the system a greater emphasis on efficiency. In 1989/90, 40 per cent of public spending is directly subjected to cash limits, 20 per cent is local authority spending which is not subject to cash limits. However, the government's main grant to them, the rate support grant, is subject to cash limits and this imposes a corresponding pressure on the local authorities. The remaining 40 per cent consists of demand-led services such as social security benefits where expenditure is determined by the number of claimants once the rates of benefit have been fixed by the government.

Providing the government is able to hold the spending departments close to the cash limits imposed, the level of public spending will fall steadily as a percentage of the GDP. However, a crucial element in this is the rate of inflation. If the target is not met then one or more of the following must happen: there will have to be an increase in cash limits, a reduction in labour employed, a decline in the goods and services provided or an increase in their prices.

THE PUBLIC SECTOR BORROWING REQUIREMENT/ DEBT REPAYMENT

Because the level of government expenditure has, for many years, exceeded the money which is obtained from taxation and other forms of revenue, it has been necessary for the government to borrow money. The amount which the public sector as a whole – the central government, local authorities and public corporations – has to borrow is known as the public sector borrowing requirement (PSBR). It is an important concept because of its impact on the economy both in terms of fiscal and monetary policy. This section will examine its composition and its impact on the economy.

There are three major sources of government borrowing: from businesses and individuals in the U.K. private sector, from the U.K. banking sector and from overseas. Of these, the first is the most important, to the extent that the government has at times over-funded, i.e. borrowed more than it needs from the non-bank private sector, in order to be able to repay debts owing to the other two sectors. Borrowing from the non-bank private sector can take a number of forms: gilt-edged securities, national savings investment, and local authority bonds all being examples of this. Borrowing from the banking sector and external borrowing includes all such transactions with the banking sector and the residents of other countries respectively, including in the latter category not only official government borrowing – sales of government securities overseas – but also changes in the U.K.'s official reserves.

In the 1960s the PSBR averaged approximately 3 per cent of GDP. Since reaching nearly 10 per cent of GDP in 1975/76, great attempts have been made to reduce it. From a PSBR in 1988/89 of £11,067m (3·8 per cent of GDP), government financing in 1989/90 changed to a planned surplus of £11,600m (− 2.6 per cent of GDP). This has been termed "Public Sector Debt Repayment" (PSDR), with the Bank of England able to re-purchase some of the outstanding government stock. This surplus is the outcome of restraints on public expenditure combined with a rise in the level of economic activity (i.e. increased revenue from income tax, sales taxes, and corporation tax) and privatisation proceeds. The maintenance of a surplus is clearly susceptible to any economic recession.

The PSBR/PSDR is also of importance in the government's fiscal policy. A positive PSBR means that the government is a net injector of spending into the circular flow of income. The multiplier operates on this and the effect will be, according to the analysis developed in Chapter 33, to raise the level of national income. What will be of importance in such circumstances are the relative marginal propensities to consume of the people from whom income is taken in tax and those to whom it is given by the government. Even a budget having no effect on the PSBR can be reflationary if it takes money from high income earners with low marginal propensities to consume and gives it to those with higher marginal propensities to consume. This will have the effect of raising the level of consumption in the economy.

QUESTIONS

1. Analyse the main types of government spending set out in Table 35.1 in the light of the criteria presented for government spending at the start of the chapter.

2. What are the arguments for and against a reduction in the level of spending by the government in the economy?

3. Analyse the Community Charge in the light of the criteria for assessing taxes presented in the last chapter.

4. Under what circumstances would an increase in the PSBR be advantageous to the economy?

5. Discuss the arguments for and against the privatisation of parts of the public sector.

6. What are the likely effects on the economy of any planned fall in capital expenditure by the public sector?

CHAPTER 36

INTERNATIONAL TRADE

INTRODUCTION

International trade is the exchange of goods and services between countries. Trade across national frontiers arises from the fact that the world's resources are unevenly distributed. Some countries are richly endowed with minerals, others have none. Some have mild climates suitable for the cultivation of a variety of crops, others have not. Some have workers skilled in the use of machinery, others have a shortage of skilled workers. In such circumstances, most countries prefer to concentrate production on those goods and services to which its resources are best suited. The U.K. could grow its own oranges, but it chooses to purchase them from other countries, as the cost in terms of home resources would be too high. So the world economy, like most domestic economies, is characterised by *specialisation* and *exchange*, with each country *importing* those goods and services which it can purchase more cheaply abroad, and *exporting* part of home production to pay for them.

In this chapter we shall examine how such specialisation and exchange arises, and the advantages it brings. We shall also consider why it is that many countries restrict the free movement of goods and services across frontiers, and the methods adopted to achieve these restrictions.

THE LAW OF COMPARATIVE ADVANTAGE

The claim that specialisation and exchange increase the living standards of those involved is based on a theory which dates back to the early nineteenth century – the law of comparative advantage.

We begin with two simple economies, which we shall call Urbania and Ruritania. We assume that each country has the same amount of land and labour available, and that each devotes half these resources to wheat production and half to the production of cars. We shall ignore differences in currencies and measure the total output produced in the same units. Table 36.1 illustrates the position before specialisation.

We can see from the figures that Urbania is more efficient at producing cars than wheat, and that this situation is reversed in Ruritania. In this

Table 36.1: Total production before
specialisation.

	Wheat	Cars
Urbania	4	10
Ruritania	12	6
Total	16	16

case we say that the former has an *absolute advantage* in car production
and that the latter has an absolute advantage in wheat cultivation.

If each country now specialises in that product in which it has an
absolute advantage, total output will increase. Table 36.2 shows the
position after such specialisation (we have assumed that each country
simply devotes all its resources to the production of one good, and that
total output in each industry doubles as a result, i.e. constant returns to
scale exist).

Table 36.2: Specialisation in the absolute
advantage case.

	Wheat	Cars
Urbania	–	20
Ruritania	24	–
Total	24	20

It is clear that specialisation has increased total production in this
case. *The law of absolute advantage states that if each country has an
absolute advantage in the production of a particular product, total output
will increase if each specialises in that product.*

We can now modify the example to show that specialisation and trade can
benefit both countries, even if one has an absolute advantage in both goods.

Table 36.3: Output before specialisation.

	Wheat	Cars
Urbania	12	1?
Ruritania	4	2
Total	16	14

Now Urbania is more efficient at producing both goods. However, its
relative or *comparative advantage* is greatest in car production, as it is six
times as efficient as Ruritania in this area, but only three times more
efficient in the cultivation of wheat. If Urbania now specialises in the

Table 36.4: Specialisation in the
comparative advantage case.

	Wheat	Cars
Urbania	–	24
Ruritania	8	–
Total	8	24

production of cars and Ruritania devotes all its resources to wheat
production, we have the position shown in Table 36.4.

We have gained 10 cars but we have lost 8 units of wheat in the
process. Are the countries better off? The answer depends upon the cost
of cars in terms of wheat, or their *opportunity cost*. In Urbania, the
opportunity cost of 1 car is 1 unit of wheat, as we can see by examining
Table 36.3. In Ruritania, the opportunity cost of 1 car is higher, at two
units of wheat. Therefore a gain of 10 cars would have cost 10 units of
wheat in Urbania and 20 units of wheat in Ruritania. So the actual loss
of only 8 units of wheat means that total output per unit of resources
has increased. We can see this more clearly if we now allow the countries
to trade. Urbania will require wheat in exchange for some of its cars.
The next question is, how many cars should she give up in order to
acquire (say) 6 units of wheat?

Without trade, as we have seen, Urbania could gain 1 wheat unit by
sacrificing 1 car. Obviously she would require an exchange rate which
gave rise to more wheat than this, for the loss of 1 car. Ruritania, on the
other hand, would not be willing to give up more than 2 units of wheat
for 1 car, as it could achieve this without trade. So the exchange rate
must lie between 1 car = 1 wheat and 1 car = 2 wheat. *For specialisation
to benefit both countries the exchange rate must lie between the opportunity
cost ratios.*

Let us assume that trade takes place at a rate of 1 car = $1\frac{1}{2}$ wheat,
and that Urbania exchanges 4 cars for 6 units of wheat. The final
position is outlined in Table 36.5.

Table 36.5: The distribution of goods
after specialisation and exchange.

	Wheat	Cars
Urbania	6	20
Ruritania	2	4
Total	8	24

If we now compare the distribution of goods shown above with the position as illustrated in Table 36.3, we can see that both countries have gained from trade. Urbania may have lost 6 units of wheat but it has gained 8 cars, but without specialisation it would have only gained 6 cars for the same sacrifice of wheat. Ruritania has gained 2 cars at a cost of 2 units of wheat. Again, the cost would have been higher (at 4 units of wheat) before specialisation.

We can now generalise from the above example to the real world, where many countries trade in a wide variety of goods. *The law of comparative advantage states that if each country specialises in the products in which it has the greatest comparative advantage, trade will be beneficial to all concerned.*

QUALIFICATIONS TO THE LAW OF COMPARATIVE ADVANTAGE

1. Trade will only take place if the opportunity costs differ. If they were identical the exchange rate that would benefit both countries would not exist.

2. We have ignored transport costs, and in practice they may be large enough to offset any potential gains due to the existence of differing opportunity cost ratios.

3. We assumed constant returns to scale. In practice it is likely that some resources are better suited to one occupation than another, giving rise to decreasing returns to scale as they are moved to increase the degree of specialisation.

4. The factors of production are not as mobile in practice as our example suggests. In the nineteenth century the U.K. had a substantial comparative advantage in textiles, but this had disappeared by the middle of the twentieth century. Labour, in particular, tends to be immobile, and the necessary transfer of resources away from the textile industry may be a long and painful process, involving heavy long-term structural unemployment.

FURTHER ADVANTAGES FROM INTERNATIONAL TRADE

(a) Increased Competition
International trade increases competition, which means that prices are likely to be lower than they would otherwise be. This is particularly true when the home market is controlled by a monopoly.

(b) Lower Costs
In many industries costs per unit of output fall as output expands – the

phenomenon of *economies of scale*. Without international trade many firms would be unable to benefit from such economies, as their national markets are too small.

(c) Greater Variety
International trade allows the consumer a much greater choice of goods and services than he would have if only domestic goods were available.

THE TERMS OF TRADE

In the example used to illustrate the law of comparative advantage, the countries concerned exchanged cars for what at a rate of 1 car = $1\frac{1}{2}$ wheat. The basis on which a country exchanges its exports for its imports is known as the terms of trade. As there is a great variety of goods traded, the average price of exports is compared with the average price of imports. In addition, the figures are usually quoted in index number form, to facilitate comparisons over time. The terms of trade are expressed as:

$$\frac{\text{Index of export prices}}{\text{Index of import prices}} \times 100$$

When the index rises the terms of trade are said to have *improved* as the price of exports has risen in relation to the price of imports. If the prices of imports rise in relation to the prices of exports, the index will fall because the terms of trade have worsened.

THE EFFECTS OF A CHANGE IN THE TERMS OF TRADE

(a) Living Standards
If the price of exports rise in relation to the price of imports, more goods can be imported and so there is an increase in the goods available for consumption. A doubling of export prices, for example, would mean that twice as many goods could now be imported. This is why a rise in the terms of trade is considered an improvement in a country's trading position with the rest of the world.

(b) The Balance Of Payments
The terms of trade are a measure of the change in the *prices* of imports and exports, whereas the balance of payments are a measure of the *value* of imports and exports, i.e. price multiplied by the quantity sold. So the effect on the latter of a rise in the terms of trade depends upon the responsiveness of demand to a change in price; in other words, *the price elasticity of demand*. Demand is likely to be inelastic in the short run, so

an improvement in the terms of trade will benefit the balance of payments as more will be spent on exports, even though their relative price has risen. Demand will generally be more responsive to price changes over the longer term, and this may mean a deterioration in the balance of payments following a rise in the terms of trade.

(c) Foreign Markets

One country's exports are another country's imports. So a rise in the United Kingdom's terms of trade will be accompanied by a corresponding fall in the terms of trade of those countries trading with the U.K. If, as a result, the amount of income these countries receive for *their* exports falls, they in turn may reduce any future demand for U.K. exports. Many developing countries faced this problem in the 1970s, as they were forced to pay substantially more for a major import – oil – whilst their own export earnings fell, as the developed world's demand for non-oil products dropped.

WHAT CAUSES A CHANGE IN THE TERMS OF TRADE?

The price of any good will usually change if the conditions of demand or supply change, and exports and imports are no exception. We can illustrate this by examining recent changes in the U.K.'s terms of trade, which are shown in Table 36.6.

Table 36.6: The United Kingdom's Terms of Trade (1985 = 100).

Year	Export Prices (1)	Import Prices (2)	Terms of Trade (1 ÷ 2) × 100
1979	61·4	62·4	98·4
1980	70·0	68·5	102·2
1981	76·2	74·2	102·7
1982	81·4	80·2	101·5
1983	88·0	87·5	100·2
1984	95·0	95·5	99·5
1985	100·0	100·0	100·0
1986	91·8	96·0	95·6
1987	95·5	98·5	97·0
1988	94 5	97·6	96·8

Source: Annual Abstract of Statistics.

1. Supply Changes

If the supply of a commodity falls, its price will usually rise. Conversely, an increase in supply will lead to a fall in price. Possible causes of supply changes in internationally traded goods include:

(a) Poor harvests, which are the main cause of price changes in agricultural products.

(b) Deliberate action by producers to restrict supply, with the intention of increasing income if demand is inelastic. In 1973 the Organisation of Petroleum Exporting Countries (O.P.E.C.) reduced the supply of oil on western markets, with this aim in mind. The price of oil imports rose sharply as a result, and the U.K.'s terms of trade fell in 1974 as a consequence.

(c) Political unrest in a country which is a main supplier of a particular product may cause a rise in price of that product, both as a direct result of any reduction in supply and as a consequence of panic buying by countries wishing to secure future supplies.

(d) Changes in the exchange rate. If the pound falls in value against other currencies, the price of imports will rise. This will lead to a fall in the terms of trade, although the price of exports will rise as many have an imported raw materials content.

2. Demand Changes

If the demand for a product increases, its price will usually rise. A reduction in demand will normally cause a fall in price. Possible causes of a change in the demand for internationally traded goods include:

(a) World growth. If the major western economies are experiencing an upturn in the economic cycle, the demand for raw materials is likely to rise considerably. As the supply of many primary products is inelastic, this will cause a rapid rise in the price of these raw materials. In this way the terms of trade of the developed world will often fall during periods of rapid growth.

(b) The growth of substitutes. Demand for a major export may fall if a close substitute appears on the market. Thus the demand for natural fibres was affected by the growth of synthetic substitutes, and, more recently, the demand for oil has fallen as more and more customers have turned to cheaper sources of energy, such as coal.

VOLUME OF OVERSEAS TRADE

Table 36.7 shows the volume of exports and imports in index terms, with 1985 as the base year. The noticeable feature is the large surge in the volume of imports in 1988 while exports increased very little. Part of the increase in imports is accounted for by the purchases abroad of capital equipment for British industry and part by the inability of U.K. firms to meet the growing demand for consumer durables. Preliminary figures for 1989 show a levelling off in imports and a rise in the level of exports.

Table 36.7: U.K. Volume Import–Export Index Numbers.

	1984	1985	1986	1987	1988
Exports	94·7	100	104·0	109·1	110·7
Imports	96·9	100	107·1	114·6	129·5

Source: Annual Abstract of Statistics 1990.

RESTRICTIONS ON INTERNATIONAL TRADE

The law of comparative advantage shows that free trade benefits all concerned. In practice, international trade is rarely free, and a variety of barriers to trade exist. Such *protectionist* measures include:

1. Tariffs
These are taxes or *customs duties* imposed on imported goods at the port of entry. Tariffs raise the price of imports, and demand is likely to fall as a result. Note, however, that if demand for the product is inelastic, the total spent on the product will actually rise.

2. Quotas
In this case the authorities limit the import to a given quantity. This reduction in supply will lead to a rise in price of the imported good, but, unlike tariffs, it is the firm selling the good which benefits, rather than the Government.

3. Exchange Controls
The problem with both tariffs and quotas is that the total spent on the import is not controlled. One device which succeeds in achieving this is exchange control. The authorities may impose limits on the amount of foreign currency that residents can hold, thereby introducing a ceiling on spending on imports from particular countries. Such measures are very common in Eastern European economies.

4. Subsidies
If an exporting country subsidises its production, prices can be below the costs of production. So international trade is not free, as prices do not reflect opportunity costs.

5. Embargo
In some cases a complete ban is placed on a good. This may be for health reasons, e.g. dangerous drugs, or for political reasons, e.g. many countries refuse to trade with South Africa.

6. Administration
Some countries make it very difficult for foreign goods to enter home markets by imposing strict technical requirements on products, or by increasing the paper-work involved in clearing customs. This type of restriction is very difficult to prove, and as a result became more prevalent in the 1970s and 1980s. The most blatant example occurred in 1980, when the French authorities introduced a new customs office for Japanese video equipment in the middle of France!

WHY DO GOVERNMENTS RESTRICT TRADE?

1. To Protect Employment
Governments may restrict the flow of imports into the home market if they are concerned about the level of unemployment in the economy. The reasoning is that if consumers cannot buy foreign goods, they will be forced to turn to domestically produced substitutes and in this way employment in home industries will be maintained. The problem with such a policy is that it becomes self-defeating if all countries adopt it. As one reduces its imports, others retaliate by reducing theirs, so affecting the former's exports. The end result can only be a fall in the total volume of trade, and a rise in unemployment world-wide.

2. To Protect Particular Industries
British consumers benefit from international trade if they can purchase imported goods at a lower price than they have to pay for domestically produced alternatives. Workers in the home industries concerned, however, may lose their jobs as a result. In theory the displaced workers should move to those industries in which British firms have a comparative advantage.

In practice, of course, things are rarely that simple, as labour tends to be immobile between occupations. Therefore governments often bow to pressure from industries facing strong foreign competition and introduce restrictions on imports. Such restrictions raise the cost of living for all consumers, including those working in the protected industries.

3. To Correct a Balance of Payments Deficit
As we shall see in Chapter 37, a prolonged excess of imports over exports cannot be sustained for a long period of time. To eliminate such balance of payments deficits, the authorities concerned may take action to restrict the total amount spent on imports.

4. To Protect an "Infant Industry"
A newly established industry may have higher costs than its foreign

competitors in its early stages of growth, but it may experience economies of scale as output expands, and thereby achieve lower costs than its international rivals. It can be argued that protection will eventually benefit the consumer under such circumstances, as prices will be lower in the long run if the home industry is allowed to reach maturity. Unfortunately, such "temporary" protection often turns out to be permanent.

5. To Prevent "Dumping"
"Dumping" is the sale of goods abroad at a price below the cost of production. Consumers will obviously benefit from such a policy in the short term. However, the exporter may be trying to eliminate domestic competition and thereby secure a monopoly position in the long run. Governments may restrict imports if they suspect dumping, although it is very difficult to prove in many cases.

6. Strategic Factors
Governments may protect certain industries from foreign competition if they are considered to be of vital importance to the national interest. This explains why many countries will maintain steel production and shipbuilding, even though this is at a cost of heavy subsidies.

7. To Raise Revenue
The authorities may levy some tariffs simply to raise additional revenue for the state.

THE U.K. AND FREE TRADE

The U.K. has traditionally been associated with a policy of free trade, except in those circumstances in which there is a world-wide move towards protection. There has also been strong external influences on the U.K., making for freer trade.

1. The European Community (E.C.)
The U.K. joined the European Economic Community (as it was then known) in 1973, and as a result has removed all tariffs on goods from the other members states. There is a common external tariff on goods from non-member states. We shall examine the effects of membership in more detail in Chapter 40.

2. The European Free Trade Association (E.F.T.A.)
The U.K. was a member of this association before it left to join the E.C. It is similar to the latter in that no tariff barriers exist between members states, but, unlike the E.C., each country is free to maintain its own individual tariffs against goods originating outside the free trade area.

The present members are Norway, Sweden, Austria, Switzerland and Iceland.

In 1972 the E.C. signed an agreement with E.F.T.A. members, setting out a timetable for the elimination of tariffs between the two trading blocs. All tariff barriers were finally removed on 1 January 1984, so creating the largest free trade area in the world. British firms now have free access to a market of well over 300 million consumers.

3. The General Agreement on Tariffs and Trade (G.A.T.T.)

Most of the Western nations are members of G.A.T.T., which was set up in 1947 with the aim of reducing barriers to trade. Members meet periodically to agree on tariff reductions, and as a result the general level of tariffs has fallen.

THE U.K.'S TRADING PATTERNS

International trade is very important for the British economy. Exports contributed about 24 per cent of National Income in 1988, compared with 13 per cent in Japan, and only 8 per cent in the U.S.A. This means that the U.K. is a very "open" economy, and is therefore easily affected by recessions in the major world economies. In addition, it is vital that the U.K. remains competitive internationally, as so much employment depends upon maintaining and expanding foreign markets.

The traditional picture of U.K. foreign trade was that of a country exporting manufactured goods to pay for imported food and raw materials. This is no longer the case, with the U.K. now mainly importing and exporting manufactured goods. Table 36.8 sets out the major exports and imports by commodity, showing the change in the composition of items over the last 10 years. Major changes have occurred on the export side; e.g. in 1972 less than 3 per cent of export earnings came from minerals and fuels; by 1981 around 20 per cent of earnings came from the sale of North Sea oil, though by 1988 this had dropped to 7·5 per cent. Manufactured and semi-manufactured goods still accounted for nearly 70 per cent of visible exports in 1987.

On the import side we can see the increase in the importance of foreign manufactured goods in the U.K. economy. Manufactured goods accounted for nearly 50 per cent of imports in 1987, compared to nearly 40 per cent in 1981 and over 30 per cent in 1972. Food, beverages and tobacco declined in the same period, from a fifth of the total to one ninth. The figures imply that the U.K.'s comparative advantage in the production of manufactured goods is declining, with other countries making inroads into the U.K. market. This is borne out by an examination

Table 36.8: Exports and Imports by commodity group
(1972, 1981, 1987).

Exports (%)	1972	1981	1987
Food, beverages, tobacco	6·8	7·1	7·0
Basic materials	3·4	2·6	2·8
Minerals, fuels	2·6	18·9	11·0
Semi-manufactured goods	32·4	25·8	28·1
Manufactured goods	51·9	42·7	48·4
Imports (%)	1972	1981	1987
Food, beverages, tobacco	21·0	12·4	10·8
Basic materials	11·1	7·0	6·0
Minerals, fuels	9·3	14·3	6·5
Semi-manufactured goods	25·6	24·1	26·9
Manufactured goods	31·6	39·0	48·6

Source: Annual Abstract of Statistics.

of the U.K.'s share of world exports of manufactured goods, which reveals a fall from 20 per cent in the early 1950s to around 4 per cent in the 1980s.

Table 36.9 sets out the U.K.'s trade by area for the same period.

One notable feature is the growth of importance of the oil exporting countries as a market for British goods. This reflects the increase in their income in the 1970s, as a result of the rapid rise in the price of oil. However, the most striking fact about U.K. trade is how European it is, with nearly 60 per cent of all exports going to European countries in 1987. We can also see from the table that the E.C. is the U.K.'s single

Table 36.9: U.K. Trade by Area
(1972, 1981, 1987).

Exports (%)	1972	1981	1987
E.C.	30·2	46·8	49·4
Other W. Europe	16·4	14·3	9·6
N. America	16·5	16·0	16·3
Other Developed	10·0	6·6	5·1
Oil Exporting	6·8	13·5	6·6
Rest	20·0	17·2	12·9
Imports (%)	1972	1981	1987
E.C.	33·8	43·5	52·7
Other W. Europe	17·0	15·5	13·7
N. America	16·0	14·8	11·5
Other Developed	10·6	6·5	7·8
Oil Exporting	7·6	7·3	1·8
Rest	14·9	12·5	12·5

Source: Annual Abstract of Statistics.

most important market. Trade with the E.C. has grown very substantially since 1972. Exporters did very well up to 1981 but in more recent years imports have increased substantially relative to exports.

QUESTIONS

1. Explain the law of comparative advantage. What other advantages arise from international trade?

2. Define the terms of trade. How are they usually measured? What effect would a fall in the terms of trade have on the U.K. economy?

3. Account for the main changes in the U.K.'s terms of trade in the last ten years.

4. Why do governments place restrictions on international trade?

5. What restrictions can governments place on international trade?

6. Describe and account for the main change in the U.K.'s foreign trade in the last ten years.

CHAPTER 37

THE BALANCE OF PAYMENTS

INTRODUCTION

The Balance of Payments is a statement of the United Kingdom's monetary transactions with the rest of the world. There is a continuous flow of such transactions, but it is conventional to present the balance of payments on a monthly, quarterly or annual basis.

Any transaction which gives rise to a money claim on a foreign resident is called a credit, and entered with a plus sign in the accounts. Any transaction which gives rise to a money claim on a U.K. resident is regarded as a debit and is recorded with a negative sign. Thus the sale of a Rolls-Royce abroad would be noted as a credit on the balance of payments, and the purchase of a Japanese car in this country would be recorded as a debit. All transactions are valued in sterling, with any deals in foreign currency converted to sterling at the appropriate exchange rate.

THE STRUCTURE OF THE BALANCE OF PAYMENTS

As the balance of payments is merely an accounting record, its presentation depends upon how the authorities choose to classify the items involved. Since 1986 the data has been structured as follows:

1. The Current Account.
2. Net Financial Transactions (on capital account).
3. Change in Official Reserves.
4. Balancing Item.

Table 37.1 shows the United Kingdom's balance of payments for 1988:

1. THE CURRENT ACCOUNT

This account measures the flow of goods and services between the U.K. and her trading partners. As Table 37.1 shows, it is divided into two parts.

Table 37.1: U.K. Balance of Payments 1988.

		£m
A. VISIBLES – Exports (credits)		80,602
– Imports (debits)		− 101,428
		− 20,826
B. INVISIBLES – Exports (credits)		87,233
– Imports (debits)		− 81,024
		+ 6,209

	£m	
of which:		
Services balance	4,165	
Interest, profits, dividends	5,619	
Transfers	− 3,575	
	6,209	

C. CURRENT balance (C = A + B)		− 14,617
D. Transactions in external assets		
Investment overseas by U.K. residents		
Direct	− 15,219	
Portfolio	− 9,718	
Bank lending	− 19,261	
Other lending	− 3,035	
	− 47,233	
E. Transactions in external liabilities		
Investment in U.K. by overseas residents		
Direct	7,346	
Portfolio	4,639	
Bank borrowing	33,856	
Official & other borrowing	6,487	
	52,328	
D + E = Net financial transactions		+ 5,095
F. Changes in official reserves (increase)		− 2,761
G. Balancing item		+ 12,283
		NIL

Source: U.K. Balance of Payments 1989.

a. Visible Trade

This is the term given to the export and import of tangible goods, that is goods that can physically move across frontiers. In the table both are valued at their cost on embarkation or "Free on Board" (F.O.B.). Imports are often recorded with the costs of insurance and transportation added, and this basis is known as "Cost-Insurance-Freight" (C.I.F.).

The difference between the value of visible exports and the value of visible imports is known as the *Visible Trade Balance* or the *Balance of Trade*. The balance of trade is said to be in surplus when visible exports exceed visible imports. If imports exceed exports a deficit is said to exist. Table 37.1 indicates that there was a deficit on visible trade of £20,826 million in 1988.

b. Invisible Trade

The use of the term "balance of trade" to refer solely to trade in goods is somewhat misleading, as trade also involves the purchase and sale of services. If an American tourist comes to London, the effect of his spending here is just as important to the balance of payments as if he purchased British goods in America. In each case the U.K. would gain dollars. However, the accounts treat the former case as an "invisible" item as no goods actually cross national borders.

Invisible exports mainly involve the sale of services by U.K. firms or individuals to foreign residents. Such services include:

(i) The use of British ships and aircraft by foreign companies.
(ii) Foreign firms or individuals using British banks or insurance companies.
(iii) Spending by tourists in the U.K.
(iv) Spending by foreign governments on their embassies in the U.K.

Any profits or dividends flowing into the U.K. are also classed as invisible exports, as are private or government transfers of income.

The purchase of a service abroad by a U.K. resident is classed as an invisible import. Thus any British holidaymakers who venture across the Channel are spending on imports, just as if they had bought French goods in the U.K. The loss of sterling is the same in each case. Payments by the Government to the E.C., or for the upkeep of British troops abroad, would also come under the heading of invisible imports.

Table 37.2 shows the invisible account for 1988 in more detail. The figure for each item represents the net effect on the Balance of Payments. The figures show that the U.K. earns a substantial amount of foreign currency from the sale of financial services. This reflects the importance of the City of London as a major financial centre. Profits, dividends and interest are also in strong surplus, and this is a result of the large sums of British capital invested overseas in the past.

The *current account balance* is arrived at by adding the invisible

Table 37.2: The Invisible Account 1988
(net effect)

	£m
Government services	− 1,833
Sea transport	− 576
Civil aviation	− 862
Travel	− 2,042
Financial & other services	+ 9,478
Profits, dividends and interest	+ 5,619
Transfers	− 3,575
TOTAL INVISIBLE BALANCE	+ 6,209

Source: Balance of Payments C.S.O. 1989.

balance to the balance of trade. In 1988, there was a very unfavourable current account position. It should be clear that a deficit on the balance of trade need not lead to a current account deficit, as an invisible account surplus may offset it. Indeed this has been typical of the U.K. in many post-war years.

2. CAPITAL TRANSACTIONS

International payments also arise from the movement of capital. There are a variety of restrictions on such movements, but in general capital will move to that country where the rate of return is greatest. We can see that over £47 billion of investment funds left the U.K. in 1988. Such investment may be *long term* or *short term*. The former occurs when residents of one country acquire productive resources in another country. This can involve the setting up or purchase of a factory (*direct investment*) or the purchase of shares in an overseas company (*portfolio investment*). Short term flows occur when international currencies are switched from one country to another in pursuit of a higher rate of interest. London is one of the major banking centres in the world, and as a result there is a thriving market in all leading currencies. These short term flows can be extremely volatile and a sudden outflow can have a destabilising effect on the exchange rate. For this reason such funds are often known as "hot money".

Although an outflow of British funds abroad will have a negative effect on the capital account now, it should have a positive effect in the future via the invisible account. By the same token, an inflow of foreign capital will benefit the balance of payments in the short term but will give rise to an outflow of profits and dividends in the long run.

British banks may also borrow and lend in foreign currency and this would be classified in the capital account. The other major item is foreign borrowing by private sector firms and the nationalised industries.

3. OFFICIAL FINANCING

The Balance of Payments is an accounting device and as such it must balance. If a deficit on the current account is not matched by a surplus on the capital transactions, the overall deficit must be paid for. Reserves would have to be run down or foreign currency borrowed from abroad. Similarly, an overall surplus could be used to repay past loans or to increase reserves of foreign currency.

4. BALANCING ITEM

An adjustment known as the *Balancing Item* is also made. This reflects the fact that there are errors and omissions in the figures. Spending by tourists, for example, is estimated using sample surveys and is therefore unlikely to be completely accurate.

The "Balancing Item" has been growing considerably in proportion to the other figures, in recent years. Indeed, the *cumulative* (i.e. unresolved) balancing item since 1975 now amounts (at February 1990) to more than £54 billion. The Bank of England has expressed the belief that the balancing item is made up mostly of unrecorded capital inflows. Whatever the causes of the balancing item, the U.K.'s balance of payments in 1988 was certainly not as bad as it seemed to be. Despite dreadful trade figures, nearly £3 billion was added to the official reserves.

RECENT CHANGES IN THE BALANCE OF PAYMENTS

The U.K. has traditionally run a deficit on visible trade and a surplus on invisible trade. The position of the total current account in any one year simply depended on whether the surplus on the invisible account was large enough to offset the deficit on the visible account.

1. Invisible Trade

There is still a surplus on the invisible account but is falling as a percentage of the total current account. One reason for this is the increasing competition that the City of London faces from the other leading financial capitals. A second reason is that many companies involved in the extraction of North Sea oil are foreign owned, and as a consequence there has been a large outflow of profits and dividends on the invisible account.

2. Capital Flows

Despite the large current account surplus in 1981 the total currency flow was negative. The position in 1982 was similar, and this implies large capital account deficits in each year. An important factor here was the abolition of exchange controls in 1979, which allowed the free flow of British investment funds from the U.K. The subsequent increased acquisition of foreign assets will benefit the economy in the future as profits and dividends flow back to this country.

THE PROBLEM OF A PERSISTENT CURRENT ACCOUNT DEFICIT

A current account deficit means that consumption in the economy is greater than production. A country cannot live beyond its means in such a fashion for any length of time, as the deficit must be paid for.

One method of covering the deficit is to run a capital account surplus. However, this involves costs, as a surplus on the capital account means that foreign residents are acquiring British assets. This will give rise to an outflow of profits and dividends in the future. There is also a danger that foreign companies may close down U.K. subsidiaries with little regard for the effects of such a move on local employment. An additional problem is that interest rates may have to rise to attract foreign funds into the U.K. High interests rates are likely to depress total spending in the economy, thus leading to a fall in output and a rise in unemployment.

If the capital account does not cover the current account deficit the authorities must resort to official financing. This would involve running down reserves or borrowing foreign currency. A loss of reserves cannot continue indefinitely and foreign borrowing means the payment of interest and, in the case of the I.M.F., the possibility of conditions imposed with the loan.

Therefore, most governments will take action if there is a persistent deficit on the current account. This action involves policies to increase the value of exports and to reduce spending on imports.

MEASURES TO DEAL WITH A PERSISTENT DEFICIT

1. Deflation
As the economy expands demand for imports increases. This demand comes from two sources – consumers and firms. Consumers will increase spending on most goods as their income rises, and this will involve imported goods as well as home goods. Firms will be purchasing raw materials to increase production in order to meet this increased demand, and again the level of imports will rise as some raw materials are imported. Thus if the government took measures to reduce total demand

in the economy, spending on imports would also fall. Such a deflation may be induced by an increase in interest rates, a rise in the level of taxation or a reduction in government expenditure.

The main problem with this policy is that home output and employment are also likely to be reduced. If 30 pence in every £1 is spent on imports, a reduction of £1 in income will reduce spending on imports but will also reduce spending on domestic goods by 70 pence. So a deflationary policy imposes severe costs in terms of lower output, lower employment, and reduced growth. Some firms may be able to switch from the depressed home market to foreign markets, but this will take time and involve costs.

2. Currency Depreciation

A currency which falls in value in relation to other currencies is said to have depreciated in value. Such a depreciation reduces the price of exports in terms of foreign currency and increases the cost of imports in terms of the home currency. So if £1 = $2 a British car costing £10,000 will cost $20,000 in the U.S.A. A fall in the value of sterling to £1 = $1.50 will reduce the price of the car to £15,000 in America. Similarly a computer costing $20,000 in the U.S.A. will sell for £10,000 if imported into Britain at the higher rate of exchange, but at £1 = $1.50 it will be sold for £13,333. Therefore the demand for exports is likely to rise and the demand for imports is likely to fall. However, this may not improve the balance of payments as it is the total amount spent on imports and exports which is important, rather than the quantity sold. So the demand for exports has to be elastic, otherwise the reduction in the price of exports will actually reduce total export earnings and make the current account deficit worse. We can see this by extending the above example.

If 100 cars were sold at a price of $20,000 each, total earnings would be $2,000,000. Let us assume that demand is elastic and that when the price falls to $15,000, 200 cars are sold. Total export earnings would now rise to $3,000,000. If, on the other hand, demand was inelastic the number of cars sold might only increase to 120. In this case total export earnings would fall to $1,800,000. Thus the higher the elasticity of demand for exports the better.

Similarly, the higher the elasticity of demand for imports, the greater the fall in total sales of imports following a price rise. Note that in the case of imports, *any* fall in demand will reduce the total amount of foreign currency needed to pay for imported goods. So we can state that, in general, the higher the sum of the elasticities for exports and imports, the more beneficial the effect on the balance of payments of a currency depreciation will be.

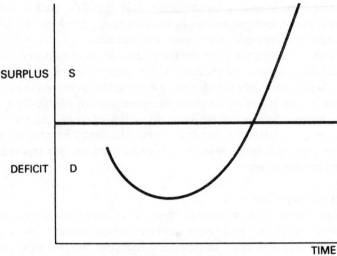

Figure 37.1: The "J" Curve.

Given that the elasticities are favourable, there is still likely to be a time lag between any currency depreciation and its effects on demand. In the short term, therefore, the deficit might actually get worse, as exporters are receiving a lower price for each item sold and importers are paying more for each item purchased. This effect is known as the "J" curve, from the pattern that emerges if the effect of a depreciation on the balance of payments is plotted on a graph. Fig. 37.1 illustrates this.

Other problems can arise which lessen the beneficial effects of a fall in the value of the currency. Many exports have an import content in that some of the raw materials used in production may be purchased from abroad. When sterling falls against other currencies, these imported goods rise in price and will therefore push up the price of the final product. In the same way, labour costs may rise if workers react to higher import prices by asking for higher wages to maintain the real value of their incomes.

A final problem concerns the supply of exports. Firms must have the capacity to increase their output to meet the increased demand from abroad. A currency depreciation is not likely to succeed in improving the current account if there are supply constraints, such as full employment or a shortage of essential raw materials. For this reason deflation often accompanies a currency depreciation, as the government reduces home demand to encourage industry to switch to foreign markets.

3. Import controls

Various methods – quotas, tariffs and exchange controls – can all be used by the authorities in an effort to reduce spending on imports and thereby arrest a decline in the current account. (These are dealt with in Chapter 36.) The problem with such policies is that they cushion ineffici-ent industries from competition and raise the cost of living for the consumer. There is also the possibility of retaliation by those countries affected by the controls, thus cancelling out any advantage gained.

It is clear that all three methods outlined above involve substantial costs to the economy. The only viable long run solution to a persistent current account deficit is to tackle the root cause of the problem. This is that costs per unit of output are too high, thus making imports more attractive than domestic goods and pricing exports out of foreign markets. Only when the population as a whole is prepared to accept that its living standards can only rise as fast as the growth of real output will the balance of payments cease to be a major problem for the policy maker.

QUESTIONS

1. "The balance of payments must always balance." Explain this state-ment.

2. Distinguish between the visible trade balance and the invisible trade balance. Which items contribute most to the U.K.'s surplus on invisible trade?

3. What are the advantages and disadvantages of running a capital account deficit?

4. Explain and account for recent changes in the U.K.'s balance of pay-ments.

5. Why is a persistent current account deficit a problem? What action could the authorities take to improve the current account balance?

6. Account for the growth of international debt in recent years. Why is the size of the debt a problem?

CHAPTER 38

EXCHANGE RATES

INTRODUCTION

In international trade, the exchange of goods gives rise to a complication which is absent from international trade. This is that most countries have their own currencies. In the U.K. goods are exchanged for pounds, in France for francs, and in the U.S.A. the medium of exchange is dollars. Therefore a British firm selling goods in France will normally require payment in sterling since it cannot pay its workforce in francs. This means that the French importer has to exchange francs for sterling, and this requires an *exchange rate*, i.e. the price of one currency expressed in terms of another.

How is this exchange rate determined? One method is to allow the price of the currency to move freely in response to changes in demand and supply. This is known as a *floating* exchange rate. Alternatively, the exchange rate may be *fixed* (usually within certain narrow limits), which means that the government concerned determines the price of the currency. In this chapter we shall examine both approaches and consider the advantages and disadvantages of each.

FLOATING EXCHANGE RATES

Under a floating exchange rate the currency is simply regarded as just another commodity, with its price determined in the foreign exchange market by the forces of demand and supply. Most of the transactions in this market are undertaken over the telephone, with commercial banks, merchant banks and foreign exchange dealers all involved in buying and selling the world's major currencies. Taking sterling as an example, we shall examine how the foreign exchange market would determine the exchange rate of the pound against the dollar.

The export of U.K. goods and services gives rise to a *demand for sterling* on the foreign exchange market. Foreign firms and individuals will require pounds if they wish to import items from this country. Similarly, foreign residents will have to exchange their own currency for sterling if they wish to invest capital in the U.K. One would expect that in both situations the demand for sterling would increase as the price of sterling falls. This gives rise to the conventional downward sloping demand curve. A complication arises here, due to the activity of speculators. These are dealers who, acting for clients or on their own behalf, switch from other currencies into sterling in the hope that the pound is about to rise in value, and so enable them to purchase more of their original currency. In these circumstances the demand for sterling might increase as the price rises, thus giving rise to an upward sloping demand curve. However, the demand for sterling for normal trade purposes is likely to predominate in most cases, and this implies that the demand curve shown is not unreasonable.

A demand for imports in the U.K. will give rise to a supply of pounds on the foreign exchange market, as the appropriate foreign currency will have to be purchased in order to pay for the imports. The purchase of foreign assets by U.K. residents will also give rise to a supply of sterling, and a demand for foreign currency. Again, as in the case of demand, speculators may also supply sterling if they fear a fall in the exchange rate against other currencies. Normally one expects the supply of a good to rise as the price rises, but in this case the supply curve could be upward or downward sloping, depending on the elasticity of demand for imports. As sterling rises in value, the price of imports falls, thus leading to a rise in demand. However, if demand is inelastic the total spent on imports will decline, and this means a reduction in the supply of sterling necessary to pay for the imports.

The exchange rate for the pound against the dollar can now be determined. It will simply be that rate at which dealers on the foreign exchange market find that the demand for sterling equals the supply. In Figure 38.1 we can see that this will be at a rate of £1 = $1.50. At an exchange rate above this, dealers will find that they have an excess of sterling on their hands, and will reduce the price in order to sell these additional pounds. At an exchange rate below the equilibrium price, dealers will find that an unsatisfied demand exists, and so they will bid up the rate in order to bring more sterling onto the market. Therefore, in a free market, the price of sterling against other currencies will be that price at which the demand for sterling equals the supply.

Fluctuations in the exchange rate will occur if the demand or supply of sterling changes. The value sterling will fall against other currencies (a *depreciation* in the exchange rate) if the supply of sterling increases at the existing rate of exchange. Such an increase might be caused by a rise in the demand for imports or an increase in the rare of interest abroad. Conversely, the pound will rise in value on the foreign exchange market (an *appreciation* in the exchange rate) if the demand for sterling increases

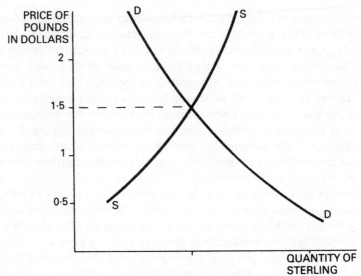

Figure 38.1: The Market Price for Sterling.

at the existing equilibrium rate. A rise in the U.K. interest rates relative to other countries or an increase in exports would bring forth such an increase in demand. In general, a balance of payments surplus will cause an appreciation in the exchange rate and a deficit will cause a depreciation in the exchange rate.

FIXED EXCHANGE RATES

Floating exchange rates have been the exception rather than the rule in the twentieth century. However, there have been two distinct systems of fixed exchange rates and we shall examine each in turn.

1. The Gold Standard

For most of the nineteenth century, and the early part of the twentieth century, the value of the major world currencies has been fixed in terms of gold. Each country was also prepared to exchange its currency for this given quantity of gold, thereby effectively determining the value of one currency in terms of another. So in 1900, the Bank of England would have exchanged about $\frac{1}{4}$ oz. gold for £1 sterling and the U.S.A. would have exchanged $\frac{1}{20}$ oz. gold for one dollar. Therefore, one pound was worth around five dollars, and if the exchange rate moved from this value gold would be shipped from one country to another, so re-establishing the equilibrium rate.

In theory, such an exchange rate system leads to an automatic correction of any balance of payments disequilibrium. Let us assume that the U.K. has a deficit on its trade with the U.S.A. There would be an outflow of gold from the U.K. to pay for this deficit. As the money supply is backed by gold in each country, there will be an expansion of the supply of money in America and a contraction of the money supply in the U.K. From the Quantity Theory of Money we remember that prices move in proportion to the amount of money in circulation. Thus there will be a rise in prices in the surplus country and a fall in prices in the deficit country. This would result in a rise in demand for U.K. goods and a fall in demand for American products, thereby eliminating the deficit on U.K. trade with the U.S.A.

The adjustment process outlined above never worked as smoothly in practice as the example implies. One problem stemmed from the fact that prices tend to be rather "sticky" downwards, and as a result it was output and employment that fell in deficit countries. This meant that the elimination of a deficit might be a long and painful process. Another difficulty was that surplus countries were often reluctant to inflate their economies following an inflow of gold, thereby prolonging the basic imbalance in price levels which had led to the original disequilibrium.

The gold standard collapsed in the early 1930s, when many countries suspended the outflow of gold in the face of severe unemployment. The U.K. was no exception, going off the gold standard in 1931.

2. The Bretton Woods System

In 1944 the allied nations met at Bretton Woods in New Hampshire, to try to organise a system of exchange rates which would be stable enough to encourage a growth in international trade after the war, and flexible enough to avoid the problems that had led to the collapse of the gold standard.

A system of managed exchange rates emerged, under the auspices of the newly created International Monetary Fund (I.M.F.). All currencies were to be fixed in value in relation to the dollar, which in turn was fixed in terms of gold, with the authorities in the U.S.A. willing to exchange gold for dollars. So the dollar was "as good as gold" and as a result it became acceptable in exchange in international trade. Each government could allow fluctuations of 1 per cent each side of the par or "peg" value, but was expected to prevent movements outside these limits. Adjustments in the exchange rates were allowed if a "fundamental disequilibrium" emerged in a country's balance of payments, with an upward change known as a *revaluation* and a downward change known as a *devaluation*. The I.M.F. was also willing to lend foreign currency to any country experiencing temporary payments difficulties, obtaining the finance by levying a "quota" on member countries. It was hoped that such a facility would avoid the necessity of frequent changes in exchange rates.

The "adjustable peg" system worked very well in the next twenty years. Indeed, many economists argue that the sustained growth in living standards experienced by the developed world in this period can be attributed to the rapid expansion of world trade, which in turn was greatly aided by stability in the exchange rate markets. The Bretton Woods system began to show signs of strain in the late 1960s, and finally came to an end in 1971, when the U.S.A. suspended the convertibility of the dollar. Finance ministers of the major economies met at the Smithsonian Institute in Washington in December 1971, in a last-ditch attempt to save the fixed exchange rates, but by the end of 1972 most exchange rates were floating.

The collapse of the "adjustable peg" system was inevitable, as it was based on a fundamental contradiction. This centred on the role of the dollar within the system. On the one hand, an increasing supply of dollars was needed to finance the rapid growth in world trade, as it was the main medium of exchange between countries. On the other hand, the dollar was also the main reserve currency, held because governments had confidence that it would keep its value. A persistent deficit on the American balance of payments was necessary if the supply of dollars was to increase, but this conflicted with the dollar's role as a store of value. So for the system to work the dollar had to be both plentiful in supply *and* scarce, an obvious impossibility!

Several other factors were involved. It had been hoped that countries with persistent balance of payments surpluses would revalue their currencies, and that those experiencing prolonged deficits would devalue. However, countries in the first group, notably Japan and West Germany, were reluctant to remove the advantage that an undervalued currency gave them in world markets. Similarly, some countries in the second category, like the U.K., refused to devalue because they were convinced that such a move amounted to some kind of national disgrace. Heavy deficits and surpluses existed for long period as a result of this unexpected rigidity in the system.

FIXED OR FLOATING EXCHANGE RATES?

The question now arises: which system of exchange rates is preferable? Each has its advantages and disadvantages.

(a) The Advantages Of Floating Exchange Rates

The main advantages of floating exchange rates is that they remove the balance of payments as a policy problem. The currency will automatically move to a price which keeps the balance of payments in equilibrium. If there is an excess of imports over exports, there will be a corresponding excess supply of sterling at the existing exchange rate. The exchange rate will depreciate as a result, making exports cheaper and imports dearer. This will cause a rise in demand for exports and a fall in demand for imports, thereby removing the deficit on the balance of payments.

It should be noted that equilibrium in the balance of payments does not mean that the current account will be balanced, as it is the overall currency flow which determines the exchange rate. In addition, a change in the value of the currency on the foreign exchange market will change the terms of trade, and the response of the volume of goods sold depends upon the relevant elasticities. So it is possible that a deficit or surplus may not be eliminated for some time.

A second advantage of a floating exchange rate is that the country concerned can pursue an independent monetary policy. It has no need to keep reserves of foreign currency and this means that the domestic money supply will be unaffected by changes in reserves.

(b) The Disadvantages Of Floating Exchange Rates

A major disadvantage of floating exchange rates is that they increase the risks involved in international trade. Under this system, a buyer purchasing goods from abroad has two prices to watch – the foreign price of the commodity *and* the price of the foreign currency. For example, let us assume that one pound currently exchanges for two dollars, and that a British firm is purchasing goods from America at $200 each. Therefore, the British firm will have to pay £100 to import the goods. If the exchange rate suddenly fell to, say, one pound equals one dollar and fifty cents, the firm would have to provide £133·33 to import the same items. So the existence of the possibility of a sudden change in the exchange rate adds uncertainty to the business of exporting and importing. Critics of floating exchange rates claim that this will reduce the total volume of trade, and thereby reduce the benefits arising from the theory of comparative advantage.

Traders can reduce the risk of adverse movements in the exchange rate by dealing in the *forward market*. This is a market in which people agree to exchange currency at a future date (e.g. three months) at a fixed rate. So in our example, the British firm could be certain of the price they must pay by buying dollars now, for delivery in the future. Traders will usually have to pay a higher price for foreign currency delivered in the future, but the additional cost can be regarded as an insurance premium against the possibility of losses, due to fluctuations in the external value of the currency.

A second disadvantage of floating exchange rates is that speculative buying and selling may cause large fluctuations in the value of the currency. If, for example, it is felt that a currency is overvalued, dealers will begin to reduce the price on the foreign exchange markets. However, this may develop into a wave of speculative selling, thereby driving the exchange rate down very quickly. Some economists argue that speculators perform a useful function, in that they are always willing to make a market in a currency, and that this will actually reduce fluctuations in the exchange rate. This may be true in the long run, but at times a "herd" instinct appears to operate in the market, leading to sudden changes in the price of a currency for no apparent reason.

A third disadvantage follows from this. A fall in the exchange rate may set up a vicious spiral, whereby inflation rises as a result of the currency depreciation, so giving rise to a further wave of selling on the foreign exchange market, which in turn gives a further push to inflation, and so on. The authorities may have to take drastic action, in such circumstances, to convince the market that inflation will be brought under control.

(c) The Advantages Of Fixed Exchange Rates

The first advantage of fixed exchange rates is that they impose a degree of certainty in international payments, removing the risk of loss due to unexpected changes in the foreign exchange price of a good. If a holidaymaker is planning to go to Italy in six months time, he has a problem when exchange rates are floating – whether to purchase lira now, in case the pound depreciates, or to wait, in the hope that he will be able to obtain a better exchange rate in the future. This is not a problem under fixed exchange rates, as the rate will be the same in six months as it is today.

Advocates of fixed exchange rates also stress the degree of discipline which this imposes on governments. If the authorities inflate the economy too quickly, inflation is likely to rise, as well as spending on imports. The balance of payments will go into deficit as a result, forcing the government to take measures to reduce demand in the economy. If the exchange rate was floating, no such pressure would have existed, as the currency would have fallen in value and this would have remedied the payments deficit. The *purchasing power theory* of exchange rate determination underlines this approach. This states that the exchange rate will eventually adjust to take account of variations in inflation between countries.

If one pound currently exchanges against two dollars, and the price level in the U.K. now doubles, the pound will fall in value until a new exchange rate of one pound equals one dollar is established. Therefore, it is argued, if a country wants to maintain the external value of its currency, it must ensure that its inflation rate is no higher than that of its major competitors.

(d) The Disadvantages Of Fixed Exchange Rates

To remedy a balance of payments deficit, a country must reduce the price of its goods and services in relation to its main competitors. There are two methods of achieving this. The first method is to reduce the value of the currency abroad, thereby reducing prices *externally*. The second method is the one adopted under fixed exchange rates, and that is to deflate the economy in order to influence the *internal* price level. This deflation, as we saw in Chapter 37, imposes costs in terms of output and employment. Therefore, advocates of floating exchange rates stress that fixed exchange rates may make the balance of payments a major policy constraint, particularly if the government is prepared to defend the existing rate at all costs. This seems to have been the case with the Labour Government from 1964 to 1967, who ran the economy at a level below capacity, in order to cure a balance of payments deficit. The pound was eventually devalued, but the economy's growth rate suffered from the authorities' willingness to persevere with an overvalued exchange rate.

A second criticism of fixed exchange rates is once again concerned with the activities of speculators. When exchange rates are fixed, and are seen to be overvalued, speculators cannot lose in that the exchange rate has to fall eventually. So if they sell at the existing rate they may force a devaluation, enabling them to make a capital gain when the currency is bought back at a lower price. If the central bank resists the pressure, the speculator has lost nothing in that he can buy the currency again at the same price. This contrasts with speculation under a floating exchange rate, where the number guessing the movement of the rate correctly will be matched by those who guessed wrongly.

"DIRTY FLOATING"

Although most exchange rates are no longer fixed, they are not allowed to float freely on foreign exchange markets. Governments intevene to prevent undue fluctuations in the value of the currency. If the authorities wish to prevent a rise in the exchange rate they must be prepared to mop up the excess demand for the currency by supplying more of it at the

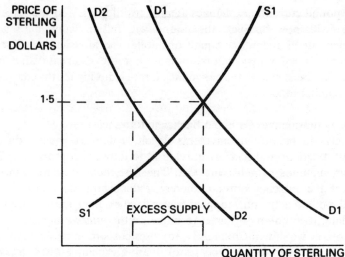

Figure 38.2: Intervention in the Foreign Exchange Market.

existing exchange rate. Conversely, the government must be prepared to buy up any excess supply of the currency if they wish to prevent a fall in the exchange rate. This last case is illustrated in Figure 38.2.

The equilibrium exchange rate in the market is £1 = $1.50, where the demand curve D_1D_1 meets the original supply curve S_1S_1. We now assume that the demand for sterling falls (perhaps due to a fall in demand for exports) and that the new demand curve is D_2D_2. It is clear that there is an excess supply of sterling at the existing exchange rate, and that in a free market the currency would depreciate. If the authorities wish to maintain the original rate they must be prepared to purchase this excess supply by selling dollars from the official reserves.

This example shows the limitations on a government's ability to maintain an exchange rate in the face of market pressure for a change. Reserves must run out eventually, thereby removing the authorities' means of supporting the currency. So governments are likely to enter the market in cases where there are temporary fluctuations in the exchange rate, rather than set out to defend a particular value of the currency at all costs.

THE EUROPEAN MONETARY SYSTEM

As it became evident that the era of managed exchanged rates was over, the countries in the E.C. began to fear the consequences of freely floating currencies. They were particularly concerned that the payments system implicit in the Common Agricultural Policy (C.A.P.) would prove unworkable if the value of each currency was continually changing. So in March 1972, they adopted a regime of fixed exchange rates within the E.C., with each currency allowed to move a maximum of 2·25 per cent from the par value. Movements beyond this limit were to be prevented by government intervention in the market. The system was known as the "snake", because the European currencies could slither up and down in value against the other world currencies.

The scheme proved unworkable, with the U.K. pulling out within two months and the franc and lira leaving in the next two years. The main problem stemmed from the fact that currencies cannot be fixed in value against each other if the economies of the countries concerned are performing differently. If one member is experiencing lower inflation and faster growth than its neighbours, that country's currency is inevitably going to rise in value against the other currencies. In this case it was the mark which proved to be the currency in demand, with the result that the other governments had to continually defend their currencies by intervening in the foreign exchange markets, as described in Figure 38.2. It is hardly surprising that most of those concerned gave up and left the "snake".

In 1978 the E.C. countries decided to try again. This time each currency was to be fixed in value against a "basket" of other currencies, rather than fixed in value against each other. It was hoped that this would minimize the damage if one currency proved to be in great demand, as it would only be part of the "basket" and sudden price movements would thus be dampened down. This "basket" of currencies was the basis of the European Currency Unit (Ecu) whose role originally was to be that of a unit of account within the E.C., with the possibility of its developing as a medium of exchange between member states.

From 13 March 1979, each country was expected to maintain a fixed rate between its currency and the Ecu. Fluctuations of up to $2\frac{1}{4}$ per cent each side of parity were allowed, with Italy given slightly wider limits. The new Exchange Rate Mechanism (E.R.M.) is the major part of the European Monetary System (E.M.S.), and it has worked surprisingly well, only one major re-alignment of the exchange rates being needed in 1983.

Although the U.K. is a member of the E.M.S., the Government has not yet decided to join the E.R.M. It was felt that the pound might have come under speculative pressure, forcing the authorities to constantly run down reserves to maintain the pound's value in the system, and to deflate the economy in order to prevent balance of payments problems.

More recently, there have been moves within the E.C. for achieving closer monetary union. Following discussion of the Delors Report in June 1989, a three-stage approach to European Monetary Union (E.M.U.) was agreed by the Council of Ministers. The first stage was aimed at establishing a single market in goods, services and capital (see Chapter 40). A prerequisite would be that all member states would be required to take part in the E.R.M. of the E.M.S. The first stage should begin on 1 July 1990, though no date was fixed for its completion.

The E.M.S. is essentially a system of fixed parities between the exchange rates of the E.C. member countries. Its basis is the Ecu, a weighted index of the currencies of E.C. countries including the U.K. Each currency has a central rate, expressed in Ecus, and the central bank concerned must maintain the value of its currency within $2\frac{1}{4}$ per cent either side of this value. When a currency reaches the limit of this margin the relevant central bank must take action to move towards its central rate, with other member countries assisting by changing the value of their own currencies.

Since such adjustments involve the buying and selling of currencies, each country deposits 20 per cent of its gold and currency reserves with the European Monetary Co-operation Fund (E.M.C.F.) in exchange for Ecus with which to assist its currency and the currency of others. The E.M.C.F. will provide loans of varying duration to member countries to enable them to buy back their currency if it falls below its central rate. The parities are formally fixed although they can be renegotiated to allow for different trading situations and parities are changed by agreement of all members.

Factors favouring participation in the E.R.M. can be stated as follows:

(a) Trade will be facilitated through the greater stability in exchange rates.
(b) Speculation against E.C. currencies may be less de-stabilising; the drastic devaluations associated with previous fixed exchange systems (e.g. Bretton Woods) can be avoided.
(c) Financial discipline will be imposed upon the member governments by the need to keep within the E.M.S. parities.
(d) Multilateral action to stabilise exchange rates will be less harmful than the use of high interest rates or market intervention when one country has to stabilise its currency alone.

The arguments against U.K. participation in the E.R.M. may be stated thus:

(a) Loss of control by the U.K. Government over monetary policy in the attempt to maintain exchange rate stability and parity. Thus, if the U.K. faces inflation and exchange rate appreciation, the authorities might be obliged to cut interest rates to reduce the exchange rate at the expense of higher inflation.

(b) The use of a floating exchange rate to restore balance of payments equilibrium would be lost forever.

(c) The factors affecting sterling are greater than those affecting the rest of the E.C. currencies: for example, the status of sterling as a petrocurrency and the U.K.'s continued trade with non-E.C. countries, especially those from the Commonwealth.

Time and again the U.K. government's view has been that the it will do so when the "time is right". It wants to see structural changes in the U.K. sufficiently advanced and the U.K. inflation rate much lower in line with that of the other leading E.C. countries. Specifically, it has been stated Britain will not join the E.R.M. until:

- the U.K. inflation rate is significantly lower;
- there is freedom of capital movement in the Community;
- real progress has been made towards completion of the single market;
- there is freedom of financial services and strengthened competition policy.

THE INTERNATIONAL MONETARY FUND

The I.M.F. was originally founded to "facilitate the expansion and balanced growth of international trade", and to "promote exchange rate stability and maintain orderly exchange arrangements among members". Although the emergence of floating exchange rates has rendered the latter aim redundant, it still plays a vital role in promoting trade expansion by enabling countries with balance of payments difficulties to borrow foreign exchange. Without this facility, those countries with payments problems would resort to the various barriers to trade discussed in Chapter 36.

The Fund now has over 150 members, and each pays a quota which is determined by its share of world output and trade. Members pay in their own currency an amount equal to 75 per cent of quota, and the remaining 25 per cent in reserve assets. Each country can then draw foreign exchange to meet balance of payments difficulties. The first 25 per cent of the quota can be drawn without conditions, but any borrowing above this carries increasingly rigorous conditions. These are designed to support the members' efforts to reduce balance of payments deficits,

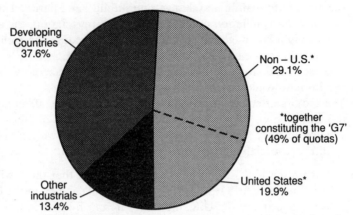

Figure 38.3: I.M.F. members and their quotas, as per cent of total.

Source: Economist, 6 February 1988.

and usually include measures to deflate the economy concerned along with the depreciation of the exchange rate. The I.M.F. has therefore acquired the reputation of a policeman, particularly in the third world, in that governments which have allowed the economy to go out of control have been forced by the I.M.F. to remedy the situation.

Quotas are reviewed every five years, and are important as they determine voting rights as well as the amount of foreign currency that can be borrowed. The U.K.'s share of the Fund's resources has steadily declined, reflecting the decline in the U.K.'s share of world trade. The U.S.A. now has 19·9 per cent of the votes, instead of the 32 per cent it had in 1952, but this understates its importance in the I.M.F., since a majority of 85 per cent is required for most decision, so giving the United States a veto.

An important achievement of the I.M.F. has been the creation of an artificial currency to finance expanding international trade, namely the Special Drawing Rights (S.D.R.s). These were introduced in 1970, because fears were expressed that there was a danger of a shortage of world liquidity, and that it was unwise to rely on a steadily increasing supply of dollars to finance the growth of trade. S.D.R.s are reserve currencies in themselves, and member countries can transfer them to pay for international debts. S.D.R.s are now made up of a combination of five of the world's major currencies: the dollar, the yen, the pound, the franc and the mark. The S.D.R. is important because it was the first form of international money which is independent of the supply of gold in the world, or the amount of any one currency in existence.

In conclusion, it may be instructive to put the I.M.F.'s role as an international source of loans in perspective, by comparing it with the world's major banks. In terms of outstanding international loans in 1981, it ranked as the twenty-eighth largest bank with outstanding loans of $14 billion. However, most of this lending is to the non-oil developing countries, many of whom would find it very difficult to borrow from the commercial banking system given the experience of the banks during the 1970s and 1980s.

QUESTIONS

1. Explain how the value of sterling on the foreign exchange market is determined.

2. How did the gold standard operate? What problems prevented the elimination of balance of payments deficits under this system?

3. Explain how the "adjustable peg" system worked. Why did it break down?

4. Compare the advantages and disadvantages of fixed and floating exchange rates.

5. How might the U.K. authorities prevent a fall in the value of sterling against other currencies? Is there any limit to intervention by the authorities?

6. Examine the arguments for and against the U.K.'s membership of the E.M.S.

CHAPTER 39

THE INTERNATIONAL DEBT PROBLEM

In the 1980s much attention focused on the external debt problem that confronts many poor countries. The two main groups of countries which have faced serious problems in servicing debt are the "middle income debtors", and the much poorer countries of sub-Saharan African.

The middle income debtors are Argentina, Bolivia, Brazil, Chile, Colombia, Ecuador, Ivory Coast, Mexico, Morocco, Nigeria, Peru, the Philippines, Uruguay, Venezuela, and Yugoslavia.

Sub-Saharan Africa includes all African countries south of the Sahara, with the exception of Nigeria, the Ivory Coast, Namibia and South Africa.

Table 39.1: The main borrowers.

	Total debt end 1985 $bn	Debt per head (1985 $)	G.D.P. per head (1985 $)
15 middle income debtors	449	840	1,450
Sub-Saharan Africa	73	220	280

Source: Economic Progress Report, July 1987.

Table 39.2 sets out debt owed to the main creditors by the most important debtors.

Table 39.2: The main creditors and debtors ($bn end 1985).

	Multi-lateral agencies	I.M.F.	O.E.C.D. countries Banks	Export credits	Official aid	Other	Total
15 middle income debtors	32	17	308	52	10	30	449
Sub-Saharan Africa	16	6	13	19	8	11	73

Source: Economic Progress Report, July 1987.

A large part of the total outstanding debt is owed to various American and European banks. The main worry is that the sheer size of the sums involved will result in a default by a major borrower. Such an occurrence would lead to the insolvency of some of the world's largest commercial banks. The consequences of banks failures on such a scale could include a massive fall in employment and world trade. The 1930s, saw just such a sequence of events, and a repetition must be avoided.

THE GROWTH OF INTERNATIONAL DEBT

Bank lending to these poorer countries had increased steadily in the 1960s and 1970s, for a number of reasons.

1. Developing countries needed foreign capital to finance development programmes, as their own financial markets could not generate the sums required. A substantial amount of this capital was used to build up the infrastructure, including spending on roads, railways and power supplies.

2. The 1970s saw two major oil price rises, in 1973 and 1979. In both instances the non-oil developing countries were left with huge balance of payments deficits, as they could not reduce their demand for oil in the short term. The balance of payments must always balance, as we have already noted, and so the deficits on current account were financed by foreign borrowing on the capital account.

3. A high proportion of this foreign borrowing was from commercial banks, who were increasingly willing to lend in currencies other than their own domestic currency. It must be remembered that the counterpart to the non-oil countries deficits were the huge surpluses of the oil exporting countries. The latter were deposited with the international commercial banks, thus providing them with the funds to lend. This process became known as "re-cycling".

The debt problem worsened considerably in the 1980s, as two other factors emerged, both connected with the second major oil price rise.

4. The developed countries reacted to the increased price of energy by deflating their economies to prevent inflation. This resulted in a fall in output and employment in most of them. Consequently, world trade declined and the Third World countries, in particular, found that they could not generate sufficient funds from exports to re-pay past borrowings.

5. Over eighty per cent of foreign debt is denominated in dollars, and a significant part of the loans were at variable interest rates. This meant that debtor countries were dealt a double blow when the United States decided to adopt a stricter monetary policy in 1981. The resultant rise in interest rates also led to a significant rise in the value of the dollar against other currencies. So debtor countries not only had to pay more

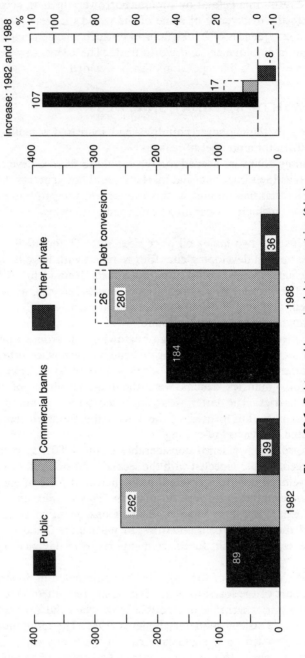

Figure 39.1: Debt owed by main debtor countries ($ bn).

Source: Institute of International Finance.

in interest, they also had to pay more of their own currency to acquire the necessary dollars.

MIDDLE INCOME DEBTOR COUNTRIES

Since 1982, the exposure of commercial banks to the major debtors has risen by 17 per cent (after allowing for the debt reduction that has taken place, mainly via debt/equity swaps). But the exposure of governments, export credit agencies and international financial institutions has risen by 107 per cent: see Figure 39.1.

At meetings of the I.M.F. and the World Bank in 1988, agreement was reached on development of a strategy in relation to middle income debtors, to place more emphasis on debt reduction. It was stated that the primary responsibility for solving their economic problems must be with the debtor countries themselves ". . . through fundamental domestic economic reforms."

The increased exposure of governments, together with the I.M.F. and the World Bank had provided an injection of funds enabling the banks to rebuild their balance sheets while receiving interest payments virtually in full. The next phase of the debt strategy was intended to lead to actual debt reduction.

PROSPECTS

The international banking community has so far managed with some financial assistance to deal with the problem and widespread debt repudiation has been avoided. The banks have been increasingly willing to re-schedule debts, rather than call a default on a loan. However, the possibility of defaults remain, with all the uncertainty that this entails for international financial order. This is because debtor countries must adopt deflationary policies to reduce their import bills and generate revenue from exports. The resulting social pressures on governments could prove intolerable, with populist movements coming to power with a mandate to repudiate all international debts.

QUESTIONS

1. What are the chief causes of the international debt problem?
2. In determining whether to increase lending to a particular country what factors would the lender pay regard to as most important?

CHAPTER 40

THE EUROPEAN COMMUNITY

In a previous chapter we saw that the E.C. is the largest market for British exports, and that it has grown in importance in this role in the last eighteen years. In this chapter we shall examine the E.C. in some detail, bringing out the advantages and disadvantages of Britain's membership. The discussion will concentrate on the economic implications of the E.C., as an analysis of the political consequences of membership is beyond the scope of this study.

ORIGINS AND DEVELOPMENT

In 1952, Belgium, Holland, Luxembourg, Italy, France and Germany joined together to form the European Coal and Steel Community. Its aim was to promote industrial expansion by creating a common market in coal and steel, free from any restrictions on movement of these goods between member states. Encouraged by the success of this venture, the "Six" decided to extend the notion of a "common market" to include *all* goods and services traded. In 1957 they signed the Treaty of Rome, establishing the European Economic Community.* Its aims were:

  1. The elimination of customs duties and quotas between member states.
  2. The establishment of a common tariff against goods from outside the Market.
  3. The free movement of the factors of production within the E.C.
  4. Common policies for agriculture, transport and competition.

The U.K. declined to join the E.C. at its inception, but by the early 1960s opinion in the U.K. had moved closer towards the idea of membership. However, it was not until 1 January 1973 that the U.K. became a member, along with the Irish Republic and Denmark. Greece joined in 1981, bringing the community up to ten member states and by early 1985 the chief barriers to the admission of Spain and Portugal had been overcome.

---

* The word "Economic" was later deleted reflecting the E.C.'s wider aims.

THE INSTITUTIONS OF THE EUROPEAN COMMUNITY

1. The Council Of Ministers
This is the main decision making body in the E.C. Each country is directly represented by a government minister at all meetings of the Council, with the nature of the meeting determining which particular ministry is represented, e.g. agriculture ministers when farm policies are on the agenda, finance ministers when economic affairs are being discussed, and so on. Decisions on all essential matters have to be unanimous, giving each country a veto on major policy decisions. This often leads to situations where one country may be willing to support another on a particular vote, in return for similar support on another issue.

2. The Commission
The Commission is charged with ensuring that approved policies are actually carried out, and it employs civil servants for this purpose. In addition, the Commission is expected to draft policy and present ideas to the Council. The commissioners themselves are appointed for four years from within the member states, and are expected to look after the interests of the E.C. as a whole, rather than to represent particular national interests.

3. The Parliament
This is mainly a consultative body, directly elected by the voters in each member state. It can question the Commission and the Council on their activities, but in practice it tends to have little direct influence over the decision makers.

4. The Court Of Justice
The Court is completely independent of member states and from the other institutions. It interprets community law, and its decisions override any one country's decisions. Individuals and institutions can appeal to it for judgement.

EXPENDITURE AND REVENUE

The E.C. is intended to be self-financing, in that revenue from member states is derived on the basis of an agreed formula, and that this is sufficient to cover total spending in any one year. The main areas of expenditure are:

1. The Common Agricultural Policy (C.A.P.)

This accounts for the bulk of Community spending. Guaranteed prices are set for various commodities, and the authorities are pledged to intervene in the market to prevent prices falling below these guaranteed levels. This usually means the purchase of excess supply by the Community, and its storage awaiting a rise in price, or its export to markets outside the E.C. Duties are also levied on foodstuffs entering the E.C., in order to bring prices up to the levels operating in the Community. In this way farmers are protected from the wild swings in prices which usually characterise agricultural markets. It is also hoped that this will encourage investment in the agricultural sector and so lead to growth in long term productivity. To this end, financial assistance is also given to farmers for drainage schemes and the consolidation of holdings into larger units.

Table 40.1: The European Community Budget (% of total).

	1981	1987
EXPENDITURE		
Agriculture	66·0	61·4
Regional Aid	10·6	8·9
Development Aid	4·3	2·6
Social Fund	3·9	6·9
Administration	3·7	4·7
Other (incl. research)	11·5	15·5
REVENUE		
VAT contributions	49·9	62·8
Customs duties	34·7	26·8
Agricultural levies	9·5	5·7
Other (incl. surplus from previous year)	5·9	4·7

Source: Europa Year Books, 1983 and 1988.

2. The Social Fund

This exists to mitigate the effects of the reallocation of resources which inevitably follow the development of the Community. Financial aid is given to schemes which help to retrain workers whose previous skills are now obsolete.

3. Regional Development

The Community has set up an Investment Bank, whose function is to finance regional development and to assist with modernisation programmes.

4. Administration

Funds have to be set aside to cover the running costs of the community, including the salaries of the civil servants employed by the Commission, the salaries of the members of the European Parliament and the staff of the Council of Ministers.

There are three main sources of revenue to finance the above expenditure. Each country has to pay into the Community budget an amount equal to 1 per cent of its VAT revenues, alongside all customs duties levied on goods entering the E.C., and any funds raised by imposing taxes on imported foodstuffs. Such a formula for payments ensures that those countries with the largest incomes will pay the largest contributions, although the *net* contribution obviously depends upon how much each country benefits from Community expenditure in relation to this contribution.

U.K. MEMBERSHIP: THE ADVANTAGES

1. Economics Of Scale

The total population of the E.C. is over three hundred and twenty million, which is nearly six times the total population of the U.K. This means that each firm in the U.K. has a much larger potential market,

Table 40.2: Markets compared.

	European Community	U.S.A.	Japan	U.K.
Population (million)	324	246	123	57
G.D.P. (billion Ecu)	3,856	3,993	2,205	608

Source: Economic Progress Report, October 1988.

where freedom of access is guaranteed. Given such a market, firms can produce at output levels which give rise to greater economies of scale. So consumers should benefit from the lower costs that result.

2. Greater Scope For Specialisation

The creation of a free trade area allows more scope for the application of the principle of comparative advantage. The production of particular commodities can now be concentrated in those areas best suited to it, rather than the situation existing before the formation of the E.C., where production was duplicated in each country under widely different degrees of efficiency.

3. Increased Competition

The removal of tariff barriers exposes the industries in each country to a much greater degree of competition. Although this has its disadvantages it may stimulate the creation of a more efficient industrial sector, as firms abandon the "sleepy" outlook which lack of direct competition encourages.

4. Aid To The Regions

If faster economic growth does result from the formation of a free trade area in Europe, it is argued that this provides greater opportunities to channel resources into those regions of the Community which have incomes per head well below the E.C. average. Without the stimulus to growth which the Community provides, the rate of expansion of each country alone would be insufficient to provide the level of aid required.

THE U.K. MEMBERSHIP: THE DISADVANTAGES

1. Some Loss of Economic Freedom

Apart from the arguments concerning the loss of political sovereignty which membership gave rise to, the U.K. has forfeited some independence in economic policy. This is most apparent in relation to the balance of payments. One method of curing a persistent deficit is to impose tariffs and quotas on imports. This is obviously not a policy option with regard to any fellow member of the Community.

2. Higher Food Prices

As we have seen, the Community guarantees certain agricultural prices and taxes any imported foodstuffs to bring prices up to the levels existing in the E.C. Consumers suffer from this policy if world food prices are lower than the guaranteed prices. This has generally been the case for most foodstuffs, as the prices paid to farmers are often set at a level which keeps the inefficient in production.

3. Trade Diversion

The creation of a free trade area with a common external tariff (a customs union) should lead to an expansion in international trade. However, if the common tariff is too high, it merely protects the inefficient producers within the E.C. from the competition of the more efficient producers outside the customs union. This is known as trade diversion, and will result in a loss of welfare as imports are diverted from low cost to high cost sources. The operation of the Common Agricultural Policy (C.A.P.) may result in such welfare losses.

4. The U.K. Contribution

The U.K. has emerged as the second largest net contributor, even though it is seventh in terms of income per head within the Community. There are two main reasons for this imbalance, one concerned with the revenue side and one connected with Community spending. To take the

Table 40.3: United Kingdom's
net contributions to the E.C.
(£ million).

Year	Net contribution (credits *less* debits)
1978	1,364
1979	1,626
1980	1,783
1981	2,188
1982	2,878
1983	2,994
1984	3,213
1985	3,804
1986	2,812
1987	4,066
1988	3,556

Source: U.K. Balance of Payments 1989.

latter first, it was pointed out that the bulk of E.C. spending is on the C.A.P. (about 60 pence in every £). Britain has a very small but efficient farming industry in relation to the other eleven member states, with only about 3 per cent of the working population employed in agriculture. As a result the U.K. receives far less direct benefits from the operation of the C.A.P. than those countries with a large proportion of the population involved in agriculture.

On the revenue side, Britain still imports a greater supply of foodstuffs from outside the E.C. than the other member states. This means that the U.K. has to levy taxes on these imports to a greater degree than other countries, and the proceeds from these taxes are paid into the Community budget. This, combined with the reason outlined above, explains why Britain remains a net contributor to the community.

"1992" – A SINGLE EUROPEAN MARKET

As the 1980s progressed it became increasingly recognised that insufficient had been done to weld member states' individual markets into one growing and flexible market in which resources are used to greatest advantage. The European Commission therefore drew up a programme of measures to achieve this. The wide-ranging programme includes, inter alia:

– creating open markets in information technology and communications;
– removing all remaining controls on capital movements;

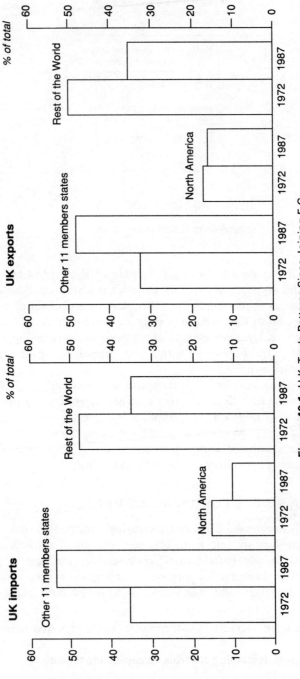

Figure 40.1: U.K. Trade Patterns Since Joining E.C.

Source: Economic Progress Report, October 1988.

- removing artificial barriers to trade resulting from differences in trade mark and patent laws; and
- removing frontier controls, subject to retaining necessary safeguards for security, social or health reasons.

Agreement has already been reached which will lead to:

- abolition of exchange controls throughout the Community (the U.K. effectively abolished these in 1979);
- professional people being able to practice in other member states without having to requalify every time;
- removal of barriers to the provision of non-life insurance services in other member states; and
- abolition of permits and quotas in the road haulage industry.

The practical implementation of these measures will require several years. Closer monetary union is also a key part of the proposals: these have been outlined in Chapter 37.

As a whole, benefits are likely to be felt over time in terms of increased growth, lower prices and higher employment. The European Commission has estimated that there could be a net increase over a period of years of around 2 million jobs throughout the Community.

There is much disagreement as to how the various aims might be achieved. In general, the U.K. Government believes that individual measures should be designed and influenced within a clear framework which allows markets as much freedom as possible and avoids unnecessary bureaucratic intervention. Thus, in relation to the proposed harmonisation of VAT and excise duty rates, the U.K. Government consider that the Commission's proposals are unnecessary. They argue that by reducing customs controls at frontiers on most products, market forces would then produce convergence in indirect tax rates over time. Restrictions on tobacco and alcohol, are likely to continue to be necessary for reasons of health policy.

In the U.K., the Labour Party has significantly changed its stance – to a strongly pro-E.C. policy. It is especially supportive of the proposed Social Charter which provides for a framework of worker protection as well as for consultative arrangements between management and the workforce. The U.K. Government is opposed to the introduction of the Social Charter, on the grounds that by imposing additional burdens on employers it will tend to increase the numbers of persons unemployed.

THE FUTURE OF THE EUROPEAN COMMUNITY

Given the major political changes in Central and Eastern Europe, there may be big changes in the E.C. One possibility is the offering of associate status, i.e. partial membership, to some of these countries; with the possibility of full membership being available in individual cases at some later date.

QUESTIONS

1. Outline the development of the E.C. and explain the functions of the main institutions.

2. What are the main sources of revenue for the E.C.? How is this revenue spent?

3. Compare the advantages and disadvantages of U.K. membership. How might a different pattern of expenditure help the U.K.?

CHAPTER 41

LOOKING AHEAD: THROUGH THE 1990s

The changed political scene in Europe offers considerable trading opportunities. There is a good prospect of a fully-functioning single market
of 320m people in the European Community. To this might be added the
potential trading links with 140m people in Central and Eastern Europe
together with some 40m people in the European Free Trade Association
(E.F.T.A.); making a total market of 500m people.

The U.K. itself staged something of an economic revival from the
middle 1980s, though less than was claimed at the time. By the end of
the 1980s, there was rising inflation and a massive balance of payments
current account deficit in 1989 of some £20 billion. It is now clear that
there was a failure

    (a) to control consumer demand from about 1987
and (b) to bring about an adequate improvement in the performance of
    manufacturing industry.

The share of manufacturing in the U.K. economy is lower than in any
other major industrial country. John Wells of Cambridge University has
calculated that elimination of the external deficit would require a 15 per
cent expansion of supply. Moreover, that expansion must occur relative
to the growth of demand. If, for example, the deficit were to be closed
over 5 years and the demand for manufactures were to rise by as little as
$2\frac{1}{2}$ per cent per annum then manufacturing output must rise at an
annual rate of 6 per cent per annum.

Weakness on the manufacturing side is the more significant given the
increasing competition being faced in invisibles (e.g. banking, insurance
etc.) and the noticeable falling off in their contribution to the balance of
payments.

Fundamental to any improvement in the economy is the level of and
quality of investment. Overall, in 1990 the level of investment has merely
recovered from its low levels in the early 1980s and is no higher that it
was for much of the 1970s. Furthermore, the composition has shifted
away from manufacturing. During the 1980s, gross domestic fixed capital
formation improved 34 per cent in real terms; whereas manufacturing's

share of fixed capital formation fell from 18 per cent in 1979 to 13 per cent in 1988.

Undoubtedly there was an improvement in labour productivity during the 1980s, though in 1990 there are clear signs that much lower levels of improvement are being achieved. This has coincided with a period of rising wage settlements. The inevitable effect will be to reduce company profitability and thus to lessen the incentive and the means for further investment. Part of the industrial problem is a shortage of certain labour skills, due in no small measure to a failure to provide adequate training facilities in the country as a whole.

There has been a marked decline in the personal savings ratio accompanied by a high level of consumer credit. The Government is committed to heavy dependence on interest rates as a means of monetary control: the 1990 Budget Statement forecasts only 1 per cent growth in Gross Domestic Product for 1990/91.

It is apparent that much remains to be done in improving the flexibility of labour markets and the supply of skilled labour; in raising the level of investment; and in improving the quality and reliability of U.K. products. Furthermore, major deficiencies in the infrastructure in the U.K. (e.g. rail system) need major investment to make possible the exploitation of the undoubted market opportunities.

MULTIPLE CHOICE TEST NO. 3

Answers are on page 372.

1. In the Kingdom of Octavia, the marginal propensity to consume is two-thirds. If, in a period of heavy unemployment, the Government decides on additional state spending in order to achieve an increase in National Income of £15 billion, how much money should it inject into the system?
   (a) £5 billion
   (b) £2 billion
   (c) £10 billion
   (d) £12 billion

2. The term "Balancing item" is to be found
   (a) in company annual accounts
   (b) in Balance of Payments statistics
   (c) in Bank of England statements of monetary aggregates
   (d) in U.K. National Income Accounts

3. An example of progressive taxation is
   (a) value added tax
   (b) stamp duty on property
   (c) excise duties on alcohol and tobacco
   (d) Income tax

4. An improvement in a country's terms of trade signifies that
   (a) an improvement in the balance of payments will ensue in the longer term
   (b) the index of export prices is rising relative to the index of import prices
   (c) an increased value of goods has been exported
   (d) import prices are falling

5. Which of the following would *not* reduce the money supply?
   (a) the introduction of consumer credit controls
   (b) the raising of domestic interest rates

    (c) the purchase of reserve currencies by the Bank of England with the aim of preventing an appreciation of sterling

    (d) an effective control on the level of bank deposits in a country subject to exchange control

6. With $C = 10 + 0.7Y$ and the level of income changing from £70 billion to £80 billion, the increase in consumption and the revised average propensity to consume (apc) respectively would be
   (a) £9 billion and 0·78
   (b) £6 billion and 0·8
   (c) £7 billion and 0·79
   (d) £7 billion and 0·825

7. The J Curve refers to
   (a) the relationship between inflation and unemployment
   (b) the recession and boom cycle in the economy
   (c) the consequence of a devaluation with deeper deficit followed by an improving balance of payments
   (d) a decline in product demand followed by an upswing

8. When inflation is at a high level
   (a) nominal interest rates will also be high
   (b) the real rate of interest will be higher than the nominal rate
   (c) public expenditure will already be falling
   (d) the share market is likely to be rising

9. An increase in real wages in the economy
   (a) will make tax increases inevitable
   (b) implies a corresponding increase in discretionary spending power
   (c) is the result of increased output
   (d) means that earnings have increased faster than the retail price index

10. A rise of 3 per cent in labour productivity within the U.K. will necessarily
    (a) increase the competitiveness of U.K. exports
    (b) raise the level of gross national product
    (c) raise the level of company profitability
    (d) facilitate the payment of higher factor rewards

11. A rising foreign exchange rate for country X will
    (a) result in a rise in X's RPI
    (b) be likely to raise the employment level in X
    (c) favour those holidaying in X from abroad
    (d) ease inflationary pressures within X

12. A PSDR of £12 billion will
    (a) bring about a reduction in the level of employment
    (b) add to inflationary pressures
    (c) lessen the need for tax revenue
    (d) reduce the level of debt funding costs

ANSWERS TO MULTIPLE CHOICE TEST NO. 1

1. (d)
2. (c)
3. (b)
4. (c)
5. (a)
6. (d)
7. (d)
8. (c)
9. (c)
10. (d)
11. (d)
12. (a)

ANSWERS TO MULTIPLE CHOICE TEST NO. 2

1. (c)
2. (b)
3. (a)
4. (c)
5. (b)
6. (b)
7. (d)
8. (c)
9. (d)
10. (a)
11. (a)
12. (c)

ANSWERS TO MULTIPLE CHOICE TEST NO. 3

1. (a) £5b × (1/1 − 0.67) = £15b
2. (b)
3. (d)
4. (b)
5. (c)
6. (d) Increase in consumption = £10b × 0·7 = £7b.
   Consumption £10b + (£80b × 0·7) = £66b
   Average propensity to consume = £66b/£80b = 0·825
7. (c)
8. (a)
9. (a)
10. (d)
11. (d)
12. (d)

INDEX

equilibrium price 30
equilibrium 281
E.R.M. = Exchange rate mechanism
European Community 294, 325, 356
European Monetary System 346
European Free Trade Association 325, 365
European Monetary Union 348
exchange control 211, 323
exchange equalisation account 211
exchange rate mechanism 347
exchange 51

factor mix 77
factors of production 13, 55, 137
final product method 241
finance corporations 229
finance houses 229
firm size 90
fiscal policy 290
Fisher, I. 194
fixed exchange rates 340
fixed/variable costs 98
floating exchange rates 338
foreign exchange market 223
forward market 343
free goods 2
Friedman, M. 194
full employment 288
functions of money 181

GATT = General Agreement on Tariffs
    and Trade
gearing 68
General Agreement on Tariffs and Trade
    294, 326
George, H. 167
giffen goods 35, 53
gold standard 340
government stocks 219
Gresham's law 179
gross domestic product 240
gross national product 245

housing investment 276

ICFC 71
imperfect competition 123
import controls 337
income effect 53
income elasticity 46
income tax 296
incomes policies 150
index-linked stocks 220
indirect product 55
indirect tax 295, 298
industrial inertia 106

inelastic demand 39
inferior goods 35, 53
inflation 248
inflationary gap 285
infrastructure 276
inheritance tax 297
injections 254
insurance companies 227
integration 94
inter-bank market 222
intermediation 200
International Monetary Fund 341, 349
international trade 316
interest 154, 188, 236
inventory/stocks, 275
investment 154, 253, 271
investment appraisal 160
investment companies 228
invisible trade 331

J curve 336
joint supply 37

Keynes, J. M. (Lord) 20, 189, 256, 280
kinked demand curve 125

labour 13, 143
land 13, 163
laws of economics 10
leakages 253
lender of last resort 209
LIBOR = London Inter-Bank Offered
    Rate 235
life-cycle hypothesis 268
LIFFE = London International Financial
    Futures Exchange
limited companies 67
liquidity preference 190
loan guarantee scheme 71
local authorities 309
local authority market 221
localisation 61, 106
location of industry 103
London International Financial Futures
    Exchange 223
long run/short run 77
long run 100, 114, 119, 128

macroeconomics 10
management buy-outs 72
margin 4
marginal cost 99
marginal efficiency of capital 273
marginal product 79, 135
marginal propensity to consume 260
marginal revenue 117